Essays in Fiscal Federalism

RICHARD A. MUSGRAVE, *Editor*

GREENWOOD PRESS, PUBLISHERS
WESTPORT, CONNECTICUT

Library of Congress Cataloging in Publication Data

Musgrave, Richard Abel, 1910- ed.
Essays in fiscal federalism.

Reprint of the 1965 ed. published by Brookings Institution, Washington, issued in series: Studies of government finance.
Includes bibliographical references and index.
1. Intergovernmental fiscal relations--United States.
2. Intergovernmental tax relations--United States.
I. Title. II. Series: Studies of government finance.
[HJ275.M8 1977] 336.73 76-49481
ISBN 0-8371-9366-4

Originally published in 1965 by The Brookings Institution, Washington

Reprinted with the permission of The Brookings Institution

Reprinted in 1977 by Greenwood Press, Inc.

Library of Congress Catalog Card Number 76-49481

ISBN 0-8371-9366-4

Printed in the United States of America

THE BROOKINGS INSTITUTION is an independent organization devoted to nonpartisan research, education, and publication in economics, government, foreign policy, and the social sciences generally. Its principal purposes are to aid in the development of sound public policies and to promote public understanding of issues of national importance.

The Institution was founded December 8, 1927, to merge the activities of the Institute for Government Research, founded in 1916, the Institute of Economics, founded in 1922, and the Robert Brookings Graduate School of Economics and Government, founded in 1924.

The general administration of the Institution is the responsibility of a self-perpetuating Board of Trustees. The trustees are likewise charged with maintaining the independence of the staff and fostering the most favorable conditions for creative research and education. The immediate direction of the policies, program, and staff of the Institution is vested in the President, assisted by the division directors and an advisory council, chosen from the professional staff of the Institution.

In publishing a study, the Institution presents it as a competent treatment of a subject worthy of public consideration. The interpretations and conclusions in such publications are those of the author or authors and do not purport to represent the views of the other staff members, officers, or trustees of the Brookings Institution.

BOARD OF TRUSTEES

Foreword

PRINCIPLES OF PUBLIC FINANCE apply very largely to a hypothetical "unitary" fiscal system in which there is only one government with taxing and spending powers. But the assumption of a unitary system is obviously not applicable to a federal system like that in the United States and in many other countries. Problems of public finance do not arise in relation to government in general, but rather to particular units of government at different levels. This volume, which incorporates summaries of five dissertations by students of Professor Richard A. Musgrave, reexamines some of the principles of public finance in this multi-unit context.

The manuscript was reviewed by a reading committee consisting of James M. Buchanan of the University of Virginia, Sam B. Chase, Jr., of the Brookings Institution, and James A. Maxwell of Clark University. The authors also benefited from the assistance of Professor Musgrave and a number of their colleagues in preparing their dissertations, including James Friedman, Peter Mieszkowski, and Duncan Campbell, who provided helpful suggestions on the paper by Stanley Engerman; William G. Bowen for his comments on the paper by Robert W. Rafuse, Jr.; Burton Weisbrod for his comments on W. Irwin Gillespie's paper; Edwin S. Mills for his advice on the paper by William C. Birdsall; Carl F. Christ for his comments on the Gillespie and Birdsall papers; and James Kindahl for his assistance on the Engerman and Gillespie papers. The manuscript was edited by Verrick O. French.

Richard A. Musgrave is Professor of Economics at Harvard University. The work on this study was done under his supervision at The Johns Hopkins University and Princeton University. The project was part of a special program of research and education on taxation and public expenditures, supervised by the National Committee on Government Finance and financed by a special grant from the Ford Foundation. In addition to assistance from the National Committee on Government Finance, Mr. Gillespie's work was supported by a Ford Foundation Doctoral Fellowship and Mr. Birdsall's work was supported by the Committee on Urban Economics of Resources for the Future and the Committee on Public Affairs of The Johns Hopkins University.

The views expressed in this book are those of the authors and are not presented as the views of the institutions with which the authors are affiliated, or the views of the National Committee on Government Finance or its Advisory Committee, or the staff members, officers, or trustees of the Brookings Institution, or the Ford Foundation.

ROBERT D. CALKINS
President

October 1965
Washington, D.C.

Studies of Government Finance

Studies of Government Finance is a special program of research and education in taxation and government expenditures at the federal, state, and local levels. These studies are under the supervision of the National Committee on Government Finance appointed by the trustees of the Brookings Institution, and are supported by a special grant from the Ford Foundation.

MEMBERS OF THE ADVISORY COMMITTEE

Contents

Authors' Tables and Figures

Engerman

Rafuse

Bridges

RICHARD A. MUSGRAVE*

Introduction

THIS VOLUME CONTAINS FIVE ESSAYS dealing with fiscal federalism and multi-unit public finance. They are based on Ph.D. dissertations prepared under the sponsorship of the Brookings Institution's program in Studies of Government Finance, which is financed by a grant from the Ford Foundation. Four of the dissertations were prepared under my direction at the Johns Hopkins University, and one at Princeton.

The traditional approach to fiscal theory has been in the context of unitary government. Reflecting the centralized nature of British finances, Adam Smith's work dealt with the fiscal needs of the prince, and the funding of national public works. His successors were concerned with the retarding effects of public finance, again at the national level. The continental discussion of the late 19th century continued in this tradition. The general theory of tax and expenditure determination was seen in unitary terms, and it failed to penetrate to regional or level considerations. Following the advent of the new income theory of the 1930's, the Keynesian renaissance in the economics of public finance focused on government finance as a tool of stabilization, thus directing attention once more to the central level. Notwithstanding occasional discussions of such matters as grants, tax sharing, or fiscal equalization, no frontal attack

* Harvard University.

on the problems of fiscal federalism (the fiscal relation between hierarchically ordered units) or multi-unit finance (the fiscal relation between coordinate units) was undertaken. Yet recent years have shown a trend away from the unitary bias, and for good reasons.

The student of American public finances cannot escape the fact that our fiscal structure is highly decentralized. Over one-third of total and more than one-half of civilian fiscal affairs are conducted at the state-local level. Moreover, the state-local share in public expenditures will probably increase as civilian programs, customarily administered at lower levels of authority, are expanded relative to national defense. The fact that state-local revenue sources are not readily amenable to expansion will tend to create a growing imbalance between the location of expenditure responsibility and that of taxing power. As this takes place, our traditional forms of fiscal federalism will have to be reconsidered and adapted to changing needs. Should there be a transfer of expenditure functions, allowing for the increasingly national importance of outlays in education, for example? Or should ways be found to use the federal revenue system in support of state-local expenditures? If so, what forms should this support take, to what functions should it apply, and to what levels of government should it be directed? What degree of fiscal centralization will or should be involved in such a process? The answers to these questions, to be sure, involve political as well as economic reinterpretations of fiscal federalism, but there is no doubt that economic analysis can make an important contribution.

Across the Atlantic, fiscal thinking in multi-unit terms has been stimulated by the movement for European economic integration. There the problem is one of rearranging and synchronizing the tax structures of associated countries, so that economic frontiers can be eliminated and efficiency gains from tariff reduction can be realized without being offset by distorting tax differentials. This problem raises the issue of tax shifting in the open economy, and thus the tools of fiscal and trade analysis are brought together. Similarly, there arise the questions of how stabilization policy may be made to work in the open economy, and how the interests of domestic and balance-of-payments stability may be reconciled.

Quite apart from these forces of institutional change, there are good theoretical reasons for reorientation of fiscal thinking in multi-unit terms. The very theory of social wants, difficult though it may be, remains at the core of fiscal economics. Certain wants cannot be satisfied through the market, but must be provided for by government because the resulting benefits accrue to all members of the "group," independent of individual contributions. Membership in the group, however, frequently depends on spacial considerations. Street cleaning services in Bangor, Maine, are of little interest to residents of Palm Beach, Florida. National defense services, on the other hand, concern both groups relatively equally. Thus various types of public services concern various regions; and if the supply of such services is to be determined by the preferences of the beneficiaries, as it essentially has to be in a democratic system, fiscal service units should reflect the regional impact of benefits. Application of this principle is complicated by the fact that benefits may not be homogeneous throughout an area, but may taper off with increasing distance from the center. Similarly, benefits rendered by existing political units (for example, counties or states) may spill over to the outside, and benefits rendered on the outside may spill inward, resulting in problems of inter-unit adjustment.

A further case for a multi-unit fiscal structure arises from the fact that individual preferences differ. It follows from the nature of social goods that services are consumed in relatively equal amounts by members of the beneficiary group. Since the cost is shared among the members, it is in the interest of the individual to associate with others whose preferences for social goods are similar to his own. Thus, people with high preference for public services may join together in one service area (a suburb, for example), while people with low preferences may gather in another. To the extent that this is feasible, the provision for social wants may be subjected to a quasi "market" mechanism, and the existence of multiple fiscal units may again prove advantageous by virtue of being efficient.

Finally, economies of scale may permit certain public services to be rendered more cheaply by a multiple system than by a single unit of government. There are various economic reasons why an efficient rendering of public services may require multiple governmental units; fiscal analysis should be of help in deciding what constitutes an efficient structure.

Similar considerations ensue if the problem is approached from the revenue side. A regional structuring of public services along the lines just discussed requires that taxpayers who enjoy benefits incident to a particular region bear the costs of those benefits. The problem of regional benefit incidence and overlap thus has its counterpart in regional burden incidence, as well as in the export and import of tax burdens. It follows that various taxes are appropriate for various levels of government and that the determination of "appropriateness" depends upon the regional incidence of the tax burden. The problem of tax shifting in an open economy—hitherto touched on only in the theory of international trade—thus assumes crucial importance in fiscal theory as well.

It would be naive, of course, to expect that the prevailing fiscal structure can be made over in the image of such an "efficient" pattern. The broader outlines of our federalist fiscal structure, as well as the vast variety of state-local patterns, are the result of manifold historical forces; and the economist is hardly free to rebuild the system in the interest of economic efficiency. Moreover, considerations of economic efficiency are but one among various criteria which include social and political considerations as well. Nevertheless, economic analysis can provide guidelines for the patterns of change in the broader fiscal relations among federal, state, and local levels of government, and for the degree of responsibility which the federal government should assume for the provision of public services at the lower levels. Analysis can also guide the revision of fiscal units at the lower levels as, for example, in the restructuring of service units in the expanding metropolitan area, or the consolidation of school districts.

The essays presented here address themselves to some aspects of this question. Two deal with fiscal policy as a stabilization device, and both of these challenge traditional positions. Engerman reconsiders the view that stabilization policy must be conducted largely on a nationwide basis, and that regional leakages render pinpointing of expansionary measures in high unemployment areas ineffective. His analysis shows that regional variations in unemployment are substantial, that regional orientation of fiscal measures is more effective than is frequently assumed, and that the degree of effectiveness depends upon the particular causes which are responsible for the regional variations.

Rafuse takes a second look at the widely held view that the cyclical behavior of state and local finances tends to accentuate rather than alleviate the instability of the economy. While this "perversity hypothesis" may account for conditions during the 1930's, the record since World War II suggests that the hypothesis may now be more misleading than helpful in understanding the fiscal behavior of the state-local sector. Owing to the sharp and persistent upward trend in the level of state and local expenditures in the postwar period, and to the limited—but improving—income elasticity of state-local receipts, the budgetary behavior of these governments in the aggregate has been stabilizing during every postwar recession. During the upturns, however, the overall fiscal impact has accentuated inflationary pressures. Receipts have been stabilizing throughout the period, but expenditures have been destabilizing during the expansions. If departures from trend only are considered, expenditures as well as receipts are found to be stabilizing during the upturns.

Studies in the distribution of the tax burden have long recognized that both the state-local and the federal level must be included in a comprehensive picture. The conclusion has been that a regressive state-local structure combined with a progressive federal structure yields a U-shaped overall pattern. Gillespie's study shows that this general picture is changed considerably if expenditure benefits are included, and if the distribution of net benefits or net burdens is considered. A substantial share of the expenditures of the federal fiscal structure—especially those for national defense—result in general benefits which cannot be allocated readily to individuals. Thus limitation of distributional analysis to the question of taxes is reasonable. At the state-local level, however, expenditures generally permit benefit imputations to individuals, and distributional analysis is more interesting if conducted on a net benefit-burden basis. Since many state-local services provide benefits that favor lower income groups, a strongly "pro-poor" benefit structure is combined with a moderately "pro-rich" burden structure, leaving a net pattern that on the whole favors lower income groups. A comparable analysis is more difficult at the federal level, but assuming that the benefits from "general" expenditures are proportional to income, the net distribution also proves favorable to the lower-middle income groups, although to a lesser extent than at the state-local level. Thus inclusion of expenditure benefits not only reverses the role of the two levels, but (on the assumption of proportionality for general benefits) it shows the overall fiscal structure to be more favorable to lower incomes than the tax structure alone.

The fourth paper deals with the interrelationship of fiscal structures at various levels of government. Bridges examines the treatment of state-local nonbusiness taxes under the federal individual income tax. While the practice has been to permit the deduction of such taxes, recent discussion has questioned whether an allowance is justified, and whether, if granted, it should take the form of a tax credit rather than a deduction. To answer this question, the implications of various techniques are considered with respect to revenue (state-local as well as federal), distributional implications, and effects on state tax policy. The author's conclusion is that a tax credit for state-local income taxes would be preferable to a deduction, and that deductibility of most other nonbusiness taxes should be disallowed.

A final paper deals with the demand for public goods as expressed through the political process. Various studies have attempted to explain expenditure levels by functions in terms of need, or according to economic, urban, and demographic characteristics. Fairly good fits are obtained but such functions mix supply and demand factors and do not lend themselves readily to interpretation in terms of community preference. Birdsall attempts to focus more directly on public preferences by analyzing voter responses to state referenda in New York State. He endeavors to explain voter responses by cities in terms of the economic, demographic, and other characteristics of particular electorates. This is essentially a pioneering effort and although the results are not conclusive, a number of interesting methodological problems are laid open.

While these studies range widely over questions of multi-unit finance and fiscal federalism, I hope that individually and collectively they will contribute in some measure to a better understanding of problems in both fields.

STANLEY ENGERMAN*

Regional Aspects of Stabilization Policy

MOST WRITERS on cyclical stabilization are concerned with the movements of national aggregates and the responses of these national aggregates to the policies of national fiscal and monetary authorities. They explicitly or implicitly assume either that these responses affect the national economy in ways which are uniform (however defined), or that specific industrial or regional responses do not concern the policymaker. Deliberately selective policies intended to affect specific industries or areas are said by such writers to be "structural" policies, as distinguished from cyclical stabilization policies.

This paper is an examination of the implications, for cyclical stabilization policy, of regarding the nation as a network of related regions rather than as one market. The first section indicates the extent and causes of regional variation in cyclical patterns, and the manner in which these causes affect the efficiency of regional stabilization policies. The second is an analysis of the formulation of sta-

* University of Rochester. This essay is based upon the author's dissertation, "Postwar Regional Cycles and their Implications for Fiscal Policy" (Johns Hopkins, 1962).

bilization targets and policies when the regional distribution of cyclical unemployment is uneven and when the regional distribution of changes in employment resulting from fiscal and monetary policies concerns the policy maker. This concern would be greatest either when regional differentials in unemployment rates are large, so that some regions are at a "distress" level, or when the national unemployment rate is close to, but above, a maximum socially acceptable level, so that the pattern of unemployment differentials is a crucial factor in determining the compatibility of "full" employment with price level stability. This section also makes use of a simple model of interregional trade to compare the levels of efficiency of various fiscal policies in achieving specified goals. In a final section, some estimates of efficiency are derived on the basis of input-output data.

Since this study is focused on the unemployment aspect of stabilization, it employs a sectoring of the economy by geographic regions. A similar sectoring is not as relevant to a discussion of other aspects of stabilization policy. In the discussion of inflation, for example, sectoring by industries has been found most practical,[1] but the argument that a similar breakdown should be used in analyzing policies to reduce unemployment ignores differences between the two problems. Inflation tends to be more evenly diffused than unemployment, and, among regions, there are larger intra-industry differences in unemployment than in prices because goods are more mobile than labor, especially in the short run. Thus, a regional approach seems more appropriate to a discussion of unemployment than to a discussion of inflation.

Regional Differences in Unemployment

An analysis of the postwar period indicates considerable variations in regional behavior. Although the findings are more suggestive than conclusive, they are useful in placing the subsequent discussion in the context of the recent United States experience. Much of the following section is covered in greater detail in Chapters II through V of my dissertation.

[1] See, for example, Charles L. Schultze, *Recent Inflation in the United States,* Study Paper No. 1, Joint Economic Committee, 86 Cong. 1 sess. (1959).

What Is a Region?

Three criteria are customarily used in the delineation of regions: factor mobility, commodity mobility, and political boundaries. Each is useful for certain purposes, and, to some extent, the regional concept in this paper will involve all three criteria. Despite imprecision in defining the nature of the ideal regional concept to be used, the problem of geographic differences in unemployment rates obviously exists under each criterion.

The first and most obvious approach to an analysis of unemployment would focus upon regions defined in terms of labor mobility. If the national rate of unemployment is a function of the locational pattern of the labor force, an increase in labor mobility would reduce the national rate, or at least narrow regional differentials in unemployment rates. Similarly, the location of any increases in demand for output leading to increased demand for labor would not be as crucial a concern in the presence of labor mobility as when such mobility is absent. Insofar as the national goal of policy is "full" employment of the labor force, the existence of different labor market areas becomes a key consideration.

A second approach to regional classification is based on the concept of the sales market area. This should prove useful to the extent that the output of firms is directed largely towards purchasing units located within a specific area. It is relevant in analyzing the spread (or spillover) of the effects of policy changes among regions. The larger the market area for products produced in regions of high unemployment, the less necessary and desirable may be pinpointed policies, and the more these regions benefit from expenditure changes occurring in other regions. A major difficulty of this approach is that the relevant market areas will differ among products so that no one set of boundaries would suffice for all purposes. However, if certain key industries were meant to be aided by policy measures, then a knowledge of the specific market area for products of the producing units in these industries would be important in determining the expected geographic incidence of policy measures.

Imprecise as this criterion may be when applied to a complicated network of transactions (particularly since the market area itself may vary with cyclical phases), it again suggests that the geographic distribution of policy effects will depend upon the location at which the measure is introduced; and that, insofar as production in any one industry may occur at several locations, the customary assumption of national uniformity of response to all policy changes is unrealistic. It should be noted, again, that this inequality of response would not be so important if labor were mobile, meaning that for policy purposes these two criteria—labor mobility and commodity mobility—are interrelated.

A third approach is based upon administrative units for policymaking. Since the important consideration here is the institutional framework within which policies are designed and implemented, this approach requires recognition of political boundaries, particularly within the context of a federal system. While such political boundaries frequently encompass areas which otherwise are not meaningful economic units, they may nevertheless be important for purposes of policy action, as in the case of state or local fiscal measures, or with respect to federal policies implemented at lower levels of government. While most fiscal policies involve direct relationships between the federal government and individual economic units, either individuals or firms, there are grant programs in which payments are made to the states *qua* states. Thus, aside from their independent roles in formulating their own tax and expenditure policies, states also serve as administrators and conduits for federal government policies.

While some recent legislation, notably that involving aid to the so-called depressed areas, recognizes labor market areas—essentially cities and their immediate suburbs—as the locale of federal policies, direct federal-regional relationships are not as common in our political system as are federal-state relationships. Although political and economic relationships between the federal and state governments are more important than those between the federal government and other political units, this fact need not be an inherent aspect of federalism as a political process.

Whatever may appear theoretically to be the most useful criteria for regional delineation in any specific case, most empirical studies use states or census regions, which are aggregated from states, as the primary units of observation. An important exception is the use of Federal Reserve districts when monetary factors are being considered. Generally, however, the greater availability of data on the state level for most economically significant variables limits most studies to states as the basis for regional classification. Much of our information about regional cyclical behavior, for example, comes from studies using states as the basic units, improper as this may seem when judged by rigorous theoretical standards.[2] As noted above, the use of states as the fundamental units of observation is justifiable in a discussion of policy measures. For this reason, the empirical study summarized below will employ state data.

Postwar Regional Cyclical Behavior

The data in the following tables were taken from state reports, prepared for the Bureau of Labor Statistics, of employment in non-agricultural establishments. They were used to calculate changes in levels of employment, and the decline from peak to trough in employment was used to indicate the rate of cyclical unemployment. Owing to difficulties in adjusting the data for seasonal variations, annual averages of employment in each state were used. Each state's employment was not adjusted for trend, but instead, observations over each cycle were averaged according to the National Bureau of Economic Research method. The following information is presented: comparisons of the timing of turning points in the annual data; the relative share of recession unemployment of three contiguous census regions; rates of expansion and decline and average annual amplitudes of state employment for the two cycles between 1949 and 1958.

THE TIMING OF TURNING POINTS. The use of annual data for a survey of behavior within the period of a business cycle is admittedly crude, particularly for a discussion of the timing of turning

[2] See, for example, the discussions of regional cycles of Rutledge Vining, "Regional Variation in Cyclical Fluctuation Viewed as a Frequency Distribution," *Econometrica,* Vol. 13 (July 1945), pp. 182-213; "Location of Industry and Regional Patterns of Business Cycle Behavior," *Econometrica,* Vol. 14 (January 1946), pp. 37-68; and "The Region as a Concept in Business Cycle Analysis," *Econometrica,* Vol. 14 (July 1946), pp. 201-18; Frank Hanna, *State Income Differentials, 1919-1954* (Duke University Press, 1959), Chap. 3; and George H. Borts, "Regional Cycles of Manufacturing Employment in the United States, 1914-1953," *Journal of the American Statistical Association,* Vol. 55 (March 1960), pp. 151-211, reprinted as National Bureau of Economic Research Occasional Paper 73 (1960).

TABLE 1. States Whose Total Employment Changed in a Direction Opposite to the Direction of Change of Total National Employment, 1949–58[a]

1949	*1950*	*1951*	*1952*	*1953*	*1954*	*1955*	*1956*	*1957*	*1958*
District of	—	—	Idaho[b]	Arkansas[b]	Arizona[c]	North Dakota[b]	Michigan	Connecticut	Arizona[c]
Columbia			Massachusetts	District of	Florida[c]			Delaware	Arkansas[b]
Kansas[b]			Pennsylvania	Columbia	Montana[b]			Georgia[b]	Florida[c]
Idaho[b]			Vermont	Idaho[b]	Nebraska[b]			Illinois	Mississippi[b]
Louisiana			West Virginia	Maine	Nevada[c]			Indiana	New Mexico[c]
Montana[b]				Rhode Island	North Dakota[b]			Iowa[b]	South Dakota[b]
New Mexico[c]				West Virginia	South Dakota[b]			Kansas[b]	
North Dakota[b]								Maine	
Oklahoma								Massachusetts	
South Dakota[b]								Michigan	
								Mississippi[b]	
								Missouri	
								Nebraska[b]	
								Oklahoma	
								Oregon	
								Rhode Island	
								South Dakota[b]	
								Tennessee[b]	
								Vermont	

Source: Bureau of Labor Statistics.
[a] The total of national employment for all industries declined in 1949, 1954, and 1958. Employment increased in all other years.
[b] Over 20 percent of the state's experienced labor force in agriculture.
[c] Growth ranking 1 to 4.

points. Nevertheless, inspection of Federal Reserve bank reports and of the various state employment agency publications, which present monthly data, substantiates the conclusion that differences in timing were usually minor.

The data show a moderately high degree of uniformity among turning points of cyclical movements in various states. This conclusion follows from Table 1, which lists those states where changes in employment for each year were in a direction opposite to that shown by total national employment. The large number of deviant states which had over 20 percent of their experienced labor force in agriculture in 1950 are noted accordingly in the table.[3] Similarly, those states whose growth rankings were 1 to 4 (from 1949 to 1958) are also noted.[4] The behavior of the agricultural states in recession years is not directly explained, however, by a difference in behavior between agricultural and industrial sectors. While agricultural income increased in 1958, it declined both in 1949 and 1954, not only at the national level but also, excepting Nebraska in 1954, in every deviant state in both years.[5] The deviance of these states may possibly have resulted from small employment samples and consequently unreliable data; thus apparent declines may simply be inaccurate measurements. In each of the highly ranked growth states, a deceleration in the rate of growth occurred in the recession years. For this reason, these apparent deviations are attributable to the failure to adjust for trend.

Special conditions affected the patterns in 1952 and 1957. The timing of the downturns for all manufacturing and for total nonagricultural employment differs in the recession phase of the cycle of 1954-58, thus rendering interpretation of that period difficult. It should be noted that the behavior of the states from the peak—whether in 1956 or 1957—to the trough in 1958 is consistent with

[3] The state ratios of labor force in agriculture to total experienced labor force are from Everett S. Lee and others, *Population Redistribution and Economic Growth, United States, 1870-1950*, Vol. 1, *Methodological Considerations and Reference Tables* (American Philosophical Association, 1957), pp. 623-31.

[4] See Table 8 for the rankings of the states by growth rates.

[5] See U.S. Department of Commerce, *Personal Income by States since 1929* (1956), pp. 146-203 for the 1949 and 1954 income changes. For the changes in the next recession see Robert E. Graham, Jr., "Regional Markets in 1958," *Survey of Current Business,* Vol. 39 (August 1959), pp. 9-24.

the behavioral patterns in the other two postwar recession periods.[6] The other period of divergence, 1952, resulted from sharp declines of about 6 percent in employment in each of three key manufacturing industries—lumber and wood products, primary metals, and textile mill products—which were important in certain of the states.[7] The deviance of states in 1952 can be explained by the declines in employment in a "key" industry in each state—textiles in Vermont and Massachusetts, primary metals in Pennsylvania, and mining in West Virginia—which exceeded the increases in all other employment. While, for reasons given above, too much importance should not be attached to the 1957 pattern, it should be noted that eight of the states are included in the fourteen-state area discussed in the next section, which includes those states in which manufacturing claims a large share of the labor force.

The conclusion suggested by this summary is that the postwar cycles, though comparatively minor by prewar standards, are still pervasive and affect nearly all of the states during a given period of time. The differential behavior of specific industries explains almost all of the apparent deviations, and since industry movements occur at about the same time, this makes tenable the previous assumption of national uniformity in the timing of cyclical behavior.

THE SHARE OF THE "MANUFACTURING BELT" IN RECESSION UNEMPLOYMENT. To indicate the unevenness of the regional distribution of unemployment in the postwar recessions and its concentration in the northeastern manufacturing region, comparisons between shares of employment and shares of recession declines in employment were made for the three recession years, 1949, 1954, and 1958. The "manufacturing belt" is a term frequently used by economic geographers to refer to the fourteen states in the New England, Middle Atlantic, and East North Central census regions.

[6] Manufacturing employment reached a peak in October 1956, and total nonagricultural employment in September 1957. Thus manufacturing employment in 1957 fell below that in 1956, while the opposite is the case with total nonagricultural employment. See U.S. Bureau of Labor Statistics, *Employment and Earnings Statistics for the United States, 1909-1960* (1961). Because of this the 1957 movement in each state was net of the divergent movements in manufacturing and nonmanufacturing employment. The possibility exists that a greater severity in decline in employment within 1957, rather than a difference in timing of the turning points, accounts for most of the divergent movement.

[7] U.S. Bureau of Labor Statistics, *Employment and Earnings Statistics.*

TABLE 2. Proportions of Employment and Employment Declines in the Fourteen "Manufacturing Belt" States in Three Recessions, 1949, 1954, and 1958

(In percent)

	Proportion of	
	National Employment (Peak Year)	*Decline in National Employment*
1949:		
Total	55.5	73.2
Manufacturing	66.8	74.6
Durable Goods	72.5	75.9
1954:		
Total	53.9	75.9
Manufacturing	65.0	81.5
Durable Goods	70.4	82.6
1958:		
Total	52.2	81.8
Manufacturing[a]	62.7	84.3
Durable Goods[a]	67.8	88.2

Source: Bureau of Labor Statistics.
[a] Peak year 1956.

Table 2 shows the share of total nonagricultural employment, manufacturing employment, and durable goods manufacturing employment in this area in each of the peak years (1948, 1953, and 1956 or 1957) and the respective declines in the recession years. The disproportionately larger share of unemployment in these states, even after adjustment has been made for differences in industrial composition, should be noted, as should the fact that their relative share increased in each recession at the same time that their share of employment was declining.

RATES OF CYCLICAL CHANGE, BY STATES. Tables 3 and 4 show the rates of expansion and decline and average annual amplitudes for each state in the cycles of 1949-54 and 1954-58. They were computed using the National Bureau method of averaging the observations over each cycle, with the terminal years given half-weight. The numbers in parentheses indicate the ranking of the state in order of magnitude of movement. Owing to variations in the timing of turning points, rates of expansion and decline were computed for

TABLE 3. Rates of Expansion and Decline and Average Annual Amplitudes, by States, 1949–54

(In percent)

State	Rate of Expansion[a]	Rate of Decline[b]	Average Annual Amplitude[c]
Alabama	(26) 13.43	(24) 2.22	(27) 5.58
Arizona	(2) 28.00	(46) +1.16	(12) 7.16
Arkansas	(30) 11.37[d]	(11) 3.86	(25) 5.72
California	(5) 22.14	(40) .48	(21) 6.02
Colorado	(6) 20.27	(31.5) 1.37	(17) 6.44
Connecticut	(14) 18.14	(16) 2.84	(11) 7.38
Delaware	(8) 20.02	(13) 3.13	(10) 8.14
District of Columbia	(39) 9.19[d]	(2) 7.38	(14) 6.75
Florida	(3) 24.79	(48) +4.33	(4) 10.53
Georgia	(13) 18.44	(27) 1.76	(19) 6.37
Idaho	(36) 9.50[e]	(10) 4.04	(20) 6.10
Illinois	(33) 10.68	(12) 3.71	(18) 6.38
Indiana	(12) 18.46	(3) 7.35	(2) 11.97
Iowa	(46) 7.45	(31.5) 1.37	(45) 3.23
Kansas	(9) 19.71	(37.5) .80	(24) 5.73
Kentucky	(21) 15.50	(7) 5.41	(6) 9.29
Louisiana	(27) 13.18	(42) .35	(43) 3.65
Maine	(40) 9.10[d]	(22) 2.28	(39) 4.17
Maryland	(17) 16.45	(28) 1.72	(23) 5.83
Massachusetts	(42) 8.17[f]	(15) 3.00	(34) 5.04
Michigan	(10) 19.29	(5) 5.96	(3) 10.78
Minnesota	(29) 11.82	(30) 1.47	(38) 4.43
Mississippi	(23) 14.58	(37.5) .80	(37) 4.45
Missouri	(25) 13.87	(14) 3.04	(16) 6.51
Montana	(48) 6.10	(44) + .53	(49) 2.05
Nebraska	(28) 12.07	(43) + .03	(46) 3.05
Nevada	(1) 32.48	(49) +6.56	(1) 14.68
New Hampshire	(44) 7.87	(39) .70	(47) 2.67
New Jersey	(24) 14.42	(29) 1.67	(32) 5.28
New Mexico	(4) 23.40	(20) 2.45	(8) 8.30
New York	(43) 8.04	(26) 1.97	(41) 3.98
North Carolina	(16) 16.48	(34) 1.14	(33) 5.26
North Dakota	(45) 7.59	(47) +1.65	(44) 3.55
Ohio	(15) 16.94	(9) 4.23	(7) 8.47
Oklahoma	(22) 15.09	(41) .39	(40) 4.16
Oregon	(31) 10.88	(19) 2.72	(28.5) 5.44
Pennsylvania	(37) 9.43[f]	(6) 5.82	(9) 8.18
Rhode Island	(41) 9.07[e]	(4) 6.09	(15) 6.57
South Carolina	(7) 20.04	(8) 4.57	(5) 9.58
South Dakota	(47) 6.79	(45) + .76	(48) 2.46
Tennessee	(18) 16.33	(33) 1.29	(30) 5.37
Texas	(11) 18.72	(36) 1.02	(26) 5.70
Utah	(19) 16.08	(17) 2.83	(13) 6.85
Vermont	(38) 9.26[f]	(21) 2.32	(36) 4.64
Virginia	(20) 15.70	(25) 2.05	(22) 5.98
Washington	(32) 10.70	(35) 1.05	(42) 3.73
West Virginia	(49) 2.79[e]	(1) 12.12	(28.5) 5.44
Wisconsin	(34) 10.22	(18) 2.76	(31) 5.32
Wyoming	(35) 10.02	(23) 2.27	(35) 4.78
National Total[g]	13.49	2.65	6.02
National Total[h]	13.89	2.70	6.17

Source: Bureau of Labor Statistics.

Note: Numbers in parentheses indicate rankings in order of magnitude of movement.

[a] Expansion = Peak minus Initial Trough ÷ Cycle Base.

[b] Decline = Peak minus Terminal Trough ÷ Cycle Base.

[c] Average Annual Amplitude = Average Annual Expansion (Expansion ÷ Number of Years in Upswing) + Average Annual Decline.

[d] Peak in 1952.

[e] Peak in 1951.

[f] Decline in 1952, peak in 1953.

[g] National total given by the Bureau of Labor Statistics.

[h] Total of state figures.

TABLE 4. Rates of Expansion and Decline and Average Annual Amplitudes, by States, 1954–58

(In percent)

State	*Rate of Expansion*[a]		*Rate of Decline*[b]		*Average Annual Amplitude*[c]	
Alabama	(12)	10.48	(27)	2.36	(15)	5.85
Arizona	(1)	25.63	(49)	+5.12	(1)	13.66
Arkansas	(25)	6.91	(45)	+ .43	(46)	2.73
California	(4)	14.56	(40)	.72	(21)	5.57
Colorado	(7)	13.01	(36)	1.34	(19)	5.68
Connecticut	(32)	6.08[d]	(12)	4.39	(23.5)	5.24
Delaware	(6)	13.80[d]	(6)	5.40	(7)	9.60
District of Columbia	(46)	3.00	(37.5)	1.06	(47)	2.06
Florida	(2)	25.49	(47)	+1.72	(3)	10.22
Georgia	(17.5)	8.16[d]	(30)	2.26	(25)	5.21
Idaho	(14)	9.75	(37.5)	1.06	(31)	4.31
Illinois	(31)	6.09[d]	(7)	5.34	(18)	5.72
Indiana	(27)	6.54[d]	(5)	7.00	(11)	6.77
Iowa	(40)	3.98[d]	(25.5)	2.53	(42)	3.26
Kansas	(47)	2.83[d]	(17)	3.21	(43)	3.03
Kentucky	(15)	8.80	(15)	3.47	(13)	6.40
Louisiana	(8)	12.77	(18)	3.20	(9)	7.46
Maine	(42)	3.54[d]	(9)	5.21	(29)	4.38
Maryland	(13)	9.86	(29)	2.29	(20)	5.58
Massachusetts	(41)	3.91[d]	(14)	3.72	(36)	3.82
Michigan	(26)	6.67[e]	(1)	15.12	(2)	11.71
Minnesota	(28)	6.52	(33.5)	1.67	(35)	3.84
Mississippi	(20)	7.77[f]	(44)	+ .33	(44)	2.92
Missouri	(45)	3.22[d]	(25.5)	2.53	(45)	2.88
Montana	(22)	7.54	(22.5)	2.76	(22)	5.27
Nebraska	(48)	2.24[d]	(33.5)	1.67	(48)	1.96
Nevada	(5)	14.23	(16)	3.32	(8)	8.06
New Hampshire	(30)	6.16	(19)	3.19	(23.5)	5.24
New Jersey	(24)	7.29	(10)	4.94	(10)	7.37
New Mexico	(3)	17.79	(48)	+4.09	(4)	10.02
New York	(35)	5.54	(21)	2.89	(27)	4.74
North Carolina	(17.5)	8.16	(39)	.96	(37.5)	3.68
North Dakota	(39)	4.03[g]	(43)	.01	(49)	1.35
Ohio	(29)	6.36	(3)	7.73	(5)	9.85
Oklahoma	(33)	6.07[d]	(28)	2.33	(32)	4.21
Oregon	(23)	7.48[d]	(11)	4.91	(14)	6.20
Pennsylvania	(38)	4.22	(8)	5.27	(12)	6.68
Rhode Island	(49)	2.15[d]	(2)	7.84	(26)	5.00
South Carolina	(36)	5.09	(32)	1.76	(41)	3.46
South Dakota	(34)	5.75[f]	(46)	+1.18	(40)	3.47
Tennessee	(37)	4.67[d]	(24)	2.67	(37.5)	3.68
Texas	(11)	11.16	(41)	.63	(30)	4.35
Utah	(9)	12.73	(35)	1.52	(16)	5.76
Vermont	(43)	3.40[d]	(13)	3.89	(39)	3.65
Virginia	(10)	11.75	(42)	.21	(33)	4.12
Washington	(16)	8.41	(31)	1.81	(28)	4.61
West Virginia	(21)	7.55	(4)	7.25	(6)	9.77
Wisconsin	(19)	7.96	(20)	3.08	(17)	5.73
Wyoming	(44)	3.33	(22.5)	2.76	(34)	3.87
National Total[h]		7.33		3.18		5.62
National Total[i]		7.48		3.37		5.86

Source: Bureau of Labor Statistics.

[a] Expansion = Peak minus Initial Trough ÷ Cycle Base.

[b] Decline = Peak minus Terminal Trough ÷ Cycle Base.

[c] Average Annual Amplitude = Average Annual Expansion (Expansion ÷ Number of Years of Upswing) + Average Annual Decline.

[d] Peak in 1956.

[e] Peak in 1955.

[f] Decline in 1957, peak in 1958.

[g] Trough in 1955, peak in 1957.

[h] National total given by the Bureau of Labor Statistics.

[i] Total of state figures.

entire phases, but amplitudes were computed from annual averages of the behavior in each cyclical phase. If the national turning point had been used, and annual rates of expansion and decline computed, the rankings shown in the tables would be little changed. These tables, along with those in Appendix A, form the basis of the rank correlations to be discussed below.

Influence of Location

Two locational factors are important in analyzing the theories used later to explain regional differences in cyclical behavior. The first follows from the geographer's concept of the export base, with its distinction between local (or residentiary or service) industries and national (or export) industries.[8] While this dichotomy may be exaggerated in some cases, it illuminates an important distinction between (1) those (national) industries which can be directly affected by demand conditions in other regions and (2) those (local) industries which respond directly to local demand conditions, including both the final demand of local consumers and the intermediate demand of locally situated national or other local industries. Local dependence may arise either because buyers and sellers must be closely proximate, owing to high transport costs (in the case of purely local industries), or because transport costs make it efficient for local purchasers to purchase from local producers.

Trade, construction, services, and utilities are usually considered local industries, and would be classified under (2) above. Most manufacturing and mining industries are considered national, or at least multi-regional, industries, with market areas extending beyond the immediate localities in which production occurs. These would be classified under (1).[9] The important point, for our purposes, is that increases in demand for certain firms arise mainly within immediate regions, while for others, increases in demand anywhere in the nation can affect regional production. Similarly, increases in

[8] For a summary and critical evaluation of this concept see Walter Isard and Associates, *Methods of Regional Analysis: An Introduction to Regional Science* (Technology Press of MIT and Wiley, 1960), pp. 189-205.

[9] For a detailed breakdown of the New York Metropolitan Area on this basis, see Robert M. Lichtenberg, *One-Tenth of a Nation* (Harvard University Press, 1960), pp. 21-24, and Apps. B and G. The high non-local share of finance and service industries found in this study would not be expected for most other areas.

expenditures within regions may purchase goods produced either by national industries located within the region or elsewhere, or those produced by local industries. The magnitude of interregional spillover of demand will depend upon the extent of expenditures for goods produced by national industries not located within the region under consideration.

Location is important, secondly, with respect to national industries. Within an industry there tends to be a negative correlation between the flow of expenditures between two regions and their distance from each other.[10] For an industry with producing units located in several regions, any initial increases in demand by any purchasing units should result in increased sales by that sales unit located closest to the source of the increase in demand. This expectation would rise with an increase in the ratio of transport costs to the delivered price of the goods. Such an effect may not occur if there is full employment in nearby regions, but during recessions, when all plants would be likely to have some under-utilized capacity, the correlation between distance and expenditures should exist. The relationship between expenditures, distance, and cyclical conditions is usually described as the problem of the marginal supplier—that unit of production which is last in and first out as a seller within certain markets, and which benefits from demand increases in some regions only after plants nearer the source of demand have approached capacity levels of output. It is for this reason that some distinction must be made between selective industrial and selective regional policies.

Theories Used to Explain Regional Differences

The theories discussed here are used most often to explain regional differences in cyclical behavior. Sometimes they have been viewed as complementary, sometimes as substitutes for each other, and it is often difficult to determine the specific relationship intended among them. For this reason each theory will be discussed separately, and implications of each will first be explored in isolation.

[10] See Rutledge Vining, "Delimitation of Economic Areas: Statistical Conceptions in the Study of the Spatial Structure of an Economic System," *Journal of the American Statistical Association,* Vol. 48 (March 1953), pp. 44-64; and Isard and Associates, *op. cit.,* pp. 126-44.

INDUSTRIAL COMPOSITION. Regional differences in cyclical behavior are most commonly explained in terms of differences in industrial composition. This explanation is stated most succinctly by Walter Isard, although he disputes it:

> Differences in the intensity and timing of regional cycles are explained in terms of differences in the sensitivity and responsiveness of particular industries. Cycles of a regional economy are simple composites of the cyclical movement of the economy's industries, appropriately weighted.[11]

As Isard points out, this implies that regional breakdowns are not functional, since only industrial behavior is significant. Any regional differences are to be explained by a weighted average of the national behavior of the industries located in the regions, with the weights reflecting the importance of each industry in the region's industrial base.[12] Thus the existence of differences in unemployment among regions simply reflects differences in industries' unemployment. The necessary assumption is that for any one downturn (upturn) there are equal percentage declines (increases) within an industry in all regions in which it is located, so that the location of the employment declines (increases) in any one industry is independent of the location of the forces leading to the declines (increases) in demand for the output of that industry.

Wide acceptance of this hypothesis has led to a lack of concern with the regional distribution of unemployment. Since the hypothesis assumes that responses of particular industries to stabilization measures would be evenly diffused among the various locations of these industries, the location of the initial increase in demand need not be considered independently in the design of stabilization policy. All regions will benefit similarly, independent of the location of

[11] Walter Isard, "The Value of the Regional Approach in Economic Analysis," in National Bureau of Economic Research, Conference on Research in Income and Wealth, *Regional Income; Studies in Income and Wealth,* Vol. 21 (Princeton University Press, 1957), pp. 69-78.

[12] For a study of regional cycles in manufacturing employment which uses this method for computing hypothetical regional cyclical behavior, see Borts, in *Journal of the American Statistical Association,* pp. 151-211. Borts concludes that "differences are in part the result of differences in the types of manufacturing industry found in each state," but that "a change in the trend of growth alters the cyclical behavior of state industries relative to their national counterparts." *Ibid.,* p. 152.

the initial injection of expenditure changes, or of the changes in demand arising from tax changes or changes in monetary policy, insofar as these changes in demand occur in certain industries. It does not follow that aggregate policies suffice, for the appropriate disaggregation in this case is in terms of industrial sectors rather than regions. Policies which discriminate appropriately by industries will be sufficient to aid all regions. The policymaker need not discriminate regionally because the market will provide the proper regional distribution of employment changes.

Even if this hypothesis is accepted in its extreme form, the behavior of each region is a function of the industries which it contains, and regional responses would still differ for alternative stabilization measures. Since the policy alternatives may give rise to different mixes of output, the stabilization decision cannot be neutral in its effects upon regional employment. A concern with regional factors in formulating stabilization policy may still be necessary, but could, again, be implemented through industry measures. Since industries are centered regionally, these measures carry regional implications.[13]

While important, the industrial composition argument in its crudest form cannot be easily accepted, since it overlooks the locational factors discussed above. It assumes away the possibility of differences in the rates of decline in various regional locations in a given industry, as well as the distinction between national and local industries. Even if the hypothesis that national industries behave

[13] Thus proposals for excise tax variations to aid states producing consumer durable goods have been suggested as a contracyclical device. Similarly intended are proposals to reintroduce and vary consumer credit controls. Their efficiency from the regional point of view would depend upon the locational pattern of producing units as well as the price elasticities (or elasticities in response to changes in consumer credit terms) of demand for the products concerned. While possibly desirable from the aggregate national point of view, their regional impacts could be less than desirable. To the extent that production in affected industries is regionally concentrated these measures could provide for a more desirable pattern of employment changes as compared with an equivalent set of measures which are nonselective. However, an estimate of the specific magnitude of the effects would require more information concerning consumer spending habits in response to these changes. Selective industry measures applied to ubiquitous industries would not have this desired regional impact. For an interesting suggestion to make excise tax variation more effective from a regional standpoint, see Mordechai E. Kreinin, "Use of the Excise Tax as a Countercyclical Measure," *Review of Economics and Statistics,* Vol. 41 (August 1959), pp. 319-20.

similarly in each region in which they are located were tentatively accepted, there remains the fact that changes in employment in local industries are related to changes in the resident national industries. Therefore, changes in local industries over the nation as a whole are not relevant in estimating changes in local industries within any region. The behavior of these local industries in any one region is dependent upon the initial change in the resident national industries via the customary multiplier and input-output processes. Thus, the larger the change in demand in national industries, the more the actual regional change in local industries will exceed the amount predicted by using national averages.[14] Since national industries located within the same region will also be linked, the same understatement in using national averages will occur. The presence of unstable national industries in a region should modify the behavior of the usually more stable national industries.[15] Applying weighted averages in these cases causes an understatement of the employment change in those states with large initial changes in demand for the products of national industries, and an overstatement in those with smaller initial changes.

Even if we were to concentrate upon the behavior of the national industries, equiproportionate decline in all regions would be a doubtful hypothesis in its extreme form. Because of the marginal supplier relationship, the initial declines in demand would not be evenly spread among the regions. The initial incidence of a decline in demand would be more likely to fall more heavily upon some suppliers than upon others, rather than be evenly spread among all suppliers. When the possibility is considered that the initial declines in expenditures may themselves be nonuniformly distributed among regions, there is a greater probability of nonuniform declines in employment within an industry. Although the industry change may be

[14] In the case of "chronically depressed areas" the Bureau of Labor Statistics comments that "it is noteworthy . . . that even in chronically depressed areas at least a third of insured unemployment comes from [finance, services, and government]—not usually thought of as being directly subject to structural unemployment." U.S. Bureau of Labor Statistics, *The Structure of Unemployment in Areas of Substantial Labor Surplus,* Study Paper No. 23, Joint Economic Committee, 86 Cong. 2 sess. (1960), p. 25. With allowance for lags the same should be true in the cyclical case.

[15] It should be noted, however, that Borts (in *Journal of the American Statistical Association,* pp. 178-80) found this to be true in only three of the six cycles which he studied.

felt in all (or most) regions in which it is located, the magnitude of these declines should differ. For this reason, as well as the one discussed in the previous paragraph, regional cycles reflect more than simply industry cycles.

In the case of nonuniform industry declines among regions, the location of the initial expenditure increase in response to stabilization policy measures becomes more important. Since nationwide diffusion is not to be expected, pinpointed policies could be more effective in reducing unemployment than comparable policies applied on a nationwide scale. While the location of the initial expenditure increase is no doubt a consideration in discussing policy responses even when one accepts the weighted average hypothesis, different emphasis is placed here on the factors which would lead to disproportionate regional changes as opposed to nationwide diffusion. Also, to the extent that initial expenditures are made for purchases from local industries, nationwide measures may not be diffused, and the benefits in the areas of high unemployment will be reduced.

The data suggest a significant relationship between industrial composition and employment declines in the postwar period. Rank correlations between cyclical behavior of states and two indices of industrial composition—share of employment in national industries (manufacturing and mining), and in durable goods manufacturing industries—are shown in Table 5. Although the rank correlations between these measures of industrial structure and the rates of decline accord with expectations, the negative correlations between the same measures and rates of expansion do not.[16] While substantially confirming the importance of industrial structure in recessions, the states' behavior in expansions indicates that other considerations must be introduced.

[16] Since growth and industrial structure were negatively correlated in this period (a correlation of —0.39 between proportion of manufacturing and mining to total employment and growth, and —0.37 between the proportion of durables to total employment and growth), calculations were made using Kendall's Tau, which permits the calculation of partial rank correlation coefficients. The positive correlations between industrial structure and declines were slightly reduced, the positive correlations between amplitude and industrial structure were slightly increased, while the correlations between rates of expansion and industrial structure became slightly positive. The correlations between industrial structure and rates of decline are considerably greater than those between industrial structure and rates of expansion. See my dissertation, pp. 104-05.

TABLE 5. Rank Correlation Coefficients (Spearman's Rho) Between Two Indices of Industrial Composition and Cyclical Behavior in Two Cycles, 1949–54 and 1954–58[a]

	Manufacturing and Mining	*Durable Goods Manufacturing*
Rate of Expansion:		
1949–54	−0.03	−0.07
1954–58	−0.18	−0.12
Rate of Decline:		
1949–54	+0.56[b]	+0.46[b]
1954–58	+0.66[b]	+0.63[b]
Average Annual Amplitude:		
1949–54	+0.21	+0.14
1954–58	+0.23	+0.29

Source: Computed from Tables 3, 4, 9, and 10.

[a] The rates of expansion and decline and average annual amplitudes for total employment, manufacturing and mining employment, and durable goods manufacturing employment in the two cycles are:

	Rate of Expansion	*Rate of Decline*	*Average Annual Amplitude*
All Industries:			
1949–54	13.5%	2.6%	3.2%
1954–58	7.3	3.2	2.6
Manufacturing and Mining:			
1949–54	17.8	7.8	5.1
1954–58	4.7	8.1	3.2
Durable Goods Manufacturing:			
1949–54	29.3	10.9	8.0
1954–58	7.3	11.3	4.7

See Appendix A of my dissertation.

[b] Significant at the 1 percent level. For $N = 49$ the significance levels are: 5 percent, 0.28 and 1 percent, 0.37.

DIVERSIFICATION AND TRADE INVOLVEMENT. The theme of stability through diversification is one that permeates the popular literature on geographic aspects of unemployment. The presumption seems to be that by increasing the degree of diversification within a region its stability will be increased, since diversified regions will tend to have smaller cyclical swings. In the absence of reference to specific industries, it is difficult to state whether this argument is intended to be a substitute for or a complement to the previously stated industrial composition hypothesis. On the one hand, it may mean that the process of diversification alters the cyclical behavior of particular national industries in such a way that the behavior of normally unstable industries is modified when they are located within the same region. This interpretation implies that diversification brings about a different relationship among industries when located in the same region than when located separately, so that the expectations of regional differentials in employment changes would not be based upon the behavior of the component industries. It is this which must be intended when the diversification argument is stated without specific details about industrial composition.[17] On the other hand, there is the interpretation which draws an analogy between the diversification argument and the reduction of risk by diversification of portfolios, an analogy which has little merit since the necessary randomness of individual industry behavior cannot be assumed to exist.

What remains to be explained is just why diversification should change relationships among industries. An alternative approach would stress the desirability of introducing more stable national industries into regions which are characterized by large cyclical declines. The diversification argument then becomes the same as the industrial composition hypothesis, since addition of stable industries to the industrial base reduces the instability of a region, regardless of the degree of diversification. The advantage of this approach follows from the fact that the cyclical behavior of industries is not random, nor do the characteristics of the industries affected vary among cycles to any great extent. Thus, Edgar M. Hoover, a strong advocate of diversification for long-term development, states that "the character of products rather than the degree of diversification determines the impact of depression."[18] It would seem that the diversification hypothesis, as usually expressed, does not explain regional differentials, but merely rephrases the industrial composition hypothesis. In a discussion of cyclical stability an abstractly defined diversification is not a useful concept.

Nevertheless, diversification may enter into the explanation of

[17] For evidence bearing on this interpretation of diversification compare the statement of Leon Moses that "the East North Central region is probably as good an approximation to the balanced region which reality affords," with the rates of employment decline for the states in this region shown in Tables 3 and 4. See Leon N. Moses, "A General Equilibrium Model of Production, Interregional Trade, and Location of Industry," *Review of Economics and Statistics*, Vol. 42 (November 1960), pp. 373-97.

[18] Edgar M. Hoover, *The Location of Economic Activity* (McGraw-Hill, 1948), p. 287. For a similar conclusion see Irving Brecher and S. S. Reisman, *Canada-United States Economic Relations* (Royal Commission on Canada's Economic Prospects, Ottawa, 1957), pp. 69-71.

regional cyclical differentials in the following fashion. A high degree of diversification is likely to mean a relatively low marginal propensity to import. A highly diversified region would therefore find it more difficult to pass on internal declines in income to the outside via reduced imports. On the export side, depending upon the relative industrial composition of the region as contrasted with the rest of the nation, exports may or may not represent a large proportion of regional output. The larger the export share, and the greater the instability of the export industries, the more sensitive will a given region be to declining national demand; a low export share and lesser instability of those industries would mean less sensitivity. Thus diversification may lead either to greater or lesser stability, but a strong institutional factor would suggest the former alternative is more likely. Taking diversification in its usual meaning as the comparison of regional relative to national industrial structures, a diversified region (in the United States and other industrial nations) is likely to contain more industries which produce durable goods than is a nondiversified region. Since demand in these industries is cyclically unstable, and since diversification makes it difficult to export the decline in income which results from the decline in national demand, diversified regions (such as the East North Central region), with variable exports and a low marginal propensity to import, will experience greater fluctuations in employment than will a nondiversified region. Thus, the differential created by "industrial composition" factors is accentuated by the low import propensity of such a region. In this case diversification will increase the need for regionally-oriented policies.

Diversification also has an important bearing on the efficiency of a regionally-oriented stabilization policy. The more diversified a region (in that it produces a larger assortment of goods to meet its final and intermediate demands), the greater will be the effects of any increase in expenditures within the region upon internal income. Given the probable relationship between diversification and the marginal propensity to import noted in the preceding paragraph, the spillover from a diversified region will be less than the spillover from a region which specializes in a narrow range of goods. Put differently, since high diversification implies a low marginal propensity to import, the more diversified a region, the more effective expenditures made within the region will be in changing that region's level of employment. Diversification within a region not only renders regionally-oriented stabilization policy more necessary, but also tends to make it more effective.

GROWTH DIFFERENCES. An hypothesis usually intended to supplement the industrial composition hypothesis relates differences in cyclical stability to differences in growth rates. Under this theory larger declines (and smaller expansions) than expected will occur in retarding regions, while rapidly growing regions will experience smaller declines (and larger expansions) than predicted on the basis of industrial composition. Two alternative explanations are given for these expectations; one stresses supply and cost factors and the other demand aspects. The implications of these alternative explanations differ; they postulate different relationships about comparative regional cyclical behavior depending upon the magnitude of the national cycle.

The former explanation is based upon the presumption that the industrial movements which occur when regions are growing rapidly lead to the location of more efficient, lower-cost firms in the expanding regions. These firms, having lower average costs, will be better able to stay in business when prices decline. Thus, in times of falling demand their declines in production would be less than for higher-cost firms located in the regions with slower rates of growth.[19] The same result would follow if the decline in demand did not depress prices, since the lower-cost firms would be better able to absorb transport costs in recession, and thus would increase their market shares. Within an industry, then, firms located in expanding regions would suffer less than would firms in retarding regions which are the marginal suppliers. But larger expansions in retarding regions during periods of expansion would not be certain, since the more rapidly growing regions would be adding new capacity, hence their rate of expansion would not be limited by the preceding rate of decline.

The second explanation emphasizes the importance of population movements into growing regions as a source of demand for investment in housing, utilities, and other forms of social overhead capital, and/or the importance of investors' expectations of further

[19] For a statement of this hypothesis, with the implication that these firms will have greater expansions than firms in more rapidly growing regions, see Borts, in *Journal of the American Statistical Association,* pp. 181-82.

expansion in the future, thus placing a floor under possible declines in investment. In retarding regions, by contrast, neither of these exogenous demand factors is present and differences in the initial declines in demand among regions will cause intra-industry differences in employment changes among regions. The higher floor under investment demand in rapidly growing regions means that declines in demand for firms in those regions will be less than the declines of firms in regions growing more slowly.[20] It should be noted, however, that in large national declines this floor may not exist, and the previously more rapid expansion may lead to larger declines in growing regions. Unlike the explanation based upon cost differences, which would imply interregional differentials in the same direction regardless of the national cyclical amplitude, the explanation based upon the differential behavior of investment would imply larger declines in growing areas in large downturns and smaller declines when the national downturn is not substantial. That is, when the cyclical downturns do not lead to reductions in longer-term investment, areas growing more slowly will suffer from larger downturns because they lack the stabilizing factors of residential and other population-oriented expenditures and the more favorable long-term expectations associated with areas of rapid growth.

Table 6 shows that these expectations were borne out in the postwar period, when national declines were not substantial.

In both cycles there was a positive correlation between growth and rates of expansion and a negative correlation between growth and rates of declines.

The existence of regional differences in unemployment based upon differential growth rates points to a possible conflict between growth and stabilization criteria in the application of public policy. When rapidly growing regions experience the larger cyclical declines, both the stabilization of employment and the growth criteria

[20] Examination of annual changes in manufacturing plant and equipment investment, and construction contracts awarded for all types of construction, public and private, do not accord with these expectations. However, nonfarm dwelling starts had a higher rate of increase in states with smaller employment declines in both recessions studied, with a sharper rate of decline when starts turned down; see my dissertation, pp. 116-20. Thus the data on the relationship between growth and the recession behavior of investment appear inconclusive.

TABLE 6. Rank Correlation Coefficients (Spearman's Rho) Between Growth and Cyclical Behavior in Two Cycles, 1949–54 and 1954–58[a]

	1949–54	*1954–58*
Growth and:		
Rate of Expansion	+0.71[b]	+0.78[b]
Rate of Decline	−0.63[b]	−0.51[b]
Average Annual Amplitudes	+0.16	+0.32

Source: Computed from Tables 3, 4, and 8.

[a] The measure of growth used here—the relationship between cycle bases—is actually a measure of acceleration and retardation. This does not affect the conclusions since the rank correlation between growth measured in this manner and the peak-to-peak growth rates is +0.95.

[b] Significant at the 1 percent level. For $N=49$ the significance levels are: 5 percent, 0.28 and 1 percent, 0.37

are applicable to the same regions. But when declines are sharper in retarding regions, regionally-oriented policies may be necessary, since these regions may be less responsive to general monetary and tax measures than growing regions.

Similar considerations apply to the longer-run aspects of growth policy. To the extent that industrial relocation continues, the relative decline in the export base of regions growing comparatively slowly continues as well. Industry-oriented measures, therefore, may not be efficient in aiding these regions, and regionally discriminatory policies (for example, in the form of grants to state and local governments for necessary public works) may become most necessary at the very time when they are most in conflict with longer-run goals of regional adjustment. While a properly designed expenditure or transfer program may aid in spurring growth in these lagging regions, regional discrimination would also be needed to avoid the inflationary pressures of an increase in national aggregate demand large enough to accomplish the same result.

Conclusions

Cyclical fluctuations in the United States during the postwar years have been nationwide, with small differences in turning points between regions (here defined as states), but the magnitude of the movements within these fluctuations has differed considerably among regions. The foregoing discussion suggests three major conclusions about the causes of regional differentials in cyclical behavior, and the appropriateness of regionally-oriented stabilization policy.

1. The industrial composition hypothesis, in its pure form, holds that regional variations merely reflect the different weights of various industries in the industrial structure of the region. It is assumed that variations for any one industry are the same in all its locations, and specific regional forces are excluded. If correct, this would imply that regional objectives of stabilization policy can be disregarded or need be approached via industry-oriented measures. But this is not an adequate explanation. It is necessary also to consider the complications created by the difference between national and local industries, and the importance of transportation costs which affect the pattern of demand for goods produced by the national industries. These considerations introduce an explicit regional factor into the explanation of cyclical differentials, and call for concern with regional factors in the determination and evaluation of stabilization policy.

2. Diversification was found to be a relevant explanation of regional differentials only to the extent that it represents a modified form of the industrial composition hypothesis, and to the extent that a resulting low marginal propensity to import reduces the region's ability to offset cyclical fluctuations in the national demand for durable goods. This relation between diversification and propensity to import will also prove a crucial factor in determining the effectiveness of regionally-oriented policies.

3. Growth differentials were found to play an important role in accounting for differences in regional cyclical behavior, and it was suggested that specific fiscal policy measures tied to regions may be more efficient than general or industry-based policies in securing stabilization. Similarly, it was found that regionally-oriented policies may be necessary to accelerate long-term growth.

It appears that regional cyclical differentials are of considerable importance, and that they are caused to a significant degree by specifically regional (as distinct from purely industrial composition) factors. This suggests that regionally-oriented stabilization policies would be desirable if feasible. This feasibility in turn depends on the extent (absence) of interregional spillover of income creating effects. It will therefore be useful to examine a simple model of interregional trade to see what it reveals about the probable results of certain policies, and about the resultant distributions of income changes among regions.

Comparative Statics of Alternative Fiscal Programs

In this section a simple model of interregional trade will be used to compare the regional effectiveness of several fiscal programs based upon various policy targets. For purposes of expositional simplicity, the analysis assumes only two regions, but the nature of the conclusions drawn would not be changed by the introduction of more regions.

Alternative Regionally-Oriented Targets

Alternative stabilization targets may differ in the relative importance which is attached to the regional pattern of employment increases. If a policy preference for differential employment increases in different regions is introduced, interregional spillover of expenditure changes becomes a crucial consideration in the selection of appropriate policies. Spillovers may be helpful or harmful in simultaneously achieving desired targets, but in no case can they be overlooked by the policymaker.[21]

[21] The discussion that follows is in terms of targets for two regions, with the national change in employment not explicitly introduced as a policy goal. It has been suggested that a more realistic approach to this problem would be to have a preference function which includes the national unemployment rate as well as the unemployment rates in each of the regions. The policymaker would then be "trading-off" between a specific national rate and its distribution between the regions. It is possible that a higher national rate of unemployment with a more desirable distribution would be preferred to a lower national rate with a less desirable regional distribution, as in the third case of Target III-d.

In the simplest case of two regions with equal labor forces, these alternative targets can be written as:

I. $\Delta E_a + \Delta E_b$

II. ΔE_a

III. $\Delta E_a + \Delta E_b$, where $\dfrac{\Delta E_b}{\Delta E_a} = \alpha$

and a. $\alpha = 1$

b. $0 < \alpha < 1$

c. $\alpha = 0$

d. $\alpha < 0$.

ΔE is the absolute increase in employment and the subscripts a and b refer to the two regions. With labor forces of equal size, the ratio of the absolute increases in employment also indicates the ratio of the change in employment rates in the two regions.

Target I, a maximum increase in national employment, is implicit in most discussions of stabilization policy. The regional distribution of employment increases is a matter of indifference to the policymaker, since increased employment anywhere in the nation is equally desirable. This target would be most appropriate when neither region is at a "distress" level but when the national unemployment rate is high. Under such conditions there would be no great social urgency to reduce unemployment in one particular region. Moreover, increases in demand would lead to increases in employment in either region, without posing a price-stability problem. The policymaker could then afford to be indifferent to the location of employment changes—at least in the context of economic efficiency.

Target II, increased employment in one region, would be more relevant to a discussion of targets for each region treated in isolation. It is, of course, the target of any one nation in the world economy or, for that matter, the target of stabilization attempts by state or local governments. The focus of the policymaker is upon increasing employment in only one region, without concern for the effects of spillover into other regions. A policymaker concerned with the employment effects in two regions could hardly adopt this target since he could not be indifferent to the effects upon employment and prices in the other region.

The sub-targets listed under Target III would be the alternative aims of regionally-oriented stabilization policy. In each case the regional distribution of employment changes would be a key factor in the designing of the policy measures to be used to achieve these goals. Whereas Target I was specified only in terms of the national rate of unemployment, the national average would not be as important a concern under Target III as the rates in the component regions of the nation. Target III-a would call for an equal increase in employment in both regions, a policy which would be appropriate if the two regions were equally above their bottleneck rates of unemployment and both were below (or similar with regard to) their "distress" rate. Target III-a might also represent a politically necessary solution, given the feelings which could develop over a conscious policy of regional discrimination. Target III-b would be the most probable object of a regionally-oriented stabilization policy in recession periods. Employment increases in both regions would be desirable, but a greater increase in one than in the other region would be intended. This target would become more appropriate the closer the economy approached "full" employment, and the more uneven unemployment was distributed, assuming both regions were still above their bottleneck rates of unemployment.

Targets III-c and III-d would represent possible aims of a government faced with the unemployment-inflation dilemma. Increasing employment in one region would be achieved either (III-c) without changed employment in the other or (III-d) with decreases in employment in the other region. Target III-d has three possible aspects: if $|\alpha| < 1$, national unemployment would be reduced; if $|\alpha| = 1$, national unemployment would be unchanged, but redistributed between the regions; or if $|\alpha| > 1$, the national unemployment rate would be increased and its burden shifted between the regions.

Target III-c would be appropriate, in the cyclical setting, when there are significant differences in the regional unemployment rates; these would occur if the timing of regional cyclical turning points differed. As shown in the state data in the first section, above, this does not often occur. Yet during the 1956 employment decline in Michigan, which was attributable mostly to the decline in the demand for automobiles and to shifts in the placement of defense contracts, this target was a policy consideration. At that time, because of the concentrated regional pattern of production for automobiles, there was some discussion of the possible usefulness of excise tax reduction. This policy was considered unfeasible, however, because of fear of increasing the inflationary pressures in the rest of the economy. In the secular context, Target III-c is an approximation of the goal of special "depressed areas" legislation in times of cyclical expansion. By use of pinpointed construction projects, policymakers hope to maximize the increase in employment in these areas per dollar of government expenditure, while minimizing the effects upon the rest of the economy.

The discussion in the preceding paragraphs has obvious implications for the problem of stabilization policy in a common market with common fiscal and monetary policies. A country which is free to undertake its own independent policies would probably pursue Target II, aiming for domestic full employment (subject to a balance-of-payments constraint), with little concern for resultant internal effects in other nations. A common policy, however, would have to allow for external effects arising from attempts to stabilize each member, so that each member country would have to be satisfied with a less ambitious employment target. Thus, although for the common market as a whole policy might be more efficient, each member would not necessarily be better off in terms of unemployment than if left free to pursue its own policy. A similar problem is faced by each state in the United States when it proclaims its view in national policy formulation. It may then be that a more nearly equal distribution of unemployment within the nation cannot be achieved without policies designed to encourage migration to comparatively fully employed regions.

Application to Model

In the following analysis, one particular region is posed against another which represents the rest of the nation. The relative size of each region is important since it would be a determinant of the regional marginal propensities to import. That is, the smaller the region the larger would be its marginal propensity to import from another region, and the smaller would be the second region's marginal propensity to import from the region in question.

The trade model for this analysis is a standard Keynesian one:

$$
\begin{aligned}
&(1) \quad Y_a = C_a + I_a + G_a + X_a - M_a \\
&(2) \quad Y_b = C_b + I_b + G_b + X_b - M_b \\
&(3) \quad C_a = c_a Y_a \\
&(4) \quad C_b = c_b Y_b \\
&(5) \quad M_a = X_b = m_a(C_a + I_a + G_a + X_a) \\
&(6) \quad M_b = X_a = m_b(C_b + I_b + G_b + X_b),
\end{aligned}
$$

in which I and G are exogenous. Y is income, C consumption, I investment, G government expenditures on goods and services, X exports, and M imports. The marginal (= average) propensity to consume is c, and the marginal (= average) import content of expenditures (here assumed to be equal for all expenditure categories) is m. The subscripts a and b refer to the two regions. No balance of payments constraint exists, since surplus regions will be willing to hold the balances of deficit regions.[22]

[22] For illustrative purposes estimates of the upper limit to the marginal propensity to import out of consumption and other expenditures have been derived. These hypothetical computations refer to a region in which there are only individuals who provide labor services in retail stores or in the service industries. If we assume all consumer expenditures to be made within the region, the estimated income generated locally would be equal to the labor income plus the profits received by the providers of services and the owners of retail establishments. This minimum local share for services is 50.5 percent of expenditures (27.8 percent for labor and 22.7 percent for profits), and for retail purchases it is 14.7 percent (10.8 percent for labor and 3.9 percent for profits). These represent pre-tax income. The service estimates are from U.S. Bureau of the Census, *Census of Business: 1958,* Vol. VI, Part I: *Selected Services, Area Statistics, U.S. Summary and Alabama-Mississippi* (1961), pp. 1-5; and U.S. Internal Revenue Service, *Statistics of Income 1958-1959: U.S. Business Tax Returns* (1961), pp. 21, 35, 44. The retail estimates are taken from U.S. Bureau of the Census, Vol. II, Part I: *Retail Trade; Area Statistics, U.S. Summary and Alabama-Mississippi,* pp. 1-5; and U.S. Internal Revenue Service, *ibid.,* pp. 20, 34, 44. The ratio of expenditures on these two categories will depend upon the relative distribution of consumer expenditures between goods and services. The average pattern for 1958 was 61 percent for goods and 39 percent for services, a pattern in which services are slightly above their decade average. See *Economic Report of the President: January 1960,* p. 164. For this pattern the estimated local share is 28.7 percent of expenditures. For the marginal pattern estimated by Daniel B. Suits (in "Forecast-

In applying the model to the above targets, three comparisons would be of interest to the policymaker. Letting dY be the change in income, and dG the change in the government budget, with the subscripts a and b again referring to the regions, these comparisons are:[23]

$$(1)\ \frac{\frac{dY_a + dY_b}{dG_a}}{\frac{dY_a + dY_b}{dG_b}} \qquad (2)\ \frac{\frac{dY_a}{dG_a}}{\frac{dY_a}{dG_b}} \quad \text{and} \quad (3)\ \frac{\frac{dY_a}{G_a}}{\frac{dY_b}{dG_a}}.$$

The first comparison is between the effect on national income of an initial increase in expenditures (due to increased expenditures by the government or those induced by tax changes) in region a with the effect of an increase in b. The assumption, consistent with Target I above, is that the policymaker is interested only in the total increase in national income and not in its regional distribution. Regional differences in parameters are relevant only to the extent that they cause differential increases in total national income. If ratio (1) exceeds 1, the larger increase in national income will occur if expenditures are concentrated in region a. The opposite will occur if ratio (1) is less than 1. If the ratio is equal to 1, policy can be

ing and Analysis with an Econometric Model," *American Economic Review,* Vol. 52 [March 1962], pp. 104-32), in which the distribution is 86 percent on goods and 14 percent on services, the minimum estimate for the local share is 19.7 percent of expenditures. To the extent that any goods are produced within the region, and that retail and services units have intermediate demands from each other, this ratio would, of course, be higher. The estimates for investment and government expenditures will depend upon the specific expenditure pattern discussed. Estimated on-site wage income for various construction projects ranges from 27 percent of expenditures for multi-family residential dwellings to 58 percent of expenditures for highway maintenance. See Alan M. Strout, "Primary Employment Effects of Alternative Spendings Programs," *Review of Economics and Statistics,* Vol. 40 (November 1958), pp. 319-28, for estimates based on the Bureau of Labor Statistics data prepared for the 1947 Input-Output Table. While the actual regional marginal propensity to import will be a weighted average of all expenditures, for simplicity it will be assumed that it will be the same for all expenditures in these multiplier comparisons.

[23] For simplicity it is assumed that the relationship between income changes and employment changes is the same in both regions, and that a fixed relationship exists between income changes and employment changes.

indifferent (with regard to effects on national income) to the region in which expenditures are made.

The second comparison, consistent with Target II above, is directed at achieving an increase in income in region *a,* with no concern for effects upon the other region. The policymaker here must choose the region in which the expenditure change is to be made to achieve this target. If ratio (2) is greater than 1, income in *a* will be increased most by an expenditure made in region *a.* A ratio of less than 1 would mean that it would be more efficient to increase expenditures in *b*. If the ratio were equal to 1, the same increase in *a*'s income would occur regardless of where the expenditure was made, and the choice could be based upon other criteria, such as the effects upon income in region *b*. In this comparison, unlike the first, the region is important both in specifying the target and in determining the means by which the target is to be pursued.

The third comparison, which is important in determining the feasibility of the targets listed above under III, gives a measure of the spillover from an expenditure made in region *a.* The higher ratio (3), the smaller would be the spillover of income increases into region *b*. A ratio greater than 1 means that over 50 percent of the income increase has occurred in region *a,* and a ratio of 1 that the income increase is evenly divided between the two regions. Ratio (3) and the corresponding ratio for expenditures in *b,* is of particular interest, since it will determine the possibility of the achievement of a target specifying changes in both regions. If all stabilizing expenditures are to be incremental and the existing budget cannot be changed, the policy problem involves the solution of the following pair of simultaneous equations for dG_a and dG_b:

$$\frac{dY_a}{dG_a} dG_a + \frac{dY_a}{dG_b} dG_b = dY_a$$

$$\frac{dY_b}{dG_a} dG_a + \frac{dY_b}{dG_b} dG_b = dY_b,$$

subject to both dG_a and dG_b being greater than, or equal to, zero. In accord with the previous discussion of regional targets, the policymaker is looking for that combination of dG_a and dG_b which meets the goal $dY_b = \alpha dY_a$ where the desired income increases are in a fixed ratio. For any value of α this target can be achieved only if:

$$\frac{\frac{dY_b}{dG_a}}{\frac{dY_a}{dG_a}} \leq \alpha \leq \frac{\frac{dY_b}{dG_b}}{\frac{dY_a}{dG_b}}.$$

If α is equal to either ratio all expenditures will occur in one region. If α falls within the range given by the two ratios, the target can be achieved by some combination of expenditures in both regions, while if α is outside the range, the target cannot be achieved. In that case either the target must be amended, or greater flexibility in the use of budgetary means must be introduced. These may involve either a shift in expenditures between regions—a shift which still allows higher incomes in both regions than existed in an initial unemployment situation, or, possibly, some combination of taxes and expenditures which could make consistent the achievement of the two targets.[24]

In solving our model for these ratios, a distinction is drawn between expenditure programs involving imports and programs where the initial outlay is on local products only.

Expenditure Programs Involving Imports

THE FIRST RATIO. The first ratio is:

$$\frac{\frac{dY}{dG_a}}{\frac{dY}{dG_b}} = \frac{(1 - m_a)[1 - c_b(1 - m_b)] + m_a(1 - m_b)}{(1 - m_b)[1 - c_a(1 - m_a)] + m_b(1 - m_a)}.$$

The ratio will differ from 1 only if there is a difference in the two regional marginal propensities to consume. If the marginal pro-

[24] This last point would be an argument for the efficiency of equal changes in taxes and expenditures, since taxes would be collected in both regions, while the expenditures are made in only one. Thus a nationally balanced budget increase may not only be expansionary, but could have the effect of shifting income among regions and permitting different income changes in the two regions. While this point is frequently discussed in the context of the redistributional effects of the federal budget, the stabilization potential when there are differences in regional conditions should also be noted.

pensities to consume are the same in both regions, the increase in national income will be the same regardless of where the initial expenditure is made. If they differ, the increase in national income will be highest if it is made in the region with the higher marginal propensity to consume. In these cases the value of the ratio will be affected by the size of the regional marginal propensities to import. Excluding the possibility of the import propensity in each region being equal to or greater than 1, the extreme values of the ratio will occur when neither region has imports from the other. The greater the regional marginal propensities to import, the smaller will be the effect of differences in regional consumption propensities (the closer the ratio to 1).

This, of course, is the basis of the argument that (in the absence of differences in marginal propensities to consume) government expenditures in areas of labor surplus do not have a different effect upon national income than do expenditures in areas of high employment, since (given this condition) there are no differential effects upon aggregate demand. If there is no presumption that marginal consumption propensities differ with levels of unemployment, and assuming a model with constant wages and prices, the regional pattern of expenditures is a matter of indifference to the policymaker concerned only with effects upon national income and total employment. Once price and wage flexibility in an upward direction is allowed for, however, these conclusions may need to be modified to allow for the effects of differences in the levels of unemployment upon changes in prices as opposed to changes in employment.

THE SECOND RATIO. The second ratio is:

$$\frac{\frac{dY_a}{dG_a}}{\frac{dY_a}{dG_b}} = \frac{1 - c_b(1 - m_b)}{m_b}.$$

In order to increase income in *a*, an expenditure made in *a* is more efficient than an equal expenditure made in *b* if $(1 - c_b)(1 - m_b) > 0$. This condition is met unless either c_b or m_b, but not both, is greater than 1. The efficiency of an expenditure in *a* increases as c_b and m_b are smaller. If c_b is greater than 1, the two regional marginal propensities to consume cannot be equal, or the system will be unstable.[25] If c_b and m_b are less than 1, a given desired increase in Y_a can be most cheaply achieved if expenditures are made directly in *a*. It is to be noted that the relative efficiencies of the policies do not depend upon any of the parameters in *a*.

In order to obtain some idea of the sensitivity of this ratio to changes in the parameters, c_b and m_b, the ratio of

$$\frac{\dfrac{dY_a}{dG_a}}{\dfrac{dY_a}{dG_b}}$$

was computed for several hypothetical values:[26]

$m_b =$	$c_b = .7$	$c_b = .5$
0	∞	∞
.2	2.20	3.00
.4	1.45	1.75
.6	1.20	1.33
.8	1.08	1.13

In a region having a small amount of induced exports in response to expenditure changes in other regions, it would be necessary to increase expenditures. Even as the level of induced exports rises it remains more efficient to increase expenditures within that region, unless the induced exports exceed the initial expenditure.

[25] See Thomas C. Schelling, *National Income Behavior* (McGraw-Hill, 1951), p. 202. This holds for both marginal propensities to import less than 1.

[26] A marginal propensity to consume of .7 represents an approximation to the marginal propensity to consume found by Suits. See Suits, in *American Economic Review,* pp. 104-32. The marginal propensity of .5 is introduced for purposes of comparison.

THE THIRD RATIO. The "spillover ratio" is given by:

$$\frac{\frac{dY_a}{dG_a}}{\frac{dY_b}{dG_a}} = \frac{(1 - m_a)[1 - c_b(1 - m_b)]}{(m_a)(1 - m_b)}.$$

This ratio will be higher (the spillover will be less) as m_a and c_b are smaller and as m_b is larger. The ratio is independent of the marginal propensity to consume in *a*.

In order to see how this ratio varies with the different values of m_a, m_b, and c_b calculations were made using several combinations of values for these parameters:

	$c_b = .7$						$c_b = .5$				
	$m_a =$						$m_a =$				
	0	.2	.4	.6	.8		0	.2	.4	.6	.8
$m_b =$						$m_b =$					
0	∞	1.20	.45	.20	.08	0	∞	2.00	.75	.33	.13
.2	∞	2.20	.83	.37	.14	.2	∞	3.00	1.13	.50	.19
.4	∞	3.87	1.45	.65	.24	.4	∞	4.67	1.75	.78	.29
.6	∞	7.20	2.70	1.20	.45	.6	∞	8.00	3.00	1.33	.50
.8	∞	17.20	6.45	2.87	1.08	.8	∞	18.00	6.75	3.00	1.12

It is to be noted that as the openness of both economies increases, the interregional spillover becomes larger, and the restriction placed upon the pursuit of differential regional policies becomes greater. Even if both regions have equal marginal propensities to import, the higher these propensities, the less feasible differential regional policies become.

A related calculation which is of interest is the estimation of the value of region *a*'s propensity to import, which—given the other parameters—is consistent with any distribution of the income increase among regions. If, for example, the target is distribution of income equally between the regions for an expenditure made in *a*, then m_a must equal

$$\frac{1 - c_b(1 - m_b)}{2 - c_b(1 - m_b) - m_b}.$$

Using the hypothetical values of c_b and m_b, for the various combinations, m_a must equal the following:

	$c_b = .7$	$c_b = .5$
$m_b =$		
0	.23	.33
.2	.36	.43
.4	.49	.54
.6	.64	.67
.8	.81	.82

For values of m_a less than those shown, over 50 percent of the income increase will be in *a*. As is obvious, the more a region's induced exports, the greater can be its marginal propensity to import consistent with achieving a given share of the income increase.

Expenditure Programs Not Involving Imports

In order to examine the maximum possible efficiency of government expenditures in meeting regional targets, similar comparisons can be made for a different set of government expenditure programs. In the previous comparisons the marginal propensity to import from government expenditures was the same as the import propensity from all other expenditures. As one limiting case, we can analyze an expenditure program so designed that all of the initial expenditure will give rise to income only in the region in which expenditures are made, and where imports will occur only in the second round via induced consumption. Such a program could involve either creation of employment through government hiring of additional labor, or expenditures specifically designed to utilize only locally produced goods and services. While these cases are hypothetical, they permit a comparison with policies in which the import share of the government expenditures does not differ from that of the private consumption sector.

THE FIRST RATIO. The first ratio is now:

$$\frac{\dfrac{dY}{dG_a}}{\dfrac{dY}{dG_b}} = \frac{1 - c_b(1 - m_b) - m_a m_b + (1 - m_b)m_a c_a}{1 - c_a(1 - m_a) - m_a m_b + (1 - m_a)m_b c_b}.$$

This ratio will again differ from 1 only if the marginal propensities to consume in the two regions differ. If $c_a = c_b$ the effect on national income of an expenditure increase in either region would be the same; otherwise the effect would be greatest if the expenditure were made in the region with the larger propensity to consume. In the case of equal consumption propensities, the increases in national income from these "local-intensive" expenditures will be the same as in the previous case. If they differ, there will be a greater increase in national income from an expenditure in the region with the higher propensity to consume.

THE SECOND RATIO. The second ratio is now:

$$\frac{\frac{dY_a}{dG_a}}{\frac{dY_a}{dG_b}} = \frac{1 - c_b(1 - m_b) - m_a m_b}{(1 - m_a)m_b c_b} .$$

Unlike the ratio in the case of an expenditure involving imports, this ratio now depends upon the marginal import content of expenditures in *a*, although not upon its propensity to consume. This ratio will be higher the lower are m_b and c_b and the higher is m_a. It will be greater than 1 if $(1 - c_b)(1 - m_a m_b) > 0$. If m_b and c_b are less than 1 the income increase in *a* from an expenditure in *a* is larger, and the income increase in *a* from an expenditure in *b* is smaller, than in the previous case. Thus the "local-intensive" expenditures make it more desirable that expenditures be increased in the region where the income increase is needed. This can be seen by comparing the values of this ratio for hypothetical values of c_b, m_b, and m_a, shown below, with those for government expenditures involving imports:

	$c_b = .7$					$c_b = .5$				
	$m_a =$					$m_a =$				
$m_b =$	0	.2	.4	.6	.8	0	.2	.4	.6	.8
0	∞	∞	∞	∞	∞	∞	∞	∞	∞	∞
.2	3.14	3.57	4.29	5.71	10.00	6.00	7.00	8.67	12.00	22.00
.4	2.07	2.23	2.50	3.04	4.64	3.50	3.88	4.50	5.75	9.50
.6	1.71	1.79	1.90	2.14	2.86	2.67	2.83	3.11	3.67	5.33
.8	1.54	1.56	1.61	1.70	1.96	2.25	2.31	2.42	2.63	3.25

THE THIRD RATIO. The third ratio is now:

$$\frac{\frac{dY_a}{dG_a}}{\frac{dY_b}{dG_a}} = \frac{1 - c_b(1 - m_b) - m_a m_b}{(1 - m_b)m_a c_a}.$$

Unlike the previous cases, the comparison now depends upon the marginal propensities to consume in both regions, as well as upon their marginal propensities to import out of expenditures. The ratio will be higher (the spillover less) the smaller are m_a, c_a and c_b, and the larger is m_b. If m_b and c_b are less than 1, the spillover will be less than from the government expenditure involving imports. As shown by the values of this ratio for hypothetical values of c_a, c_b, m_a, and m_b, the introduction of a "local-intensive" policy widens the range in which the achievement of desired employment changes in both regions can be attained:

$c_a = .7, c_b = .7$					
	$m_a =$				
$m_b =$	0	.2	.4	.6	.8
0	∞	2.14	1.07	.71	.54
.2	∞	3.57	1.61	.95	.63
.4	∞	5.95	2.50	1.35	.77
.6	∞	10.71	4.29	2.14	1.07
.8	∞	25.00	9.64	4.52	1.96

$c_a = .5, c_b = .7$					
	$m_a =$				
$m_b =$	0	.2	.4	.6	.8
0	∞	3.00	1.50	1.00	.75
.2	∞	5.00	2.25	1.33	.88
.4	∞	8.33	3.50	1.89	1.08
.6	∞	15.00	6.00	3.00	1.50
.8	∞	35.00	13.50	6.33	2.75

$c_a = .7, c_b = .5$					
	$m_a =$				
$m_b =$	0	.2	.4	.6	.8
0	∞	3.57	1.79	1.19	.89
.2	∞	5.00	2.32	1.43	.98
.4	∞	7.38	3.21	1.83	1.13
.6	∞	12.14	5.00	2.62	1.43
.8	∞	26.43	10.36	5.00	2.32

$c_a = .5, c_b = .5$					
	$m_a =$				
$m_b =$	0	.2	.4	.6	.8
0	∞	5.00	2.50	1.67	1.25
.2	∞	7.00	3.25	2.00	1.38
.4	∞	10.33	4.50	2.56	1.58
.6	∞	17.00	7.00	3.67	2.00
.8	∞	37.00	14.50	7.00	3.25

Such policies will also have the effect of raising the level of the marginal propensity to import in a region, consistent with any distribution of income increases among regions. For an equal distribution, m_a must equal $\frac{1 - c_b(1 - m_b)}{c_a(1 - m_b) + m_b}$. This value of m_a, for hypothetical values of m_b, c_a, and c_b, is shown below:

	$c_b = .7$, $c_a = .7$	$c_b = .7$, $c_a = .5$	$c_b = .5$, $c_a = .7$	$c_b = .5$, $c_a = .5$
$m_b =$				
0	.429	.600	.714	1.000
.2	.579	.733	.789	1.000
.4	.707	.829	.854	1.000
.6	.818	.900	.909	1.000
.8	.915	.956	.957	1.000

It is interesting to note that these magnitudes of m_a makes it probable, for all but the smallest regions, that more than 50 percent of the national income increase from any "local-intensive" expenditure program will occur within the region in which the expenditure is made.

Tax and Transfer Programs

Similar comparisons for regional changes in taxes and transfers will depend upon the parameters previously discussed in the comparisons for government expenditures. While regional tax policies are generally considered difficult to administer and unacceptable on constitutional grounds, such comparisons are still significant, especially since programs may take the more feasible form of differential transfer payments.[27] The specific manner in which such taxes (or transfers, considered as negative taxes) are treated within the model will affect the nature of the comparisons. In the simplest case, that of lump-sum tax changes, the ratios will be similar to those discussed in the case of government expenditures involving imports, except for the introduction of additional terms representing the marginal propensities to consume of the two regions. These propen-

[27] For suggestions concerning regionally differentiated unemployment compensation benefits, see John Kenneth Galbraith, *The Affluent Society* (Houghton Mifflin, 1958), p. 301; and Senate Special Committee on Unemployment Problems, *Report of the Special Committee on Unemployment Problems,* 86 Cong. 2 sess. (1960), pp. 170-71—the report of the Republican minority.

sities, multiplied by the changes in taxes, will produce the initial expenditure arising from tax changes. The remainder of the terms compared will be the same as in the previous cases. If the marginal propensities to consume are the same in both regions, all three ratios will be the same as above.[28] If marginal propensities to consume differ, the first two ratios will be those shown multiplied by a factor (c_a/c_b). The effects of differences in the parameters will increase, as compared with effects in the expenditure cases.

If tax changes are introduced via variations in tax rates rather than lump sum taxes, then all ratios will depend not only upon the regional parameters, but also upon the income levels in the two regions. For equal incomes, the ratios will be determined by the parameters, as discussed in the preceding paragraph. If incomes are unequal, equal tax rate changes in either region would not provide a valid comparison since they would result in different absolute changes in the government budget. The first two ratios will thus vary with differences in regional income levels. Since the more realistic case entails nationwide tax changes, it suggests that the regional distribution of income changes may be harder to control through tax measures than through government expenditures.

The Fiscal Responses of Lower-Level Governments

An additional factor which will be important is the effect of federal policies upon the revenues and expenditures of the lower levels of government. To the extent that these governments pursue a balanced budget policy, increased income in response to federal policies will, at constant tax rates, permit an increase in their expenditures. As long as the marginal propensities to consume in the private sector are less than 1, these expenditures would provide an additional supporting effect on changes in national income resulting from federal stabilization policies.[29] For equal marginal propensities to consume, the gain in national income would then be higher if expenditures were made in the region with the higher tax and expenditure patterns.

If the import content of public (sub-federal) expenditures is the

[28] If the marginal propensities to consume are less than 1, while the ratios are the same, the absolute amounts of the income changes will be less than in the expenditure cases.

[29] See Harold M. Somers, "The Multiplier in a Trifiscal Economy," *Quarterly Journal of Economics,* Vol. 63 (May 1949), pp. 258-72.

same as that of private expenditures, the second and third ratios will be reduced. Although absolute increases in income would be higher, it would be less important to place the federal expenditure in the region in which the increase is desired, and the regional distribution of the effects of any federal expenditure would be more even. These results would hold also in the case of federal expenditures with zero import content. If the lower-level governments had lower marginal propensities to import than did the private sector, both ratios would be higher, for it becomes more efficient to increase expenditures in the region in which the increase is desired, and the spillover between regions is reduced.

Thus, if the import patterns of the public and private sectors are the same, induced expenditures of lower-level governments increase spillover and reduce the importance of the region where expenditures are initiated. If the public import propensities are lower, spillovers are reduced, and a greater concern with the regional pattern of federal expenditures is needed.

Qualifications

LAGS. The policymaker may be interested not only in the distribution of the total income change arising from a given policy change, but also in the time path of these changes within the various regions. Thus, he may desire not only that a greater income increase occur in one region, but also that it occur more rapidly there than in other regions. The use of the undated multipliers in this section precludes any comparisons of this nature, but the introduction of a lag between expenditures and income permits them. If consumption (and induced government or other private expenditures) occurs one period after the receipt of income, then "the time in which a certain proportion of a straight multiplier effect is realized is shorter than that which is required to realize the same proportion of any cross multiplier effect."[30] That is, during any moment of time a larger percentage of the final income change will have occurred in the region in which the expenditure was made than in any other. Thus not only will the total regional income increase be greater for an expenditure made within a region, but the increases will also occur more rapidly.

[30] See Michio Morishima and Yukio Kaneko, "On the Speed of Establishing Multi-Sector Equilibrium," *Econometrica,* Vol. 30 (October 1962), pp. 818-22.

BOTTLENECKS. The multiplier discussion thus far has been in terms of income and output expansion at constant prices in both regions. But, as already noted, differences in the initial levels of unemployment within regions may cause the expenditure increase to lead to bottlenecks and price rise in one region before these occur in other regions. To the extent both that this leads to increased import demands in the region with price rise and that these demands can be met from production in regions which are still below full capacity output, such regions will enjoy a larger output effect for the given expenditure change. The marginal suppliers in these regions will increase exports in the short run, thus moderating inflationary pressure in the bottleneck region and reducing unemployment in the others.

This is the argument underlying the position that, even in the absence of labor mobility, sufficiently large increases in aggregate demand will eliminate concentrations of unemployment by raising (through internal price increases) the marginal propensity to import in regions which reach full employment. The more similar the range of goods produced in these regions, and the lower the transport costs, the smaller will be the increase in prices required to raise the regional marginal propensity to import. However, if the demand for the output of localized industries is price inelastic, interregional spillover from price increases would be lessened, and some spread between regional price levels would be possible without necessarily leading to more imports from other regions.

If such a situation persists, the longer-run effect of regional differences in unemployment should be to accelerate the movement of capital and labor to the region of higher employment. If labor responded to wage differentials, mobility would narrow cyclical differentials over time. Thus, short-term and long-term effects of changes in the regional terms of trade should occur in a manner which reduces unemployment differentials over time.[31]

[31] However, an argument has been made that the short-run effects can outweigh the long-run effects, and maintain differentials. If the creation of employment opportunities due to spillover into regions of high unemployment will deter mobility (since workers respond to wage differentials only if employment is not available where currently located) in the upswing, no readjustment can occur since labor will not move when unemployment exists in all regions. Thus booms which get too large, combined with nationwide recessions, would reduce pressures toward labor mobility. If this is true, the short-run reduction in unemployment in

If there exist differences in regional industrial structures, the expected effects of price changes upon the compatibility of high employment and price stability could be positive or negative, depending upon the relationship between the patterns of demand change and the respective regional industrial structures. If the region of full employment were to increase its demands for the imports of final and intermediate goods from the other region, the pressure upon prices in the former would be reduced. To the extent that intermediate products could be obtained at constant prices, the possibility of cost-induced price increases would be reduced.

If, however, the production in the region of higher unemployment required imports from the fully employed region, or there existed final demands for products which could not be satisfied within the region, the attempt to increase employment in the former, even with the use of pinpointed regional programs, would be precluded. Any increased demands would bring about higher prices for intermediate inputs and final demand products, thus diluting the employment effects of the increase in expenditures. In this case full employment nationally could not be achieved unless some inflation were tolerated, since the effect of price increases works against full employment in the short run.

An Input-Output Analysis of Alternative Fiscal Programs

The preceding multiplier analysis suggests possible regional impacts of alternative stabilization measures, but it also raises several questions which require empirical estimation and a consideration of the existing characteristics of regional industrial structures. Unfortunately, the information necessary for empirical evaluation of the regional effects of alternative stabilization measures is not readily available. A complete study would require input-output tables

---

all regions may preclude the longer-run adjustments. See James S. Duesenberry, "The Co-ordination of Policies for Full Employment and Price Stability," in D. C. Hague (ed.), *Inflation,* Proceedings of a Conference held by the International Economic Association (Macmillan, 1962), pp. 129-46. More empirical information is required, however, before anything definitive can be said concerning the relationship between labor mobility and cyclical stability.

for each region (however defined) which allow for imports from other regions as well as for the effects of demand increases in other regions upon each region in question. Besides the customary information on technological production coefficients for each industry, such a study would require data on trade flows among regions for each industry.[32] This information would be necessary for the construction of a series of regional input-output tables suitable for the present discussion. Since it is not readily available, an existing interregional input-output table has been used instead for illustrative purposes. This table is conceptually useful, but it is somewhat imperfect for present purposes, owing to its over-aggregation on both the regional and industrial levels.[33] Nevertheless, calculations obtained from this table provide some measure of the orders of magnitudes involved.

Procedure

The Moses input-output table divides the nation into three regions: the New England, Middle Atlantic, and South Atlantic census regions are region I, the Pacific and Mountain states are region III, and the remaining states are region II. There are ten industries, and an endogenous household sector. The table allows for interregional trade, and has built a pattern of trade transactions into the matrix of production for each region. This permits the computation of the regional distribution of income changes resulting from an expenditure in any one region. Given the recent geographic distribution of unemployment, the regional breakdown of the table is not especially useful for contrasting actual with hypothetical policies, but it shows the importance of considering the regional factor in the design of stabilization policies.

The assumptions underlying input-output analysis, and more particularly, those underlying interregional input-output analysis, make caution necessary when these analyses are applied to problems of stabilization policy. These assumptions—perfect elasticity

[32] For discussions of interregional and regional input-output techniques, see Isard, *Regional Analysis*, pp. 309-74, and John R. Meyer, "Regional Economics: A Survey," *American Economic Review*, Vol. 53 (March 1963), pp. 19-54, particularly pp. 32-36.

[33] Leon N. Moses, "The Stability of Interregional Trading Patterns and Input-Output Analysis," *American Economic Review*, Vol. 45 (December 1955), pp. 803-32.

of supply in all industries, fixed production coefficients implying proportionality between labor income and product output, constant prices, and unchanging trade patterns—quite obviously reduce the strength of the particular conclusions obtained. This is even truer in the present case, because it includes an endogenous household sector with an average pattern of consumption expenditures, rather than the marginal pattern which would be desirable in a discussion of stabilization policy.[34] All of these difficulties could no doubt be eliminated, given sufficient data, and the resultant more refined measures would permit more nearly accurate quantitative solutions to the problem. But such refinements would almost certainly not alter the qualitative nature of the present findings.

The trade coefficients in the interregional table are low, thus unevenness in the regional distribution of the policy-induced income changes is to be expected.[35] Only eight of the sixty-six coefficients are above .2. These were in the following industries: agriculture, animal and products, forest products, manufactures, and petroleum and gas. For six of these, region II was the exporter. The trade coefficients in the electric power, transportation and communications, trade and finance, and service sectors were all zero, or very close to zero, which accords with what the definition of local industries would suggest. Another point of interest is the falling off of the trade coefficients with distance, the east and west having less direct trade with each other than each has with region II.

Computations of the income changes and their regional distributions were made for several alternative policy measures. The fiscal policy measures considered were personal tax reductions and various expenditure programs of federal, state, and local governments which are frequently suggested as useful for contracyclical purposes. For comparative purposes, several private construction projects which could be affected by monetary policy were included, as was a projected increase in the demand for manufactures. The method used in estimating the effects of various measures was to introduce the expenditure increase in each of the three regions separately, and then to compare the three results. This simplifies

[34] The average propensity to consume for the household sector (net of foreign transactions) is approximately .7. See App. B.

[35] See Moses, in the *American Economic Review*, p. 818, Table VI.

matters even though it does not reflect a very realistic set of expenditure measures.[36]

Results

Table 7 shows the increases in household income arising from an additional $1,000 expenditure of various types and from a $1,000 reduction in personal income taxes.[37] Essentially this table demonstrates the relationship between the region in which an expenditure is made and the regional distribution of the income changes to which these expenditures give rise. In all cases except manufacturing, the percentage of the income increase occurring in the region in which the expenditure was made is above 60 percent of the total increase for the nation. Because of the importance of on-site construction employment, the expenditures considered appear to have greater local effects than does the tax reduction. Similarly, the spillover from increasing expenditures in manufacturing appears to be greater than that from the construction expenditures considered. The differences in spillover from the alternative construction expenditure programs appear small, and the orders of magnitude of the results are similar. This result is in accord with the values estimated from the ratios of the second section, above, for low values of the marginal propensities to import in two regions. Thus Table 7 again demonstrates the importance of pinpointing stabilization measures when the regional pattern of income increases is a policy target. The advantages of such a policy are made clear when the income increases in any region from internally made expenditures are compared with the increases resulting from expenditures in other regions (ratio 2). Also to be noted is the fall-off of

[36] More realistically, the pattern for government expenditures would depend upon the nature of the initial expenditures, or upon the pattern in which grants to sub-federal governments are allocated, while the distribution of changes in disposable income from tax reductions (or transfer payment increases) would depend upon the levels of personal income (or the method of distributing the transfers). To determine the regional responses to changes in monetary policy it would be necessary to evaluate the regional effects of the policy change upon investment in the several regions. For any regional pattern of expenditure changes, the total effects would be the weighted average of the regional distributions shown by treating expenditures in each individual region separately.

[37] See App. B for a description of the methods employed in making these computations.

the increase in income as the distance from the source of the initial expenditure increases.

In summary, the calculations based on the interregional input-output table emphasize the regional concentration of a large proportion of income increases in the region in which expenditure is made (ratio 3). While political and administrative problems may make it difficult to apply regionally-oriented stabilization policy in a flexible fashion, regional selectivity clearly increases the efficiency of stabilization policy in the achievement of specific targets.

Conclusion: Regional Orientation with Central Responsibility

The major conclusions of this essay have been that employment fluctuations vary regionally, and that regionally pinpointed stabilization measures increase the efficiency of stabilization policy. But this emphasis on regional aspects does not imply as a corollary that the responsibility for stabilization should be left to regional governments. Federally directed policy is called for because the origins of differential rates of regional unemployment are largely national in character, as are effective solutions to problems of regional unemployment. Moreover, financial constraints and the possibilities of interstate mobility of individuals and businesses place major limitations on any contracyclical policies of subfederal governments. While these governments have an important role in influencing the industrial structures of their jurisdictions in such a way as to reduce cyclical problems in the longer run, they are in an inferior position to promote policies which affect unemployment in the short run.

Interdependence among regions in the national economy is an important factor in accounting for the unemployment of a state, and forces outside the political boundaries of a state have a major influence upon the magnitude of its internal movements. Because of the spillover of demand, an attempt by any one state in isolation to reduce its own unemployment may lead to unpaid-for benefits in other states, while attempts by all the states acting independently may lead to an excessive increase in demand from the national point of view. Thus, as long as stabilization measures are left to particular states, there can be no expectation of an optimal national

TABLE 7. Increases in Income and Their Distribution by Regions, Alternative Stabilization Measures

Stabilization Measure	*Region I*	*Region II*	*Region III*	*Total*
I. Type of Private Expenditure Increase ($1,000)				
a. All Residential Construction, Initial Increase in Expenditures in:				
I	$1,215.37	$ 488.40	$ 91.32	$1,795.09
	(67.7)[a]	(27.2)	(5.1)	
II	295.98	1,426.97	135.27	1,858.22
	(15.9)	(76.8)	(7.3)	
III	177.38	456.71	1,211.45	1,845.54
	(9.6)	(24.7)	(65.6)	
b. Industrial Construction, Initial Increase in Expenditures in:				
I	1,237.44	521.02	84.23	1,842.69
	(67.2)	(28.3)	(4.6)	
II	325.32	1,461.59	121.34	1,908.25
	(17.0)	(76.6)	(6.4)	
III	196.78	497.65	1,189.02	1,883.45
	(10.4)	(26.4)	(63.1)	
c. Manufacturing, Initial Increase in Expenditures in:				
I	1,044.41	695.47	105.41	1,845.29
	(56.6)	(37.7)	(5.7)	
II	461.70	1,327.35	145.47	1,934.52
	(23.9)	(68.6)	(7.5)	
III	287.41	689.88	918.57	1,895.86
	(15.2)	(36.4)	(48.5)	
II. Type of Government Expenditure Increase ($1,000)				
a. Educational, Hospital and Institutional Construction, Initial Increase in Expenditures in:				
I	1,247.55	525.16	84.72	1,857.43
	(67.2)	(28.3)	(4.6)	
II	327.89	1,473.64	122.08	1,923.61
	(17.1)	(76.6)	(6.4)	
III	198.12	500.78	1,195.38	1,894.28
	(10.5)	(26.4)	(63.1)	

Source: See text and Appendix B.

Note: Regions are defined on page 50. Percentages may not add to 100.0 because of rounding.

[a] The numbers in parentheses refer to percentages of the national income increase resulting from each expenditure increase or tax reduction.

TABLE 7. Continued

Stabilization Measure	*Region I*	*Region II*	*Region III*	*Total*
b. Army Corps of Engineer Projects, Initial Increase in Expenditures in:				
I	1,336.40	459.83	75.23	1,871.46
	(71.4)	(24.6)	(4.0)	
II	282.08	1,530.66	110.76	1,923.50
	(14.7)	(79.6)	(5.8)	
III	160.99	422.65	1,331.37	1,915.01
	(8.4)	(22.1)	(69.5)	
c. All New Highway Construction, Initial Increase in Expenditures in:				
I	1,264.32	442.28	70.68	1,777.28
	(71.1)	(24.9)	(4.0)	
II	272.80	1,450.41	104.30	1,827.51
	(14.9)	(79.4)	(5.7)	
III	155.70	407.94	1,253.44	1,817.08
	(8.6)	(22.5)	(69.0)	
d. All Highway Maintenance, Initial Increase in Expenditures in:				
I	1,461.39	438.68	70.66	1,970.73
	(74.2)	(22.3)	(3.6)	
II	260.38	1,657.28	104.41	2,022.07
	(12.9)	(82.0)	(5.2)	
III	149.91	401.32	1,455.56	2,006.79
	(7.5)	(20.0)	(72.5)	
III. Tax Reduction				
Tax Reduction of $1,000 in:				
I	838.49	436.20	71.12	1,345.81
	(62.3)	(32.4)	(5.3)	
II	239.09	1,057.28	103.94	1,400.31
	(17.1)	(75.5)	(7.4)	
III	142.14	395.01	837.80	1,374.95
	(10.3)	(28.7)	(60.9)	
(National)[b]	468.85	693.36	211.57	1,373.78
	(34.1)	(50.5)	(15.4)	

[b] 41 percent in I, 42.5 percent in II, and 16.5 percent in III. See Appendix B.

policy, for there may be either smaller or larger changes in demand than would be considered desirable.[38] In the contemporary situation, given both financial constraints and interstate strategy, the presumption that stabilization measures will be insufficient if they are left to lower-level governments appears most reasonable.

Nevertheless, the fact that the federal government is the most efficient unit for undertaking stabilization measures and for bearing their costs does not eliminate a concern with regional factors, nor does it follow that state (and local) governments have no role to play in stabilization policy. Indeed, through proper inter-level cooperation, a more efficient regional orientation can be secured than would be possible by reliance on purely federal policies, such as the letting of contracts on the basis of regional criteria (as distinguished from cost alone), the use of regionally selected public works programs, or regionally oriented variation in excise tax rates. State and local governments can function as administrative and planning units in the implementation of federally financed policies. Perhaps the most efficient policy would establish federal grants to state (or local) governments yet leave these governments considerable discretion in the choice of specific programs.[39]

[38] See J. Tinbergen, *Economic Policy: Principles and Design* (North-Holland Publishing Co., Amsterdam, 1956), pp. 172-78, for a discussion of the implications of centralized vs. decentralized policy administration.

[39] See Robert A. Dahl and Charles E. Lindblom, "Variation in Public Expenditure," in Max F. Millikan (ed.), *Income Stabilization for a Developing Democracy* (Yale University Press, 1953), pp. 347-96, for a more detailed discussion of the desirability and usefulness of this inter-governmental division of labor in stabilization policy.

APPENDIX A

Tables

This appendix contains three tables which, with Tables 3 and 4 in the text, were used to compute the rank correlations presented in Tables 5 and 6. All three appendix tables were computed from state employment data compiled by the Bureau of Labor Statistics.

TABLE 8. Ratios of Growth, by States, 1949–58

State	Growth			
	By Cycle Bases[a]		Peak to Peak[b]	
Alabama	(17)	110.03	(19)	119.87
Arizona	(3)	134.55	(1)	174.69
Arkansas	(35)	105.02	(36)	113.47
California	(5)	119.77	(5)	141.68
Colorado	(6)	115.64	(6)	136.79
Connecticut	(23.5)	107.77	(24)	117.26[c]
Delaware	(7)	114.46	(7)	135.75[c]
District of Columbia	(47)	98.29	(45)	106.30
Florida	(1)	135.09	(2)	174.61
Georgia	(12)	111.64	(12)	127.51[c]
Idaho	(33)	105.91	(21)	117.82
Illinois	(36)	105.00	(41)	109.88[c]
Indiana	(39)	104.33	(29)	116.31[c]
Iowa	(43)	103.39	(39)	110.23[c]
Kansas	(23.5)	107.77	(13)	126.65[c]
Kentucky	(29)	106.52	(25)	117.13
Louisiana	(9)	113.41	(10)	129.83
Maine	(44)	102.73	(46)	105.48[c]
Maryland	(13)	111.45	(14)	126.59
Massachusetts	(45)	102.17	(43)	106.68[c]
Michigan	(34)	105.05	(28)	116.43[c]
Minnesota	(25)	107.46	(30)	116.09
Mississippi	(16)	110.42	(17)	122.39[c]
Missouri	(40)	104.17	(37)	113.43[c]
Montana	(18)	108.29	(27)	116.67
Nebraska	(31)	105.97	(32)	115.31[c]
Nevada	(2)	134.88	(3)	166.10
New Hampshire	(32)	105.95	(42)	108.46
New Jersey	(21)	108.03	(20)	118.18
New Mexico	(4)	119.85	(4)	156.71
New York	(38)	104.52	(40)	109.93
North Carolina	(14)	110.63	(16)	123.64
North Dakota	(27)	106.67	(22)	117.67
Ohio	(26)	106.91	(31)	116.05
Oklahoma	(15)	110.50	(15)	124.40[c]
Oregon	(37)	104.95	(35)	113.51[c]
Pennsylvania	(46)	100.17	(47)	103.26
Rhode Island	(48)	96.45	(48)	99.09[c]
South Carolina	(28)	106.53	(18)	120.28
South Dakota	(22)	107.81	(33)	115.15[c]
Tennessee	(19)	108.23	(26)	117.07[c]
Texas	(8)	113.69	(8)	134.21
Utah	(10)	112.51	(9)	130.72
Vermont	(42)	103.52	(44)	106.40[c]
Virginia	(11)	111.89	(11)	127.96
Washington	(20)	108.11	(23)	117.63
West Virginia	(49)	94.70	(49)	92.83
Wisconsin	(30)	106.23	(34)	113.85
Wyoming	(41)	103.82	(38)	111.46
National[d]		107.80		117.36
National[e]		107.78		117.75

Source: Bureau of Labor Statistics.
Note: Numbers in parentheses indicate rank.
[a] Ratio of 1954–58 Cycle Base to 1949–54 Cycle Base.
[b] Ratio of 1956 or 1957 peak to 1948 peak.
[c] 1956 Peak.
[d] National total given by the Bureau of Labor Statistics.
[e] Total of state figures.

TABLE 9. Percentage of Manufacturing and Mining Employment to Total Employment, by States, 1953 and 1956

State	1953		1956	
Alabama	(18)	37.24	(19)	35.41
Arizona	(39)	20.21	(39)	21.02
Arkansas	(29)	28.41	(27)	29.47
California	(30)	28.32	(28)	28.53
Colorado	(41)	19.53	(41)	18.94
Connecticut	(1)	52.09	(1)	47.83
Delaware	(11)	43.75	(14)	39.08
District of Columbia	(49)	3.42	(49)	3.21
Florida	(45)	15.50	(45)	14.95
Georgia	(20)	35.60	(20)	35.08
Idaho	(38)	21.16	(37)	22.04
Illinois	(17)	39.82	(17)	37.78
Indiana	(3)	48.00	(4)	44.01
Iowa	(32)	27.76	(31)	26.55
Kansas	(28)	28.62	(33)	25.72
Kentucky	(23)	33.34	(21)	33.77
Louisiana	(33)	27.71	(34)	25.65
Maine	(14)	41.79	(13)	39.61
Maryland	(22)	33.69	(23)	31.58
Massachusetts	(15)	40.68	(15)	38.50
Michigan	(2)	50.49	(3)	45.03
Minnesota	(31)	28.25	(32)	26.53
Mississippi	(27)	29.77	(25)	30.45
Missouri	(24)	32.91	(24)	30.68
Montana	(42)	19.39	(40)	20.16
Nebraska	(43)	17.98	(44)	17.01
Nevada	(46)	12.99	(46)	12.79
New Hampshire	(5)	46.99	(2)	45.37
New Jersey	(8)	45.99	(10)	42.87
New Mexico	(44)	17.69	(42)	18.68
New York	(21)	34.14	(22)	31.93
North Carolina	(10)	44.80	(6)	43.70
North Dakota	(48)	7.54	(48)	7.25
Ohio	(6)	46.53	(5)	43.82
Oklahoma	(36)	24.71	(35.5)	25.04
Oregon	(25)	31.06	(26)	29.88
Pennsylvania	(9)	45.51	(11)	42.23
Rhode Island	(4)	47.98	(8)	43.37
South Carolina	(13)	42.61	(7)	43.55
South Dakota	(47)	11.98	(47)	11.30
Tennessee	(19)	36.09	(18)	35.98
Texas	(35)	25.07	(35.5)	25.04
Utah	(37)	21.25	(38)	21.72
Vermont	(16)	40.25	(16)	38.17
Virginia	(26)	30.50	(29)	28.46
Washington	(34)	26.98	(30)	27.21
West Virginia	(7)	46.19	(9)	43.08
Wisconsin	(12)	43.56	(12)	40.85
Wyoming	(40)	19.54	(43)	17.54
National		36.41		34.21

Source: Bureau of Labor Statistics.
Note: Numbers in parentheses indicate rank.

TABLE 10. Percentage of Durable Manufacturing Employment to Total Employment, by States, 1953 and 1956

State	*1953*		*1956*	
Alabama	(14)	17.88	(17)	16.57
Arizona	(33)	9.98	(33)	10.59
Arkansas	(22)	14.43	(19)	14.93
California	(13)	17.89	(13)	18.53
Colorado	(38)	7.40	(39)	7.40
Connecticut	(2)	38.91	(2)	35.93
Delaware	(25)	13.81	(29)	11.83
District of Columbia	(49)	.20	(49)	.18
Florida	(43)	6.22	(43)	6.01
Georgia	(30)	11.39	(30)	11.64
Idaho	(32)	10.91	(31)	11.50
Illinois	(6)	25.73	(6)	24.65
Indiana	(3)	36.32	(3)	32.90
Iowa	(23)	14.08	(25)	13.17
Kansas	(21)	14.82	(23)	13.30
Kentucky	(29)	12.61	(21)	14.05
Louisiana	(36)	8.99	(40)	7.05
Maine	(28)	13.03	(28)	12.54
Maryland	(12)	19.56	(12)	18.70
Massachusetts	(16)	17.70	(16)	16.78
Michigan	(1)	42.28	(1)	36.80
Minnesota	(24)	13.99	(26)	12.88
Mississippi	(26)	13.16	(27)	12.79
Missouri	(19)	15.91	(20)	14.10
Montana	(40)	6.87	(38)	8.16
Nebraska	(42)	6.46	(44)	5.14
Nevada	(45)	3.07	(45)	2.71
New Hampshire	(18)	16.55	(15)	17.32
New Jersey	(7)	25.50	(7)	23.68
New Mexico	(44)	5.73	(41)	6.62
New York	(20)	15.09	(22)	13.97
North Carolina	(31)	11.08	(32)	11.42
North Dakota	(48)	.98	(48)	.94
Ohio	(4)	33.86	(4)	31.63
Oklahoma	(37)	8.39	(36)	8.91
Oregon	(11)	22.69	(10)	21.78
Pennsylvania	(8)	25.45	(8)	23.66
Rhode Island	(10)	23.21	(11)	21.48
South Carolina	(41)	6.57	(42)	6.28
South Dakota	(46)	2.40	(46)	1.93
Tennessee	(27)	13.08	(24)	13.23
Texas	(35)	9.38	(35)	9.48
Utah	(39)	6.93	(37)	8.25
Vermont	(9)	25.39	(9)	23.28
Virginia	(34)	9.84	(34)	9.68
Washington	(15)	17.85	(14)	18.21
West Virginia	(17)	16.66	(18)	16.00
Wisconsin	(5)	27.61	(5)	26.06
Wyoming	(47)	1.49	(47)	1.59
National		20.34		19.00

Source: Bureau of Labor Statistics.
Note: Numbers in parentheses indicate rank.

APPENDIX B

Data and Methods Used in the Input-Output Analysis

This appendix is a discussion of the data and methods used in the input-output analysis. The source of the construction estimates was the study prepared by the Bureau of Labor Statistics for use in the 1947 input-output study.[40] The estimates for the bill-of-goods for manufacturing expenditures and for tax reductions are discussed below. The domestic propensities to consume for regions I, II, and III are approximately .704, .714, and .710, respectively. Because of imports from abroad, the increases in national income for expenditures differ among the regions but the differences are minor.

Construction Expenditures

The construction cost data on bills-of-goods for various construction projects were prepared on the basis of the four-digit S.I.C. classifications. The information necessary to allocate these bills-of-goods in a manner consistent with the ten-industry breakdown used in the input-output table was obtained at the Harvard Economic Research Project. Certain items of expenditures were omitted in deriving the bills-of-goods, either because of difficulties in assigning the location of recipients or of applying a consumption pattern to these expenditures, and they are omitted from the measures of the increases in national income. They are: pensions, profits after tax, interest paid, depreciation, travel expenses, and all federal, state, and local taxes.

[40] Bureau of Labor Statistics, *New and Maintenance Construction: Construction in the 1947 Inter-Industry Study* (Mimeo.), (August 1952).

Since data for the construction projects (except for all residential construction) are given at purchasers' cost, it was necessary to divide this amount into producers' value and margin (the share going to the trade and the transportation and communication sectors). This division (except for all residential construction) was made by use of the separate margins for each industry derived from the relationship between producers' value and purchasers' value for all new construction for all projects except highway maintenance, for which the relationship for all maintenance construction was used. The margins on materials were 23.6 percent and 28.6 percent, respectively. The margin was then divided between the trade and transportation sectors in accordance with the ratio for all new or all maintenance construction. Half of transportation was allocated in the region of expenditure and half in the region of production. Each bill was then distributed among the regions on the basis of the trade coefficients presented by Leon Moses, in *American Economic Review,* p. 818, Table VI. Because of the manner in which the household sector is treated, it was necessary to compute a set of final demands for the initial wage-earners on the project. This was done by multiplying wage payments by the consumption pattern shown in the matrix. The bills-of-goods applied were therefore the initial demands from each industrial sector, except households, plus the final demands from the initial incomes of the on-site construction workers.

Since the important question was the effect on household incomes, not output by industries, it was necessary to multiply the increases in output for each industry by its household income coefficient in the production matrix. These totals were then added to the initial labor income to obtain the total household income arising from each project.

Manufacturing Expenditures

To approximate the manner in which the construction estimates were made, the $1,000 expenditure increase was divided between increased demand at producers' value and the margin components, in the same ratio as manufactures purchased in all new construction. The bill was then distributed among regions in accord with the trade coefficients in Moses, *ibid.*

Tax Reduction

The final bill of goods introduced was taken from the average household consumption pattern for each region, which is distributed regionally within the matrix. The bill-of-goods for the national tax reduction was based upon the distribution of personal income by states in 1958: 41 percent in region I, 42.5 percent in II, and 16.5 percent in region III. See Graham, in *Survey of Current Business.*

ROBERT W. RAFUSE, JR.*

Cyclical Behavior of State-Local Finances

WHEN WORLD WAR II came to an end the state and local government sector was no larger a part of the American economy than it had been in the golden days of William McKinley and William Jennings Bryan. Indeed, state-local budgets were relatively smaller in 1946 than in the 1920's. During the years after the war the picture changed dramatically. By 1964 the expenditures of state and local governments were six times as large as they had been in 1946. As a proportion of the gross national product, this represented an increase from 5.3 percent to 10.8 percent during the same eighteen year period.

A sector of the economy that is as large and growing as rapidly as the state and local sector is necessarily an important determinant of the general level of economic activity. Was the inflation that plagued the American economy during the first decade after the war a result, at least in part, of state and local fiscal behavior? Were conditions during the four postwar recessions made worse by the

* George Washington University. This paper is based upon the author's dissertation, "State and Local Fiscal Behavior over the Postwar Cycles" (Princeton, 1964).

budgetary policies of state and local governments? Is the fiscal behavior of these governments likely in the future to aggravate fluctuations in the general level of economic activity? This study is an attempt to answer these questions.

The Perversity Hypothesis

Since the Great Depression many attempts have been made to define the basic characteristics of the cyclical performance of state and local governments. Unquestionably the most influential of these is a study that was published in 1944 by Alvin H. Hansen and Harvey S. Perloff.[1] The essence of their findings is expressed in a paragraph that is worth quoting in its entirety:

> The taxing, borrowing, and spending activities of the state and local governments collectively have typically run counter to an economically sound fiscal policy. These governmental units have usually followed the swings of the business cycle, from crest to trough, spending and building in prosperity periods and contracting their activities during depression. In the boom of the late twenties, they added to the disposable income of the community, and bid up prices and building costs in large-scale construction activities. In the depressed thirties, the fiscal policies of these governments exerted a deflationary rather than an expansionary effect on the economy: expenditures, and especially construction outlays, were severely reduced, borrowing was restricted, and taxes weighing on consumption were substantially increased.[2]

Thus, Hansen and Perloff conclude, since "states and localities have in fact *followed* the swings of the cycle and have thereby *intensified* the violence of economic fluctuations . . . unless their fiscal systems are planned in relation to the federal stabilization program, they are likely to nullify in large measure the national counter-cyclical activities."[3] This melancholy conclusion is the "perversity hypothesis."

Professor Galbraith has observed that the shortcomings of economics arise not so much from original error as from obsolescence. The perversity hypothesis has been challenged on both counts. Sev-

[1] *State and Local Finance in the National Economy* (Norton, 1944).
[2] *Ibid.*, p. 49.
[3] *Ibid.*, p. 199.

eral studies have suggested that the interpretation by Hansen and Perloff of the 1920's and 1930's may have been mistaken. Others have not challenged the historical interpretation, but have argued that institutional developments since World War II have brought about major changes in the cyclical performance of state and local governments. In spite of the articles that have questioned the perversity hypothesis,[4] the enduring influence of the Hansen-Perloff view is easily documented.[5]

A brief summary of the theoretical and institutional foundations of the hypothesis may help to explain its durability. Whether one believes, as do Hansen and Perloff, that state and local governments should actively pursue *counter*cyclical policies or, rather, that these governments should undertake only allocation responsibilities, which should be pursued independently of cyclical considerations,[6] the reasoning that underlies the perversity hypothesis should be of some concern. The principal points of this reasoning follow.

1. Constitutional and statutory restrictions on budget policies impair the ability of most state and local governments to pursue the traditional allocation functions. How much more serious must be the debilitating effects of these constraints on the feasibility of countercyclical policies.
2. The low income elasticity of the state and local revenue system restricts the contribution of the system to built-in flexi-

[4] Among these are studies by E. Cary Brown, "Fiscal Policy in the Thirties: A Reappraisal," *American Economic Review,* Vol. 46 (December 1956), pp. 857-79; Morton S. Baratz and Helen T. Farr, "Is Municipal Finance Fiscally Perverse?" *National Tax Journal,* Vol. 12 (September 1959), pp. 276-84; James A. Maxwell, "Counter-Cyclical Role of State and Local Governments," *National Tax Journal,* Vol. 11 (December 1958), pp. 371-76; Mabel Newcomer, "State and Local Financing in Relation to Economic Fluctuations," *National Tax Journal,* Vol. 7 (June 1954), pp. 97-109; and Ansel M. Sharp, "The Counter-Cyclical Fiscal Role of State Governments During the Thirties," *National Tax Journal,* Vol. 11 (June 1958), pp. 138-45.

[5] See John F. Due, *Government Finance,* 3rd ed. (Richard D. Irwin, 1963), p. 541; Harold M. Groves, *Financing Government,* 6th ed. (Holt, Rinehart and Winston, 1964), p. 647; A. E. Holmans, *United States Fiscal Policy, 1945-1959* (London, Oxford, 1961), p. 2; Kenyon E. Poole, *Public Finance and Economic Welfare* (Rinehart, 1956), pp. 375-85, 495-500; *The Report of the Commission on Money and Credit* (Prentice-Hall, 1961), pp. 121-27.

[6] This is the view suggested by Richard A. Musgrave, *The Theory of Public Finance* (McGraw-Hill, 1959), p. 181.

bility. If expenditures are more elastic than revenues, state and local fiscal behavior will be cyclically perverse.[7]

3. The probable leakage to other jurisdictions of employment-creating effects is likely to minimize the interest of state and local officials in the countercyclical timing of construction expenditures. Moreover, to the extent that increased or sustained spending during a depression would have to be financed by the sale of securities, the burden of the debt to the locality will be very real if, as is likely, most of the bonds are sold to outsiders.

4. The ability of state and local governments to obtain credit does not begin to compare with that of the federal government. In the 1930's the consequences of this disparity were catastrophic in many cases.

5. Intergovernmental competition is a major constraint on the freedom of action of state and local governments. Such competition probably is more effective in holding down tax rates than in improving public services.

6. The practice of earmarking revenues for expenditure only on specific functions, widespread primarily among state governments, restricts budget flexibility, which is a prime requisite for effective stabilization policy and even for adaptation to depression and inflation.

7. Finally, the sheer number of state and local decision-making units, the hundreds of thousands of elected and appointed officials, the diversity of attitudes about the role of government, all of these factors are potential sources of confusion and inconsistency sufficient to frustrate the most concerted effort to achieve some degree of stability in state and local fiscal policies.

The perversity hypothesis deserves reexamination from a number of different points of view. This paper appraises the hypothesis by means of reference cycle analysis, a study of receipts elasticities, and various measures of the overall impact of government budgets on the economy.

[7] See the perversity model outlined by Baratz and Farr, "Is Municipal Finance Fiscally Perverse?" p. 277.

Reference Cycle Analysis

The techniques of business cycle analysis developed by the National Bureau of Economic Research are useful tools for the study of the behavior of economic time series over the cycle.[8] In this section a number of National Bureau techniques are used to build up a descriptive picture of the cyclical behavior of state and local government finances during the years since World War II.

Procedures

Though it is not possible here to summarize the procedures used to derive "reference cycle patterns," the reader may refer to any one of a number of readily-available sources for information on the National Bureau techniques.[9] The heart of the analysis is the concept of the "reference cycle"—the period from trough to trough of a business cycle. The "reference dates" and durations of the postwar reference cycles in the United States, as defined by the National Bureau, are summarized in Table 1. The Bureau's identification of these turning points in the general level of economic activity is based on a consensus of the views of financial journalists, academicians, and business analysts.[10]

[8] To my knowledge, the only application of these techniques to the public sector is a study by John M. Firestone of the cyclical behavior of federal government receipts and expenditures. *Federal Receipts and Expenditures During Business Cycles, 1879-1958,* National Bureau of Economic Research Studies in Business Cycles, No. 9 (Princeton, 1960).

[9] The primary source is, of course, the classic volume by Arthur F. Burns and Wesley C. Mitchell, *Measuring Business Cycles* (National Bureau of Economic Research, 1946). Summaries of the "National Bureau method" appear in Frederick C. Mills, *Statistical Methods,* 3rd ed. (Holt, Rinehart and Winston, 1955), pp. 390-425; and in Firestone, *Federal Receipts,* pp. 3-6.

[10] The National Bureau's techniques of business cycle analysis have been the subject of vigorous controversy for several decades. The discussion appears recently to have centered on the Bureau's procedure for defining reference dates. Though this is not the place for an extended discussion of this issue, the relation between the NBER dates and the turning points in the gross national product is taken up in note 21, below. See also George W. Cloos, "How Good Are the National Bureau's Reference Dates?" *Journal of Business,* Vol. 36 (January 1963), pp. 13-32; Lorman C. Trueblood, "The Dating of Postwar Business Cycles," *Proceedings of the Business and Economic Statistics Section of the American Statistical Association* (1962), pp. 16-28; and in the same volume the discussion by Geoffrey H. Moore of the Trueblood article, pp. 34-37.

TABLE 1. Reference Dates and Durations of Business Cycles in the United States, 1945–61

Monthly Reference Dates			*Quarterly Reference Dates*			*Duration in Quarters*		
Initial Trough	*Peak*	*Terminal Trough*	*Initial Trough*	*Peak*	*Terminal Trough*	*Expansion*	*Contraction*	*Full Cycle*
Oct. '45	Nov. '48	Oct. '49	'45-IV	'48-IV	'49-IV	12	4	16
Oct. '49	July '53	Aug. '54	'49-IV	'53-III	'54-III	15	4	19
Aug. '54	July '57	Apr. '58	'54-III	'57-III	'58-II	12	3	15
Apr. '58	May '60	Feb. '61	'58-II	'60-II	'61-I	8	3	11

Sources for monthly reference dates: U. S. Bureau of the Census, *Business Cycle Developments* (June 1965), p. 67.

TABLE 2. Average Duration of Peacetime Reference Cycles, 1879–1961

Period	*Average Duration in Months*		
	Expansion	*Contraction*	*Full Cycle*
1879 to 1914	23.2	19.7	42.9
1921 to 1938	30.0	20.8	50.8
1945 to 1961	35.5	10.5	46.0

Sources: Table 1, and Firestone, *Federal Receipts*, p. 4.

As Table 2 indicates, the four postwar reference cycles were roughly comparable in average duration to the cycles of the pre-World War I period and the interwar period from 1921 to 1938. The average postwar contraction phase was substantially shorter, however, and the average expansion was correspondingly longer.

This examination of the reference cycle patterns for state-local receipts and expenditures will be more fruitful if we pause briefly at this point to consider the stability implications of certain characteristic patterns. A reference cycle pattern for the surplus and deficit series shows behavior that is stabilizing if it is bell-shaped. A pattern has such a shape if it has a positive slope during the trough-peak phase and a negative slope during the succeeding peak-trough phase. Conversely, a U-shaped reference cycle pattern—negative slope during the expansion phase and positive slope during the contraction phase—is characteristic of perverse behavior of the surplus-deficit series. A single reference cycle pattern may, of course, show perversity during an expansion and stabilizing behavior during the following contraction, and vice versa. An example of such a case would be a pattern that is a straight line with a negative slope for the surplus-deficit series. It follows from these definitions that a bell-shaped receipts pattern is stabilizing, and that a receipts pattern that is U-shaped is perverse. The reverse is true for expenditures: a U-shaped pattern is stabilizing, a bell-shaped pattern is destabilizing.

Results, Unadjusted for Secular Trend

The astounding growth of the state and local sector since the end of World War II has been noted. With very few exceptions, this growth imparts a pronounced upward tilt to the reference cycle patterns. This suggests that it might be fruitful to adjust the data by removing the secular trend. Accordingly, the results of the analysis are presented in two sections. The first summarizes the reference cycle patterns for typical categories of receipts and expenditures when no attempt is made to abstract from trend. The second section considers the patterns that are obtained for total receipts and expenditures when only deviations from trend are considered.

The reference cycle patterns for total state and local receipts (Figure 1) reflect the overwhelming growth of the sector in the postwar period.[11] Total receipts failed to decline during a single stage of the four cycles. The rate of growth was highest during the 1945-49 expansion. A slight decline in the rate of increase during contractions is apparent in all but the 1954-58 reference cycle pattern.

Total state and local receipts consist of federal grants-in-aid and state-local "own" receipts. The behavior of federal grants to state and local governments during the four postwar cycles is depicted in Figure 2. Beyond the fact that the amount of grants increased from the beginning to the end of each cycle, a reflection of secular growth in grant programs, no generalization seems appropriate. The very substantial increase in grants during the contraction phase of the 1954-58 cycle is probably the most striking aspect of the figure. Indeed, the unusual behavior of grants during the 1958 recession fully accounts for the exceptional behavior of total state-local receipts during the contraction phase of the 1954-58 cycle. This is the only case in which abstracting from federal grants affects the reference cycle behavior of state and local receipts in any important respect. As grants have never amounted to more than 15 percent of total receipts, this result is not surprising. With the possible exception of the 1957-58 contraction, the evidence does not contravene the hypothesis suggested by James A. Maxwell in 1952: "Except with respect to emergencies, federal intervention by grants has not taken account of cyclical fluctuations in business activity."[12]

[11] The receipts and expenditures series analyzed in this section are those prepared by the National Income Division of the Office of Business Economics, U.S. Department of Commerce. Though monthly data are preferable for these techniques, the National Income Division's seasonally-adjusted quarterly series are the most detailed estimates available. Quarterly data may obscure important details at turning points, but the amplitude picture presented by such data should be accurate.

[12] *Federal Grants and the Business Cycle* (National Bureau of Economic Research, 1952), p. 9.

FIGURE 1. Reference Cycle Patterns for Total State and Local Receipts, Four Cycles, 1945–1961[a]

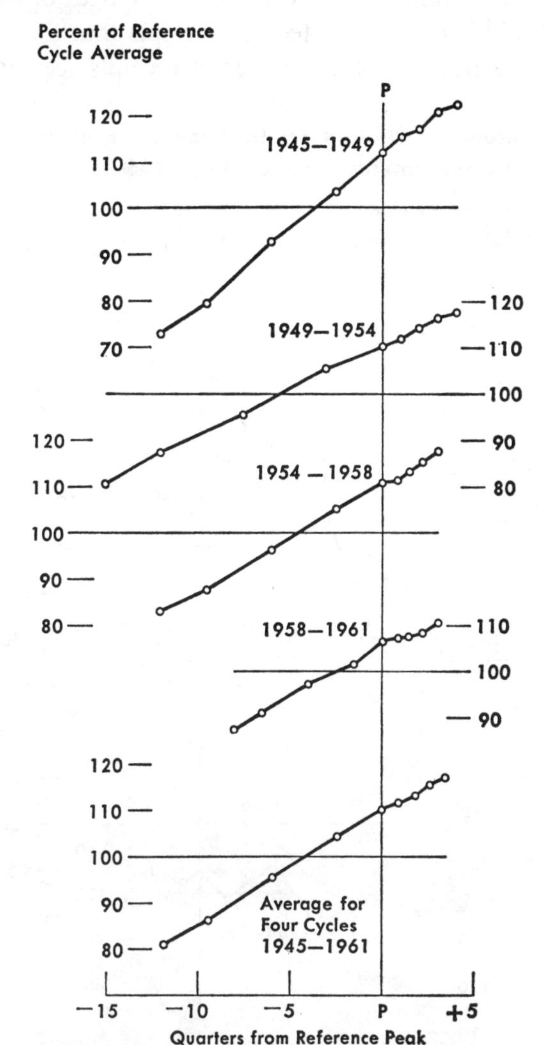

Source: U. S. Department of Commerce, Office of Business Economics, National Income Division.
[a] Current dollars, national income basis.

Total state and local government own receipts increased during every stage of every reference cycle since the end of World War II. As an indication that reference cycle averaging procedures are not obscuring the picture, it is worth noting that own receipts declined in only one quarter of the period—during the Korean War expansion in the second quarter of 1951. This behavior is so greatly at variance with the findings of studies of the behavior of the relatively income-inelastic categories of federal receipts that a breakdown of the results by a number of categories of receipts seemed appropri-

FIGURE 2. Reference Cycle Patterns for Federal Grants-in-Aid to State and Local Governments, Four Cycles, 1945–1961[a]

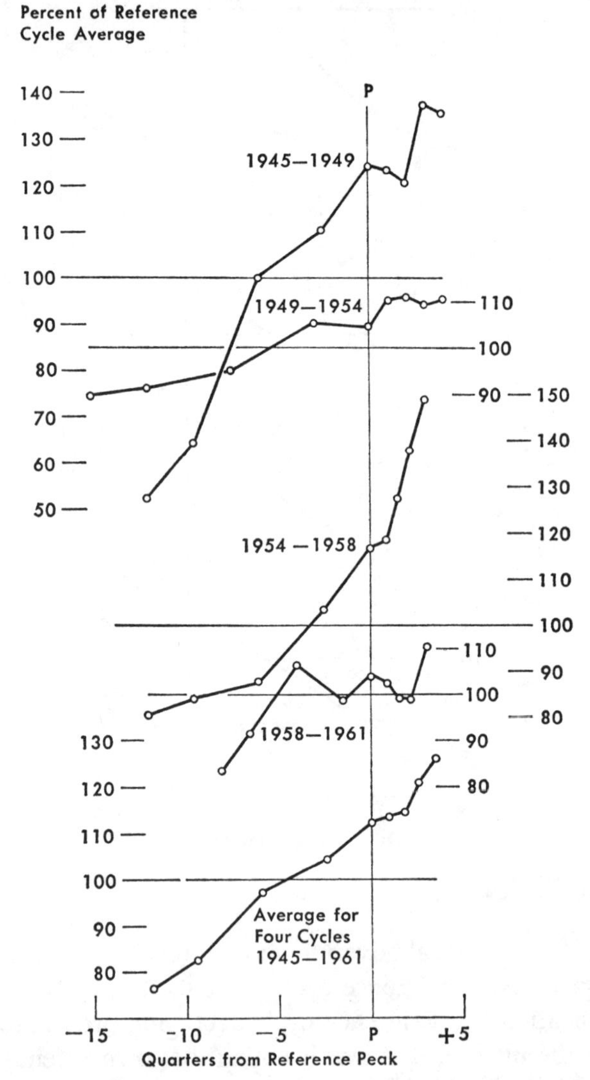

Source: U. S. Department of Commerce, Office of Business Economics, National Income Division.
[a] Current dollars, national income basis.

ate. Accordingly, the reference cycle behavior of the following classes was considered: state personal tax and non-tax receipts; local personal tax and non-tax receipts; corporate profits tax accruals; state general sales taxes; state sales taxes on gasoline, liquor, and tobacco; state and local business property taxes;[13] miscellaneous state indirect business taxes and non-taxes; and contributions for social insurance. Though they are not reproduced here, the reference cycle patterns for these eight categories of state and local

FIGURE 3. Average of Four Reference Cycle Patterns, 1945–1961, for Total State and Local Business Property Taxes[a]

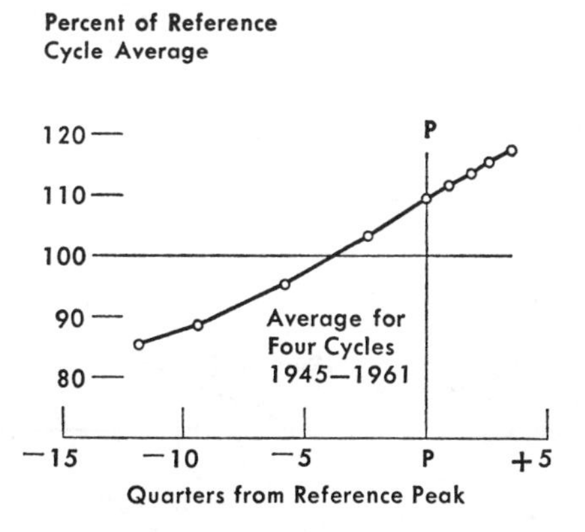

Source: U. S. Department of Commerce, Office of Business Economics, National Income Division.
[a] Current dollars, national income basis.

receipts show that considerable diversity underlies the uniform behavior of total receipts. Even though total receipts failed to decline during any reference cycle stage, five of the eight categories registered declines during one or more stages. As would be expected, corporate profits tax accruals show the most substantial and consistent fluctuations during the four cycles.

The most important single factor underlying the behavior of total state and local receipts is business property taxes. The average reference cycle pattern for this revenue category (Figure 3), which accounts for approximately 40 percent of total own receipts, exhibits little or no response to declining national income. Since the

[13] The Commerce Department includes personal property taxes in the "personal tax and non-tax receipts" category, and it classifies property taxes on owner-occupied houses as business property taxes.

patterns for the four cycles are very similar to the average, they are not reproduced.

State and local expenditures rose throughout the period, as shown in Figure 4. In the expenditure patterns for each cycle and in

FIGURE 4. Reference Cycle Patterns for Total State and Local Expenditures, Four Cycles, 1945–1961[a]

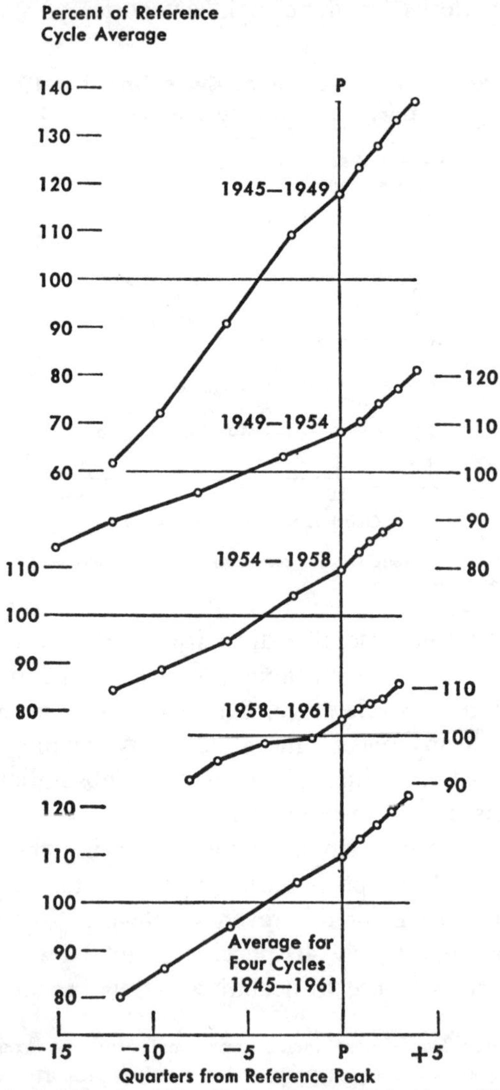

Source: U. S. Department of Commerce, Office of Business Economics, National Income Division.

[a] Current dollars, national income basis.

the average pattern a moderately higher rate of growth during contraction phases is apparent. Perhaps the most plausible hypothesis is that this pattern has resulted from the behavior of transfer payments.

During most of the postwar period transfer payments accounted for roughly 10 percent of total state and local expenditures. If transfers have been responsible for the deviations of total expenditures from a constant upward trend, the reference cycle patterns for transfer payments should be U-shaped. At the very least the patterns should exhibit a substantially higher rate of growth during contraction phases. In fact, the cyclical behavior of transfer payments has been mildly erratic. The average reference cycle pattern shows only a moderately higher rate of increase during the contraction phase. The failure of state and local transfer payments to display a significantly countercyclical pattern of behavior is not surprising. The major reason is that the data do not include unemployment compensation. Most state and local transfer payments are pensions and direct relief payments. Though some cyclical response from these programs might be expected, as Wilfred Lewis notes with respect to the behavior of federal matching grants to states for public assistance, "the cyclical sensitivity of such programs has been quantitatively insignificant."[14]

The absence of a clear-cut pattern of movement in transfer payments accounts for the fact that the reference cycle patterns for total state and local purchases of goods and services are almost exactly the same as the patterns for total expenditures. The behavior of the compensation of employees portion of state and local purchases is completely dominated by trend. The average reference cycle pattern for these expenditures, which account for nearly 50 percent of all state and local spending, shows no response whatsoever to the postwar cycles.

The second most important category of state and local expenditures, accounting for roughly a quarter of the total, is purchases of goods and services for new construction (Figure 5). The average reference cycle pattern for this class of expenditures shows a substantially higher rate of increase during contractions than during expansions. In this case, however, a considerable degree of varia-

[14] *Federal Fiscal Policy in the Postwar Recessions* (Brookings, 1962), p. 60.

tion from cycle to cycle underlies the regularity of the average pattern. The huge increase in construction spending during the first four years after the war dominates Figure 5. Most of this surge resulted from the backlogs that developed during a decade and a half

FIGURE 5. Reference Cycle Patterns for Total State and Local Purchases of Goods and Services for New Construction, Four Cycles, 1945–1961[a]

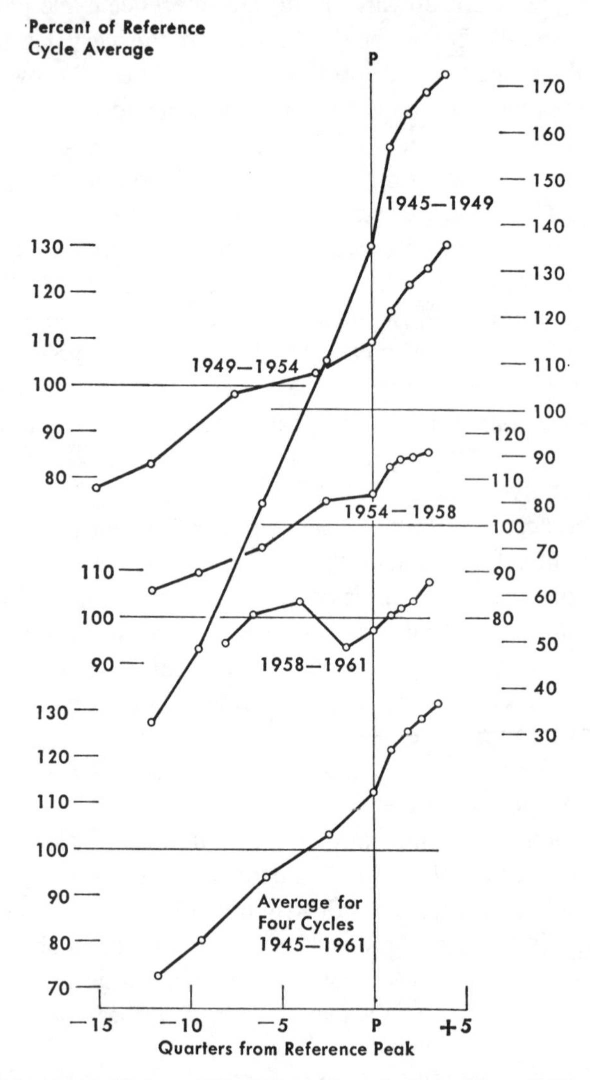

Source: U. S. Department of Commerce, Office of Business Economics, National Income Division.
[a] Current dollars, national income basis.

of depression and war. The behavior of state and local construction during the cycles of 1954-58 and 1958-61 was influenced by several rather substantial gyrations in federal grant-in-aid programs. An indication of the magnitude of the shifts in the federal programs is given by the record of grants as a proportion of total state-local construction spending. In 1956 the ratio was 9.0 percent; by 1959 it had risen to 22.4 percent; and in 1961 the grants-expenditures ratio fell back to 18.8 percent.

Quite a different picture of state and local construction activity is provided by Figure 6, which shows the reference cycle patterns for contract awards for state and locally-owned new construction. In this figure the typical expenditures pattern of acceleration during the contraction phase appears only for the 1954-58 cycle. Indeed, the contract awards patterns for the other three cycles show lower rates of increase during contractions than during expansions. Since contract awards are more amenable to adjustments by local officials than are payments to contractors for work in progress, this series may be the best available indicator of the true cyclical propensities of state and local officials. With the exception of the 1957-59 period, when the situation was distorted by major changes in federal grant programs, Figure 6 reveals a tendency toward perversity that might be expected to show up in construction expenditures if the economy enters a downturn that is any longer than those it has encountered since World War II. It has been suggested that a significant part of the economic impact of government spending occurs at stages of the spending process that precede the cash transaction.[15] To the extent that this is true, the results of Figure 6 imply that during recent cycles the expansionary effects of the acceleration in construction expenditures during contractions have been partially offset by the perverse behavior of contract awards.

Figure 7 summarizes the cyclical behavior of state and local surpluses and deficits during the postwar period.[16] Though the ref-

[15] See Murray H. Weidenbaum, "The Timing of the Economic Impact of Government Spending," *National Tax Journal,* Vol. 12 (March 1959), pp. 79-85.

[16] Since both positive and negative quantities are involved, the data in this case cannot be expressed as cycle relatives. Of course, the absolute surpluses and deficits are in fact the real interest here. Thus the reference cycle patterns in Figure 7 are calculated from data expressed in absolute rather than relative terms. For the sake of clarity the peak quarters are centered on three separate axes rather than on one as in the previous figures. With these two exceptions, Figure 7 may be read in the same way as those preceding it.

erence cycle patterns do not show perfect conformity to the swings of the cycle, their behavior is extremely interesting in view of all that has been said about the fiscal perversity of state and local finances. The expansion phase of the 1945-49 cycle is the only im-

FIGURE 6. Reference Cycle Patterns for Construction Contract Awards for State and Locally Owned New Construction, Four Cycles, 1945–1961[a]

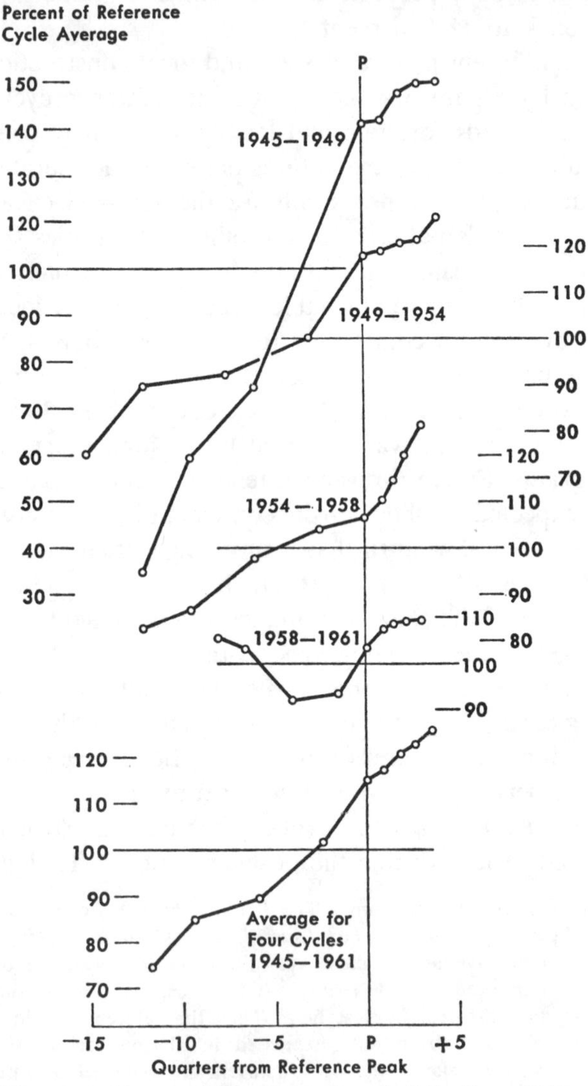

Source: U. S. Department of Commerce, Office of Business Economics, National Income Division.
[a] Current dollars.

FIGURE 7. Reference Cycle Patterns for State and Local Surpluses and Deficits, Four Cycles, 1945–1961[a]

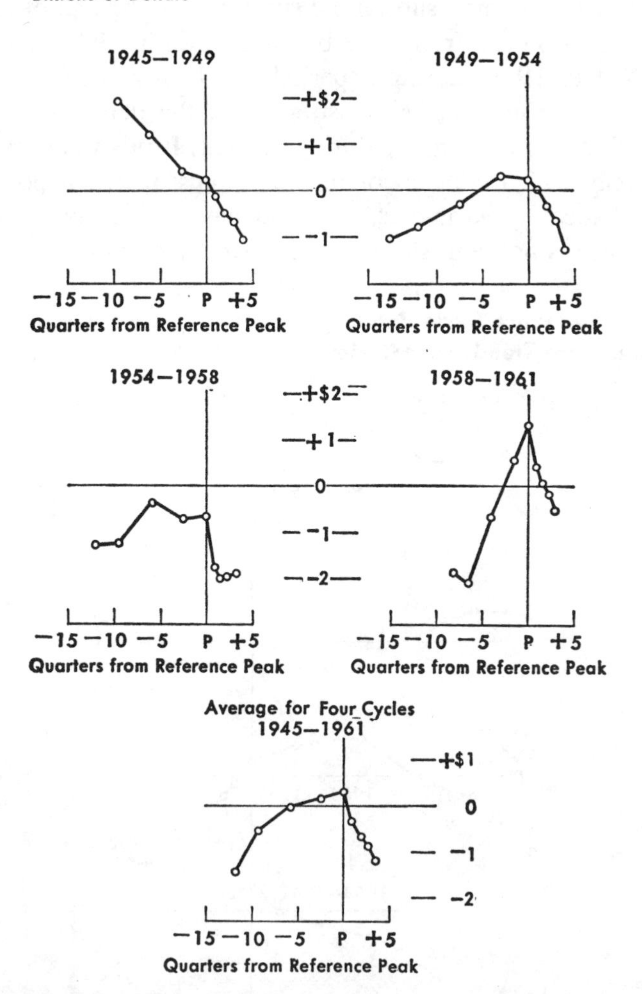

Source: U. S. Department of Commerce, Office of Business Economics, National Income Division.
[a] Current dollars, national income basis.

portant exception to a stabilizing pattern of increase during expansion and decline during contraction. The behavior during the upswing of the 1945-49 cycle is attributable to the special circumstances that obtained as a result of the war. Because of war-time restrictions, state and local spending in 1945 was 6 percent less than in

1939. While expenditures were being curtailed, the massive increase in national income during the war was lifting receipts 20 percent above prewar levels. For these reasons, state and local governments were running substantial surpluses by the end of the war. The precipitous drop from a $2 billion surplus in 1945 to a $1 billion deficit in 1949, during a period in which revenues increased almost 70 percent, reflects the strength of the demand for public services that was building up during the war. If this study were concerned only with the behavior of the surplus or deficit position of state and local governments, it would have to be concluded that the evidence is not consistent with the perversity hypothesis.

FIGURE 8. Reference Cycle Patterns for State and Local Own Receipts: Deviations from Trend, Four Cycles, 1947–1961[a]

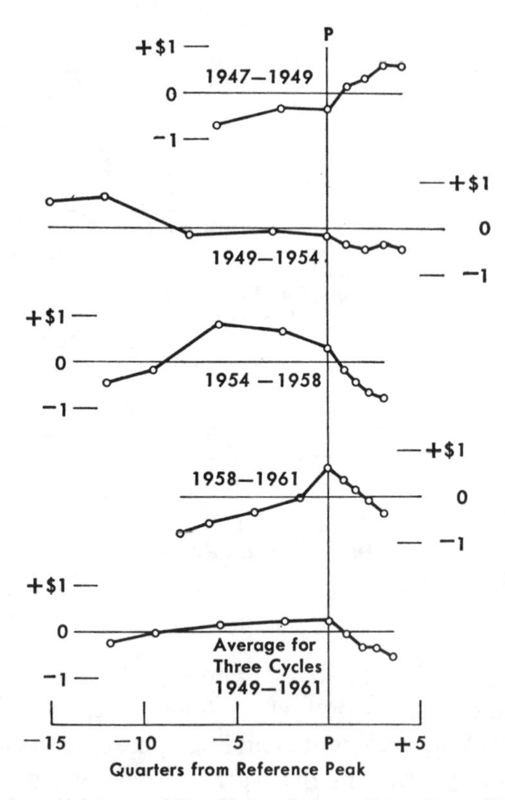

Source: U. S. Department of Commerce, Office of Business Economics, National Income Division.
[a] 1954 dollars, national income basis.

Results, Adjusted for Secular Trend

It has been noted that a slightly higher rate of increase during contractions is characteristic of the reference cycle patterns for state-local expenditures, and that receipts have tended to increase at a lesser rate during contractions than during expansions. These

FIGURE 9. Reference Cycle Patterns for Total State and Local Expenditures: Deviations from Trend, Four Cycles, 1947–1961[a]

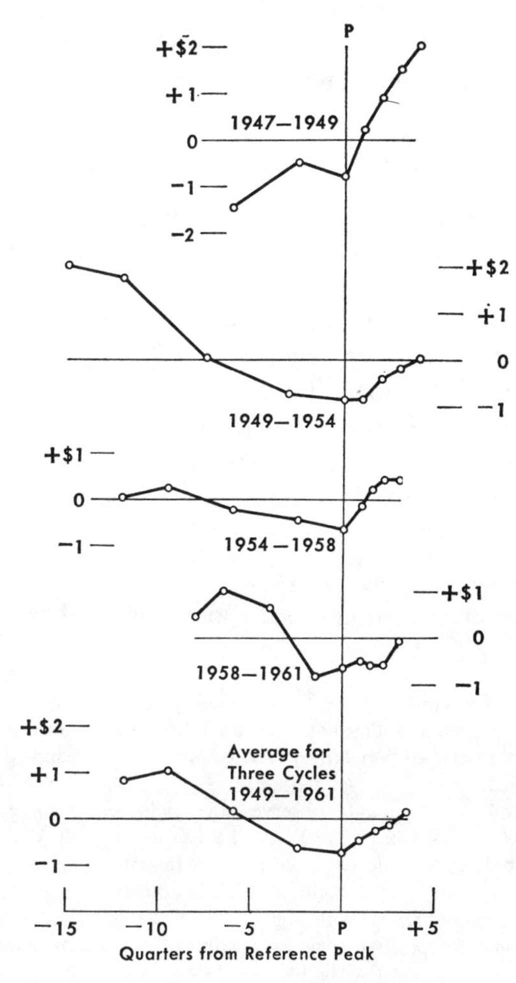

Source: U. S. Department of Commerce, Office of Business Economics, National Income Division.
[a] 1954 dollars, national income basis.

findings imply that when state and local fiscal behavior has deviated from its basic pattern of secular rise it has deviated in a stabilizing rather than a perverse direction. This point is illustrated by Figures 8 and 9. Figure 8 shows the reference cycle patterns for state and local own receipts when deviations from trend alone are considered. Figure 9 shows the patterns for deviations from trend in the case of total state and local expenditures.[17] Figure 8 reveals that the patterns of trend deviations in state-local own receipts improved with each succeeding postwar cycle to the point where, in the 1958-61 cycle, there was a nearly perfect pattern of increase during expansion and decline during contraction. On the expenditure side, in every case except the 1947-49 cycle, there was a stabilizing pattern of expansion decline and contraction rise.

Tax Yield Response, Unadjusted for Rate Changes

The behavior of a tax is stabilizing if its yield changes in the same direction as the national income. Conversely, if the marginal yield-income ratio (r_m) is negative, the behavior of the tax is destabilizing.[18] An observed change in tax collections may be an automatic (or built-in) response of yield to an income change (ΔT_b), or it may be attributable to a discretionary change in the tax law or the quality of administration (ΔT_d). Thus the observed marginal yield-income ratio, $\Delta T/\Delta Y$, may be written as the sum of the built-in and discretionary ratios:

$$r_m = \frac{\Delta T_b}{\Delta Y} + \frac{\Delta T_d}{\Delta Y}\,.$$

Ideally, an investigation of state-local fiscal behavior would use the methods that have been developed by the many excellent studies

[17] To avoid having to calculate trend values twice, the estimates used in the next section for constant dollar data are used here. Since absolute dollar magnitudes are not a matter of concern in this section, this procedure does not impair the validity of the results.

[18] Using T and Y to indicate observed tax yield and income, the marginal ratio may be defined as $r_m = \Delta T/\Delta Y$, or the change in yield divided by the income change. These criteria derive from the fact that the stability of the economy is a function of the size of the multiplier. Under most circumstances, the size of the multiplier varies inversely with the value of the marginal ratio of yield to income. The larger the positive (negative) value of r_m, the more stabilizing (perverse) is the behavior of the tax (or the tax system).

of federal fiscal policy.[19] The built-in ratio and the discretionary ratio would each be estimated for the major categories of state and local receipts. To proceed in this fashion, however, is to become involved quickly in an unhappy dilemma. Meaningful analysis of cyclical behavior during fluctuations as brief and as moderate in amplitude as those since World War II requires the use of quarterly data. But the available quarterly data are inadequate for the purpose of breaking down the observed ratio between its automatic and discretionary components. The breakdown can be estimated, however, from annual data for categories of receipts that account for about 60 percent of the total.

This section will be concerned only with the observed marginal ratio, which will be referred to as M. For this analysis the available quarterly data are quite acceptable. An attempt will be made in the next section, using annual data, to define the characteristics of the automatic behavior of state and local receipts.

A major advantage of the approach used in this section over the National Bureau Method is that the magnitude as well as the algebraic sign of the marginal ratio is significant. Moreover, if it is assumed that the values of M are additive,[20] the analysis can proceed directly from consideration of the behavior of total receipts to analysis of particular components without sacrificing comparability.

Specifically, the procedure followed in this section uses the turning points in the quarterly gross national product series to define the expansions and contractions.[21] The values of M are calculated

[19] The most recent is by Lewis, *Federal Fiscal Policy*. See also Nevins D. Baxter, "Built-in Fiscal Stabilizers in the United States," *Zeitschrift für Nationalökonomie*, Band 12, Heft 1-2 (1962), pp. 145-52; M. O. Clement, "The Quantitative Impact of Automatic Stabilizers," *Review of Economics and Statistics*, Vol. 42 (February 1960), pp. 56-61; Leo Cohen, "An Empirical Measurement of the Built-in Flexibility of the Income Tax," *American Economic Review*, Vol. 40 (May 1959), pp. 532-41, and comments by Joseph A. Pechman in the same issue, pp. 552-55; and the extensive pre-1959 literature cited by Musgrave, *Public Finance*, pp. 506, 511.

[20] For periods characterized by substantial shifts in the receipts mix this assumption may be quite illegitimate. Suppose, for example, that an increase in corporate profits tax accruals is matched by a decline in property tax receipts. Such a shift in the receipts mix is not likely to be neutral in its effect on the national income. (See, for example, Musgrave, *Public Finance*, pp. 520-22; and Lewis, *Federal Fiscal Policy*, pp. 68-77.) Such neutrality is implied by the assumption that the values of M are additive.

[21] The peaks and troughs defined by the behavior of the real GNP coincide in every case with those defined by the GNP in current dollars. Such exact coin-

TABLE 3. Real Gross National Product in the Postwar Expansions and Contractions

(1954 dollars)

EXPANSIONS

Trough Quarter	Peak Quarter	Number of Quarters of Rise	Percent Change	
			Trough to Peak	Average Annual Rate[a]
1947-I[b]	1948-IV	(7)	(+ 6.79)	(+3.82)
1949-II	1953-II	16	+28.56	+6.48
1954-II	1957-III	13	+14.33	+4.20
1958-I	1960-II	9	+12.49	+5.37
1961-I	1964-IV[c]	(15)	(+20.38)	(+5.07)

CONTRACTIONS

Peak Quarter	Trough Quarter	Number of Quarters of Decline	Percent Change	
			Peak to Trough	Average Annual Rate
1948-IV	1949-II	2	−2.35	−4.88
1953-II	1954-II	4	−3.67	−3.67
1957-III	1958-I	2	−4.38	−9.37
1960-II	1961-I	3	−1.79	−2.38

Sources: U. S. Department of Commerce, *U. S. Income and Output* (1958) and *Survey of Current Business* (July 1962, July 1964, February 1965).

Note: Parentheses indicate that the period to which the figure refers is less than a complete reference cycle phase.

[a] $GNP_t = GNP_o (1+r)^t$.

[b] The actual trough quarter is 1946-IV, but quarterly estimates of GNP in 1954 dollars are only available beginning with 1947-I.

[c] Latest date for which data were available at the time this table was completed: not a true reference cycle peak quarter.

for each expansion and contraction of the postwar period for as many receipts series as are available on a comparable, seasonally-adjusted basis.[22] Table 3 summarizes the behavior of the real GNP

---

cidence does not obtain with the National Bureau's reference cycle dates (see Table 1). The timing of the peaks is the same for three of the four postwar cycles. The exception is the GNP lead of one quarter in 1953. The situation is reversed in the case of the dating of troughs. The GNP hit bottom two quarters before the NBER trough in 1949, and one quarter early in 1954 and 1958. Only in 1961 does exact coincidence obtain. This behavior is not surprising in light of the confession by Wesley C. Mitchell that "it is usually more difficult to date the ebb of contraction than the crest of expansion." (*What Happens During Business Cycles, A Progress Report* [National Bureau of Economic Research, 1951], p. 73.)

during the postwar cycles. Figures for the expansion that is in progress as this paper is being completed are included in the table for reference purposes. No attempt is made to apply the marginal ratio analysis to the period since 1961.

Results of the Marginal Ratio Analysis

The observed marginal ratios for each postwar expansion and contraction appear in Table 4 for total state and local own receipts

TABLE 4. Values of *M* for Postwar Expansions and Contractions: Total State and Local Own Receipts

Period	Total State and Local Own Receipts	State Own Receipts	Local Own Receipts	Other Receipts[a]
Expansions:				
1947-I to 1948-IV	0.124	0.052	0.064	0.008
1949-II to 1953-II	0.065	0.028	0.028	0.009
1954-II to 1957-III	0.135	0.056	0.063	0.016
1958-I to 1960-II	0.135	0.066	0.053	0.016
Contractions:				
1948-IV to 1949-II	−0.179	−0.078	−0.105	0.004
1953-II to 1954-II	−0.102	−0.044	−0.052	−0.006
1957-III to 1958-I	−0.011	0.007	−0.022	0.004
1960-II to 1961-I	−0.121	−0.032	−0.093	0.004

Sources: National Income Division, U. S. Department of Commerce. U. S. Department of Commerce, *U. S. Income and Output* (1958), and *Survey of Current Business* (July 1962).

[a] Receipts for which no state-local breakdown is available: corporate profits tax accruals and contributions for social insurance.

and for a breakdown of the totals between the two levels of government. The positive values of *M* indicate that the behavior of receipts was stabilizing during every postwar expansion. The results also show, however, that state and local revenues behaved perversely in every contraction, with the sole exception of the 1957-58 recession, when state receipts were moderately stabilizing. In all contractions but 1953-54, corporate profits tax accruals were sufficiently stabilizing to offset the perverse behavior of social insurance contributions. State and local receipts were stabilizing to roughly the same degree during the four expansions. During the contractions, however, local receipts were substantially more perverse than state revenues. It is important to remember in this con-

[22] National income basis data. The implicit price deflators for personal consumption expenditures are used to convert all receipts data to 1954 dollars.

nection that state and local governments share about equally in total revenues.

Table 5 breaks down the expansion and contraction values of *M* for total state-local own receipts among six categories. The small increases in nearly all categories relative to the GNP in the 1949-53

TABLE 5. Values of *M* for Postwar Expansions and Contractions: Six Categories of State and Local Receipts

	EXPANSIONS			
Receipts Category	*1947-I to 1948-IV*	*1949-II to 1953-II*	*1954-II to 1957-III*	*1958-I to 1960-II*
Contributions for Social Insurance	0.009	0.006	0.012	0.009
Personal Tax and Non-Tax Receipts	0.019	0.008	0.008	0.028
Business Property Taxes	0.034	0.021	0.049	0.040
Miscellaneous Indirect Business Taxes	0.025	0.010	0.011	0.011
Sales Taxes	0.038	0.017	0.034	0.040
Corporate Profits Tax Accruals	−0.001	0.003	0.004	0.007
	CONTRACTIONS			
Receipts Category	*1948-IV to 1949-II*	*1953-II to 1954-II*	*1957-III to 1958-I*	*1960-II to 1961-I*
Contributions for Social Insurance	−0.009	−0.015	−0.004	−0.017
Personal Tax and Non-Tax Receipts	−0.046	−0.024	−0.009	−0.037
Business Property Taxes	−0.081	−0.037	−0.021	−0.072
Miscellaneous Indirect Business Taxes	−0.020	−0.017	−0.004	−0.031
Sales Taxes	−0.036	−0.018	0.011	0.015
Corporate Profits Tax Accruals	0.013	0.009	0.008	0.021

Sources: Same as for Table 4.

expansion are the most striking result. The domination of this period by the Korean War probably accounts for a good part of this finding. The average annual rate of increase in the gross national product was higher during these years than during the other three postwar expansions, and the direct controls that were imposed on consumer credit and civilian construction no doubt served to limit the growth of state and local tax bases. At the same time, the rapid increase in individual incomes may have expanded revenues rapidly enough to make state and local officials think twice about raising rates and adopting new taxes.

The magnitude of the response of total state and local revenues to change in the gross national product was identical in the two most recent expansions. From the first to the second of these, however, a number of significant changes took place. Among these were increases in the stabilizing behavior of sales taxes, corporate profits tax accruals, and personal tax and non-tax receipts. At the same time, the value of *M* decreased for business property taxes and contributions for social insurance. Compared with the 1947-48 expansion, the results for the 1958-60 period show that, with the exception of miscellaneous indirect business taxes, every source was equally or more stabilizing in the latter case.

Turning now to the results of Table 5 as they pertain to behavior during contractions, it is clear that with the exception of corporate profits tax accruals, there was a substantial movement away from perversity from the first to the third contraction. In the 1960-61 contraction, however, the negative value of *M* increased in spite of improvement in the behavior of corporate profits tax accruals and sales taxes.[23]

Do the aggregate data hide differences in the behavior of the receipts of state and local governments? Table 6 summarizes the results when the individual categories are broken down between state and local governments. The behavior of every category of state receipts except miscellaneous indirect business taxes was more stabilizing during the 1958-60 period than during any previous expansion. Moreover, since 1949 state receipts have been more stabilizing in each succeeding expansion, a trend that is explained by the behavior of sales taxes and personal tax and non-tax receipts.

On the other hand, no clear trends appear in the results for local government receipts. The difference between the results for the two most recent expansions is clearly the consequence of a decline in the value of *M* for business property taxes.

An inverse relation between the size of *M* and the magnitude of the GNP decline is apparent in the results for state as well as for local receipts. In every contraction the behavior of total state re-

[23] Note that the size of the peak-to-trough percentage decline in the real GNP (see Table 3) increased from the first to the third recession, but that the drop was substantially less in the fourth than in any of the first three.

TABLE 6. Values of *M* for Postwar Expansions and Contractions: State-Local Receipts Breakdown

EXPANSIONS

Receipts Category	*1947-I to 1948-IV*	*1949-II to 1953-II*	*1954-II to 1957-III*	*1958-I to 1960-II*
State Receipts:				
Personal Tax and Non-Tax Receipts	0.006	0.006	0.018	0.022
Miscellaneous Indirect Business Taxes	0.016	0.007	0.009	0.008
Sales Taxes: General	0.017	0.009	0.015	0.018
Miscellaneous	0.014	0.005	0.013	0.017
Business Property Taxes	−0.001	0.001	0.001	0.001
Local Receipts:				
Personal Tax and Non-Tax Receipts	0.013	0.002	0.007	0.006
Miscellaneous Indirect Business Taxes	0.009	0.003	0.002	0.003
Sales Taxes	0.007	0.003	0.006	0.005
Business Property Taxes	0.035	0.020	0.048	0.039

CONTRACTIONS

Receipts Category	*1948-IV to 1949-II*	*1953-II to 1954-II*	*1957-III to 1958-I*	*1960-II to 1961-I*
State Receipts:				
Personal Tax and Non-Tax Receipts	−0.031	−0.010	−0.006	−0.024
Miscellaneous Indirect Business Taxes	−0.014	−0.012	0.003	−0.021
Sales Taxes: General	−0.005	−0.004	0.009	0.009
Miscellaneous	−0.026	−0.016	0.002	0.003
Business Property Taxes	−0.002	−0.002	−0.001	−0.001
Local Receipts:				
Personal Tax and Non-Tax Receipts	−0.015	−0.014	−0.003	−0.013
Miscellaneous Indirect Business Taxes	−0.006	−0.005	0.001	−0.010
Sales Taxes	−0.005	0.002	0	0.001
Business Property Taxes	−0.079	−0.035	−0.020	−0.017

Sources: Same as for Table 4.

ceipts was less perverse than the behavior of local receipts. Nearly all the categories that were stabilizing in the more recent contractions were state sources.[24]

[24] Though no allocation is attempted, virtually all corporate profits taxes are levied by states, a fact that would add even more weight to the conclusion that state receipts are less perverse than are local receipts during contractions.

Total Own Receipts Adjusted for Secular Trend

Removal of trend from the gross national product series and from the state and local total own receipts series yields the marginal ratios that appear in Table 7. Without exception, during each succeeding expansion and each succeeding contraction total state and local own receipts were more stabilizing (or less destabilizing). These results mirror the finding, above, that the reference cycle patterns for deviations from the secular trend in receipts have been moving in the direction of a more stabilizing pattern.

TABLE 7. Values of *M* for Postwar Expansions and Contractions: State and Local Own Receipts

(Adjusted for Secular Trend)

Period	*Total State and Local Own Receipts*
Expansions:	
1947-I to 1948-IV	−0.174
1949-II to 1953-II	−0.011
1954-II to 1957-III	0.051
1958-I to 1960-II	0.053
Contractions:	
1948-IV to 1949-II	−0.048
1953-II to 1954-II	0.011
1957-III to 1958-I	0.038
1960-II to 1961-I	0.056

Sources: Same as for Table 4.

Two additional points deserve mention. The negative marginal ratios for the first two postwar expansions are attributable, respectively, to the fact that the GNP increased at a sub-trend rate during 1947 and 1948, and to the fact that receipts rose at a sub-trend rate during the Korean War years. Secondly, it is interesting to note that the trend-removal procedure yields a positive marginal ratio for all but the first of the postwar contractions. This, of course, is to be expected, given the results of Figure 8.

Tax Yield Response, Adjusted for Rate Changes

Changes in tax yields may be automatic responses to income fluctuations, or they may result from discretionary changes in tax laws and in the quality of administration. In the previous section this distinction was set aside in order to use quarterly data in an analysis of the behavior of the observed marginal ratio of yield changes to income changes. The crudeness of the available quarterly data made it impossible to distinguish automatic fiscal responses from behavior that originated in deliberate legislative or executive action. Annual data will be used in this section in an attempt to define the characteristics of the automatic behavior of state and local receipts.

At the beginning of the last section it was established that the automatic responsiveness of tax collections to income changes may be expressed as a built-in marginal ratio, $\Delta T_b/\Delta Y$. An alternative measure of tax behavior is the income elasticity of collections (E_T), which is defined as the percentage change in collections divided by the percentage change in income. If tax yield data are adjusted to abstract from the effects of discretionary actions by legislators and administrators, we have: $E_T = \frac{\Delta T_b/T_o}{\Delta Y/Y_o}$, where T_o and Y_o are yield and income at the beginning of the period in question. This expression may be rewritten as r_o, $E_T = \frac{\Delta T_b}{\Delta Y}$, where $r_o = T_o/Y_o$. Since the initial yield-income ratio, r_o, is always given by observation, E_T can easily be calculated from $\Delta T_b/\Delta Y$, and vice versa. Thus the built-in marginal ratio and the income elasticity of yield may be used interchangeably to measure the automatic responsiveness of yields to income changes.

The procedure used in this section to estimate the GNP elasticities of particular taxes is analogous to that employed by Harold M. Groves and C. Harry Kahn in their notable article.[25] GNP and constant rates data, expressed as first differences, are used to derive by regression analysis an estimate of the average value of E_T during

[25] "The Stability of State and Local Tax Yields," *American Economic Review*, Vol. 42 (March 1952), pp. 87-102.

ing the postwar period for each of four major state and local taxes. Since all the available data for a particular tax are used to derive a single estimate of E_T, the approach will not tell us whether the GNP elasticities have changed during the period.[26]

The behavior of yield at constant rates for a flat rate tax can be approximated from the behavior of the tax base.[27] This method will be used in the following analysis whenever it proves to be the most direct method of estimating E_T.

The following categories of state and local receipts are considered in detail: (1) state general sales taxes; (2) state and local property taxes; (3) state gasoline taxes; and (4) state personal income taxes. The first three are the most important sources of state and local revenues. State income taxes are of interest for their potential as revenue producers, though in the postwar period they have been the fastest-growing revenue source. Even though these four classes of state and local receipts are the only significant sources for which this kind of analysis is feasible, they did account for more than 60 percent of total state and local own receipts in fiscal 1961.

State General Sales Taxes

At the beginning of the postwar period the general sales tax was a part of the revenue systems of twenty-three states. By July 1, 1965,

[26] This approach assumes that the legal definition of the tax base and the quality of administration remain constant. Regrettably, no method is yet available for quantifying changes in these factors in a general analysis of state and local taxes. Thus, with a few exceptions, it has not been possible explicitly to take them into account. Since tax administration presumably has improved since World War II, and since a number of states have broadened definitions of sales tax bases, the tendency of these factors to inflate the estimates of elasticities and built-in marginal ratios derived in this study (and in other analyses) should be taken into consideration by the reader.

[27] Separating the elements of yield elasticity that are attributable to changes in the tax base from those that can be attributed to changes in the effective tax rate, we may write

$$E_T = (1 + E_t \frac{B_1}{B_0}) E_b,$$

where E_t is the elasticity of the statutory tax rate t with respect to changes in the tax base B, or $\frac{\Delta t / t_0}{\Delta B / B_0}$ and where E_b is the income elasticity of the tax base, or $\frac{\Delta B / B_0}{\Delta Y / Y_0}$. In the case of a flat rate tax, $E_t = 0$, and the income elasticity of the tax yield equals the income elasticity of the tax base.

TABLE 8. Annual Changes in State General Sales Tax Collections and Gross National Product, 1946-61

(Millions of current dollars)

Fiscal Year	Change in Collections from Previous Year				Change in GNP
	Actual (1)	Attributable to Adoption or Repeal of Tax (2)	Attributable to Changes in Tax Rates (3)	Attributable to Changes in Tax Base (4)	(5)
1946	—	—	—	—	—
1947	281.1	0	0	281.1	20.2
1948	297.6	103.4	− 21.2	215.4	23.4
1949	130.4	0	34.2	96.2	14.5
1950	61.3	23.6	78.0	− 40.3	2.5
1951	331.1	8.1	0	323.0	46.4
1952	227.3	37.6	3.5	186.2	28.2
1953	204.2	0	0	204.2	21.1
1954	107.0	37.0	18.3	51.7	2.1
1955	96.8	0	0	96.8	15.7
1956	399.8	− 24.1	149.8	274.1	32.0
1957	336.7	142.4	− 7.9	202.2	23.4
1958	134.1	0	67.8	66.3	7.3
1959	190.2	0	34.4	155.8	26.7
1960	542.5	0	204.7	337.8	27.5
1961	201.6	79.5	0	122.1	10.8

Sources: U. S. Bureau of the Census, *Compendium of State Government Finances;* U. S. Department of Commerce, *U. S. Income and Output* (1958), and *Survey of Current Business* (July 1962).

fourteen more states (not including Hawaii) had adopted this most lucrative source of revenue, and nineteen of the original twenty-three states had raised their rates.

Table 8 breaks down the year-to-year changes in sales tax yield according to the factors responsible for the changes. Column 1 shows the changes in actual collections. In the second column the portion of total ΔT that is attributable to adoption or repeal of the tax appears for each year since 1946.

The estimates of changes in collections attributable to statutory rate changes are presented in column 3 of Table 8.[28] Estimates

[28] The usual approach to rate correction is to estimate what collections would have been in terms of the most recent rate structure. To apply this procedure, however, it must be possible to derive estimates of the tax base for each year of the period. Such estimates are calculable for a given federal tax. In this case there is no way of estimating, for example, what the sales tax base for Pennsylvania would have been in 1949, since the tax was not adopted until 1952.

are calculated separately for each state, using the formula

$$\Delta T_{(\Delta t)ij} = \Delta t_{ij} \frac{B_{(i-1)j} + B_{ij}}{2},$$

where $\Delta T_{(\Delta t)ij}$ is the desired estimate for state j of the change in yield from fiscal year $(i - 1)$ to fiscal year i, Δt_{ij} is the change in the effective tax rate for state j from year $(i - 1)$ to year i, and $B_{(i-1)j}$ and B_{ij} are the implicit tax bases for state j in the respective fiscal years. For states with unchanged tax rates, of course, $\Delta t_{ij} = 0$, and the full amount of the yield change is attributable to the change in the tax base. The totals of the estimates for each state appear in column 3.

The estimates in column 4 are derived in the same way by the formula

$$\Delta T_{(\Delta B)ij} = \Delta B_{ij} \frac{t_{(i-1)} + t_{ij}}{2}.$$

In this case, if the tax rate of state j does not change during the period, then $t_{(i-1)j} = t_{ij}$, and the estimate is the same as that given by the simple formula: $\Delta T = t_o \Delta B$.

The key results of the analysis appear in column 4 of Table 8, which shows the year-to-year changes in total sales tax collections that are attributable to fluctuations in the sales tax base.

In the same way, changes in sales tax collections are broken down into three categories for each expansion period considered as a unit.[29] The results appear in Table 9. Only a few remarks are necessary concerning procedures. The estimates in column 2 are the total actual collections in each of the peak years for the states that adopted sales taxes during each of the expansions.[30] The same procedure used in deriving the estimates of columns 3 and 4 of Table 8 is used for columns 3 and 4 of the present table, the only difference being that $(i - 1)$ and i in the estimation formulas refer respectively in

[29] Since the contractions of the postwar period were all one year or less in duration, whatever light this section throws on recession relationships appears in Table 8.

[30] Four states—Connecticut, Maryland, Rhode Island, and Tennessee—adopted sales taxes during the first postwar expansion; four states—Florida, Georgia, Maine, and South Carolina—adopted such taxes during the second; two states—Nevada and Pennsylvania—did so during the 1954-57 expansion; no states were added to the roster during the final expansion period.

TABLE 9. Changes in State General Sales Tax Collections During Postwar Economic Expansions

Dates of Expansions (Fiscal Years)	Trough-to-Peak Changes in Collections			
	Actual (1)	Attributable to Adoption of Tax (2)	Attributable to Changes in Tax Rates (3)	Attributable to Changes in Tax Base (4)
	Millions of Current Dollars			
1946–48	578.7	103.4	0	475.3
1949–53	823.9	220.3	127.2	476.4
1954–57	833.3	162.8	145.4	525.1
1958–60	732.7	0	223.6	509.1
	As Percent of Total			
1946–48	100	18	0	82
1949–53	100	27	15	58
1954–57	100	20	17	63
1958–60	100	0	31	69

Source: U. S. Bureau of the Census, *Compendium of State Government Finances.*

this case to the initial and final years of the expansion. As in the earlier analysis, the estimates are built up from calculations for each individual state.

Thus, Table 9 summarizes the results of the analysis; again, the results in column 4 are the most important. It is interesting that the ranking of the expansions by the size of ΔT is different in column 4 from the ranking that appears in column 1. This is explained, of course, by the extraordinarily large proportion of the gross increase attributable to new adoptions and to changes in rates during the 1949 to 1953 expansion.

The results of Table 9 should be compared with the expansion period findings of the previous section, even though the validity of such a comparison is questionable because of differences in timing. In this section, the data used are not adjusted for price level changes. Since the analysis in the preceding section is based on adjusted data, the results of Table 9 must be translated into constant dollars, as shown in Table 10.[31]

[31] This adjustment is accomplished in three stages. First, the annual sales tax receipts totals in column 1 of Table 9 are corrected for price level changes using

TABLE 10. Changes in State General Sales Tax Collections During Economic Expansions

(Millions of 1954 dollars)

Dates of Expansions (Fiscal Years)	Trough-to-Peak Changes in Collections			
	Actual (1)	Attributable to Adoption of Tax (2)	Attributable to Changes in Tax Rates (3)	Attributable to Changes in Tax Base (4)
1946–48	n.a.	n.a.	n.a.	n.a.
1949–53	676	183	101	392
1954–57	704	141	120	443
1958–60	608	0	188	420

Sources: Table 4. U. S. Department of Commerce, *U. S. Income and Output* (1958), and *Survey of Current Business* (July 1962).

When unadjusted annual data are used to calculate the marginal ratios for the three expansions between 1949 and 1960, the results that appear in column 2 of Table 11 are obtained. Column 3 reproduces the results of the preceding section, where the marginal ratios are calculated from unadjusted quarterly data. Since the ranking of the expansions by the size of $\Delta T/\Delta Y$ is not changed by using annual data, these results lend additional credibility to the hypothesis that sales tax collections have been increasingly stabilizing from one expansion to the next since 1949. If we abstract from structural changes, the trend toward more stabilizing behavior shows up even more clearly (column 4).

Table 12 shows that most of the movement toward a higher marginal ratio resulted from an increase in the initial yield-income ratio. The income elasticity of yield remained relatively constant throughout the period from 1949 to 1960.

Given state general sales tax collections at constant rates, the

---

the implicit GNP deflators for personal consumption expenditures (excluding services). (Because these deflators are not available for 1946, the first expansion is not considered in the following discussion.) A percentage distribution is then calculated from the estimates in columns 2, 3, and 4. Finally, the expansion values of total ΔT are calculated, and the results allocated among the three categories according to the percentage distribution of the original, unadjusted data. The results of these calculations appear in Tables 10 and 11 along with the corresponding changes in the gross national product (for fiscal years, in 1954 dollars).

TABLE 11. Changes in State General Sales Tax Collections During Postwar Expansions Relative to Changes in Gross National Product

(1954 dollars)

Dates of Expansions (Fiscal Years)	ΔGNP (1)	ΔT_1[a] / ΔGNP (2)	ΔT_2[b] / ΔGNP (3)	ΔT_3[c] / ΔGNP (4)
1946–48	n.a.	n.a.	n.a.	n.a.
1949–53	45.6	0.0148	0.009	0.0086
1954–57	42.8	0.0164	0.015	0.0104
1958–60	35.0	0.0174	0.018	0.0120

Sources: Table 10, U. S. Department of Commerce, *U. S. Income and Output* (1958), and *Survey of Current Business* (July 1962).

[a] ΔT_1 = Total actual change in sales tax collections, annual data, column 1, Table 10.

[b] ΔT_2 = Quarterly data, total change in collections, divided by quarterly ΔGNP.

[c] ΔT_3 = Change in sales tax collections attributable to change in tax base, annual data; that is, column 4 of Table 10.

average GNP elasticity of the yield can be estimated. An estimate of E_T that takes into account the data for all the postwar years is given by the regression equation $Z_s = d + eX$, where Z_s is the annual percentage change in general sales tax collections, X is the annual percentage change in the GNP for the same fiscal year, d is a constant, and e is the desired estimate of E_T. The relevant yield data appear in Table 8. The dependent variable, Z_s, is the portion of the total change in general sales tax collections attributable to

TABLE 12. Marginal Yield-Income Ratio, Initial Yield-Income Ratio, and Implicit Income Elasticity of Yield from State General Sales Taxes During Economic Expansions

(Billions of 1954 dollars)

Dates of Expansions (Fiscal Years)	ΔT_3 / ΔGNP (1)	T_o (2)	GNP_o (3)	r_o (4)	Implicit E_T (5)
1946–48	n.a.	1.219	285.3	0.0043	—
1949–53	0.0086	1.806	295.8	0.0061	1.41
1954–57	0.0104	2.553	363.6	0.0070	1.48
1958–60	0.0120	3.202	401.6	0.0082	1.46

Sources: Table 11, and U. S. Department of Commerce, *U. S. Income and Output* (1958), and *Survey of Current Business* (July 1962).

the change in the tax base (column 4 divided by collections at the beginning of the fiscal year). Throwing out the datum for 1947, a step justified by the extraordinary circumstances of the postwar transition period, the least squares estimates are given by the following equation:

$$Z_s = -0.49 + 1.27X$$

$$\overline{S}_{z \cdot x} = 2.20 \qquad r_{xz}^2 = 0.878.$$

This estimate of $E_T = 1.27$ is substantially larger than those obtained by other investigators.[32] Indeed, if the estimate is re-calculated for the twenty-three states that have used sales taxes throughout the postwar period, estimates as high as 1.59 are obtained (when data for the Korean War years—1951 and 1952—are omitted).

State and Local Property Taxes

The property tax is the cornerstone of the state and local revenue system, but this status has not kept it from losing ground in recent decades. Property tax collections declined as a proportion of total state-local own receipts from 42 percent in 1946 to 38 percent in 1964, and the 1946 percentage was itself substantially smaller than the 1929 figure of 63 percent. Note, however, that the extended decline of the property tax was arrested in the early 1950's; it has held its own at roughly 38 percent of state-local receipts since 1951.

[32] Dick Netzer's estimate of the secular GNP elasticity of the state and local general sales tax base for the period 1946-57 is 0.92. He adopts an elasticity of 1.00 for his projection of collections in 1970. ("Financial Needs and Resources over the Next Decade: State and Local Governments," in *Public Finances: Needs, Sources, and Utilization* [A Conference of the Universities-National Bureau Committee for Economic Research, A Report of the National Bureau of Economic Research, Princeton, 1961], pp. 30, 38.) An analysis by David George Davies leads him to accept the hypothesis that the state personal income elasticity of state general sales tax collections per 1 percent of tax rate equals 1.00. Since the cyclical GNP elasticity of personal income tends to be less than unity, Davies' findings suggest a GNP elasticity of collections of less than 1.00 ("The Sensitivity of Consumption Taxes to Fluctuations in Income," *National Tax Journal,* Vol. 15 [September 1962], pp. 281-90). Groves and Kahn ("Stability of Tax Yields," pp. 87-102), using a regression equation of the form $\log T = \log a + e \log Y$ (where T is tax collections, Y is state income payments, a is a constant, and e is the income elasticity), estimate the income elasticity of the sales taxes of eight states for the period from the mid-1930's to the late 1940's. Their estimates range from 0.99 to 1.11, with an average of about 1.06.

TABLE 13. State and Local Property Tax Bases, Assessed Values, Collections, Effective Tax Rates, and Ratios of Assessed to "Market" Values, 1945-59

Year	Property Tax Base: Net Stock of Private Tangible Assets (Billions of current dollars) (Calendar years)	Actual Assessed Value of Taxable Property in 12 States (Millions of current dollars) (Calendar years)	Total Assessed Value of All Taxable Property in the United States		Property Tax Collections		
			1956 Actual, Other Years Estimated	As Percent of Property Tax Base (Col. 3 ÷ Col. 1)	Actual (Millions of current dollars) (Fiscal years)	As Percent of Total Assessed Value (Col. 5 ÷ Col. 3)	As Percent of Property Tax Base (Col. 5 ÷ Col. 1)
	(1)	(2)	(3)	(4)	(5)	(6)	(7)
1945	475.5	41,476	137.0	29.8	n.a.	—	—
1946	576.8	42,706	141.1	24.5	4,891	3.6	1.0
1947	692.1	47,152	155.8	22.5	5,254	3.7	0.9
1948	766.7	51,157	168.9	22.0	5,822	3.7	0.8
1949	771.1	55,218	182.2	23.6	6,490	3.8	0.8
1950	892.9	57,010	188.2	21.1	7,112	3.9	0.9
1951	979.3	61,253	202.4	20.7	7,656	4.1	0.9
1952	1,020.4	65,617	216.8	21.2	8,296	4.1	0.8
1953	1,061.0	68,999	228.0	21.5	9,017	4.2	0.9
1954	1,101.7	72,141	238.4	21.6	9,681	4.2	0.9
1955	1,184.2	76,869	253.9	21.4	10,372	4.4	0.9
1956	1,283.4	82,481	272.4	21.2	11,260	4.4	1.0
1957	1,376.0	88,499	292.3	21.2	12,323	4.5	1.0
1958	1,438.2	92,611	305.9	21.3	13,479	4.6	1.0
1959	n.a.	96,745	319.5	—	14,535	4.8	1.0

Sources: Goldsmith, *National Wealth*; Reports of State Tax Commissions and Boards of Equalization; U. S. Department of Commerce, *U. S. Income and Output* (1958), and *Survey of Current Business* (July, 1962); and U. S. Bureau of the Census, *U. S. Census of Governments: 1957, Vol. V, Taxable Property Values in the United States* (1959).

Some idea of the significance of property taxes relative to other revenue sources is given by the fact that the second most important category—state general sales taxes—yielded only 11 percent of total own receipts in 1964.

The property tax is peculiar in that the relation between yield and base is a function of two ratios—the nominal tax rate, t, and the assessment ratio, a. Thus, $T = t(aB)$, and it is possible for a community to experience simultaneously an increasing nominal rate and a falling effective rate, if a declining ratio of assessed to true market values more than offsets the effects of the rising nominal rate. A number of studies, including this one, suggest that this curious phenomenon has characterized a good part of the postwar experience in the United States.

Table 13 summarizes the evidence on which the conclusions of this section are based. Column 1 is an approximation of the property tax base for the years from 1945 to 1958 (more recent data were not available when these estimates were prepared). The estimates are derived from the comprehensive study of the national wealth of the United States by Raymond Goldsmith and the National Bureau of Economic Research.[33]

Given estimates of the underlying property tax base, and given annual property tax collections, rough estimates of the average effective tax rate in each of the postwar years can be calculated. Provision is made for a slight lag in collections by defining the effective rate as the ratio of fiscal year collections to the base in the previous calendar year. Property tax collections and the estimates of average effective rates appear in Table 13, columns 5 and 7, respectively.

The following procedure is used to estimate property tax assessments for the 1945-59 period, a step that is necessary because, to my knowledge, no series for total property tax assessments in the

[33] *The National Wealth of the United States in the Postwar Period* (National Bureau of Economic Research Studies in Capital Formation and Financing, Princeton, 1962). The Goldsmith estimate of the total net stock of tangible assets in current prices, excluding military items, is the starting point for our derivation of an approximation of the true property tax base for a given year. From Goldsmith's total are subtracted his estimates of the values of (1) public civilian structures, (2) public producer durables, (3) public lands, (4) monetary metals, and (5) net foreign assets. This calculation yields an estimate of the net private stock of tangible assets in current prices.

United States is published. Use of the reports of the tax commissions and boards of equalization of twelve states[34] permits the construction of a consistent series for each state of total property tax assessments. In each case the assessed valuation total for calendar 1956 corresponds with the figure published by the U.S. Bureau of the Census in the 1957 Census of Governments.[35] Thus the total value of assessments for the twelve states for which consistent annual series are available amounts to 30.3 percent of the total of all assessments for all states in 1956. If we assume that total assessments in the twelve states were the same proportion of the forty-eight-state total in every year of the period that they were in 1956,[36] estimates of the total assessed value of taxable property in the United States may be obtained by dividing the twelve-state totals by 0.303. These results appear in column 3 of Table 13.

Column 4 of Table 13 shows the ratio of assessed valuations to the actual value of the net private stock of tangible assets. It is interesting to note how closely these ratios compare with those calculated for 1946 and 1948 by Mabel Newcomer.[37] Though these are the only postwar years for which the ratios are estimated by Professor Newcomer, her ratio for 1946 is 24.5 percent—identical to the ratio derived here—and her ratio for 1948 is 22.9 percent—only slightly different from the estimate in this study of 22.0 percent.

Since state and local property taxes essentially are flat rate taxes, an estimate of the GNP elasticity of yield at constant rates is given by the GNP elasticity of the tax base. Two estimates of E_b

[34] Arizona, California, Georgia, Iowa, Michigan, Missouri, Montana, New Jersey, North Carolina, Texas, Washington, and West Virginia.

[35] *U.S. Census of Governments: 1957,* Vol. V, *Taxable Property Values in the United States* (1959), p. 23. Thus, for 1956, we have some assurance that the assessment figures for the twelve states are comparable as far as the Census Bureau is concerned. In addition, the fact that the 1956 data correspond with the Census Bureau compendium enables us to assume that the Census estimate of total assessments for all forty-eight states is comparable to the concept of assessments used in this study.

[36] Since this analysis was completed, the 1962 Census of Governments has been published. Its data provide a crude check on the validity of the stable proportion assumption. In 1961, assessments in the twelve states accounted for 30.4 percent of the national total (again excluding Alaska and Hawaii). (U.S. Bureau of the Census, *Census of Governments: 1962,* Vol. II, *Taxable Property Values* [1963], p. 29.)

[37] "The Decline of the General Property Tax," *National Tax Journal,* Vol. 6 (December 1953), p. 46.

are calculated from the relevant data expressed as first differences, both of which exclude the datum for 1946. The first estimate uses all the remaining data, and the second excludes data for 1947 and 1951:

$$Z_p = 2.94 + 0.78X \tag{1}$$
$$\overline{S}_{z \cdot x} = 3.95 \qquad r_{xz}^2 = 0.526.$$

$$Z_p = 2.44 + 0.82X \tag{2}$$
$$\overline{S}_{z \cdot x} = 2.69 \qquad r_{xz}^2 = 0.654.$$

Elimination of 1947 and 1951 substantially improves the fit, but both estimates of E_b are remarkably similar, lending support to the hypothesis that the GNP elasticity of property tax collections at constant rates is approximately 0.8.[38]

State Gasoline Tax Collections

In this section is analyzed the behavior of the receipts category that during the 1930's and until 1944 was the most important source of state tax receipts. Since gasoline taxes are unit taxes, the actual collections series published by the Bureau of the Census may be adjusted directly for changes in tax rates.

Gasoline tax yields at constant rates are estimated separately for each state. Given collections adjusted for rate changes, two estimates of E_T are calculated for state gasoline taxes using the data expressed as first differences. The datum for 1947 is not used in

[38] This estimate is quite a bit smaller than Netzer's constant dollars secular elasticity of 1.0 (in *Public Finances: Needs, Sources, and Utilization,* p. 30), and slightly smaller than Ernest Kurnow's cross-section estimates for all real property in 1956 of 0.9 ("On the Elasticity of the Real Property Tax," *Journal of Finance,* Vol. 18 [March 1963], p. 57). It is also substantially smaller than Benjamin Bridges' estimate of 1.0 for approximately the same period. Professor Bridges' figure is derived from a slightly different selection of Goldsmith's data than is used in this study, and he employs a different estimating procedure ("Income Elasticity of the Property Tax Base," *National Tax Journal,* Vol. 17 [September 1964], pp. 253-64). David M. Blank argues that a reasonable assumption is a secular elasticity of 0.75 to 0.8 and an "income elasticity over the cycle" of 0.2 ("The Role of the Real Property Tax in Municipal Finance," *National Tax Journal,* Vol. 7 [December 1954], pp. 321, 326), while the Groves and Kahn study suggests an income elasticity of assessments of approximately 0.2 ("Stability of Tax Yields," p. 90). A summing-up of a number of the issues in the vigorous debate regarding the elasticity of the property tax appears in a recent note by Netzer ("Income Elasticity of the Property Tax: A Post-Mortem Note," *National Tax Journal,* Vol. 17 [June 1964], pp. 205-07).

either calculation, and the second also omits the observation for 1950.

$$(1)\qquad \begin{aligned} Z_g &= 3.81 + 0.32X \\ \bar{S}_{z \cdot x} &= 1.83 \qquad r_{xz}^2 = 0.406. \end{aligned}$$

$$(2)\qquad \begin{aligned} Z_g &= 2.74 + 0.43X \\ \bar{S}_{z \cdot x} &= 1.16 \qquad r_{xz}^2 = 0.746. \end{aligned}$$

Omission of 1950 clearly gives a far better fit, and at the same time it provides a substantially higher elasticity estimate.[39] These results are more nearly the same as those of other investigators than was the case with our findings for general sales and property taxes.[40]

State Personal Income Taxes

This section summarizes the results of an attempt to define the basic characteristics of the cyclical behavior of state personal income taxes. At the beginning of the postwar period thirty-one states taxed personal incomes. None adopted income taxes between 1938 and 1961, when West Virginia and New Jersey entered the field (New Jersey's tax applies only to individuals who commute across the boundaries of the state). Indiana adopted a flat-rate net income tax in 1963. Alaska and Hawaii brought individual income taxes with them when they entered the Union. Hawaii's tax was adopted in 1901 and Alaska's in 1949.[41]

With a few exceptions (Maryland, Indiana, and Massachusetts), state personal income taxes are not levied at flat rates. In addition, special taxes, temporary reductions, and changes in rate structures, exemptions, and deductions have been frequent. For these reasons, the problem cannot be approached as it has been in other sections

[39] The best *a priori* rationale for dropping 1950 is the fact that the automotive industry sailed through the first postwar recession on the crest of its postwar boom. Thus gasoline sales were extraordinarily high while the GNP for that fiscal year reflected the general conditions of recession.

[40] Groves and Kahn present an estimate of 0.36 for the state income payments elasticity of the Wisconsin Motor fuel tax ("Stability of Tax Yields," p. 90). Duesenberry, Eckstein, and Fromm cite a long-run GNP elasticity of 0.42, which they derive from the 1957 survey of consumer expenditures by *Life* magazine. ("A Simulation of the United States Economy in Recession," *Econometrica,* Vol. 28 [October 1960], p. 780.)

[41] Advisory Commission on Intergovernmental Relations, *Tax Overlapping in the United States, 1964, An Information Report* (1964), pp. 22, 113-17.

of this study. Rather, the elasticity method is used to break down the GNP elasticity of personal income tax collections between E_b and E_t.

The base of the personal income tax is taxable income, defined here as total individual income after exemptions and deductions.[42] Dick Netzer uses quite a different concept. He defines taxable income as the Department of Commerce estimate of personal income for states with individual income taxes, "excluding estimated amounts of imputed and other nonmoney income and various types of nontaxable money income."[43] For this definition of the tax base, Netzer estimates that the "progressivity" of the 1957 state income tax system produced a "base" elasticity of yield of 1.7.[44] Netzer finds that taxable personal income rose *pari passu* with GNP, giving an E_T for that period of 1.7.

Since state income taxes typically are not flat rate taxes, it may not be assumed that $E_T = 0$. For this reason, an estimate of E_b will not be a reasonable approximation of the value of E_T.[45] Because of the complexity of the provisions of state income tax laws, no attempt is made independently to estimate E_t. Rather, an estimate of the income elasticity of "the" state income tax base is derived. This estimate of E_b, given Netzer's finding of $E_T = 1.7$, can be used to compute the implicit value of the base elasticity of yield (for my definition of the income tax base). Alternatively, given E_T and E_b, a rough estimate of E_t can be calculated for small changes in income, that is, when B_1/B_o is approximately equal to unity.

[42] If the effective tax rate is defined as the ratio of tax liability to income after deductions but before exemptions, and if the personal exemption is viewed as a zero rate bracket, then an ostensibly flat-rate tax such as Maryland's is moderately progressive over the lower end of the income range. Thus exclusion of exemptions from the tax base, a procedure that is necessary because of the way certain states define taxable income for reporting purposes, means that an important source of yield elasticity is attributed to base elasticity that properly should be attributed to E_t.

[43] In *Public Finances: Needs, Sources, and Utilization,* p. 37.

[44] Netzer's base elasticity of yield (E_B is defined as $\frac{\Delta T}{T_0} \cdot \frac{B_o}{\Delta B}$. This expression, multiplied by the GNP elasticity of the tax base, equals the GNP elasticity of the tax yield, that is,

$$E_T = \left(\frac{\Delta T}{T_O} \cdot \frac{B_O}{\Delta B}\right) \cdot \left(\frac{\Delta B}{B_O} \cdot \frac{Y_O}{\Delta Y}\right).$$

[45] See note 27.

Annual taxable income data for a number of years during which the statutory definitions of exemptions and deductions were not changed are available for three states: New York, Virginia, and North Carolina. These data can be used to calculate an estimate of the income elasticity of taxable income. Department of Commerce personal income estimates are used rather than the GNP, since a breakdown of the GNP by states is not available.

Expressing the data as first differences, estimation by least squares of the coefficients in the regression equation gives the following results:

$$Z_y = 2.37 + 1.39X$$

$$\overline{S}_{z \cdot x} = 3.17 \qquad r_{xz}^2 = 0.801.$$

The estimate of the personal income elasticity of taxable income (E_b) is 1.39. This result, coupled with the Netzer estimate of $E_T =$ 1.7, yields an implicit base elasticity of yield (Netzer's concept) of 1.2. Alternatively, the results imply an E_t of approximately 0.2 for small changes in income. These results are consistent with the established view, which is that the relatively high income elasticity of state income tax yield is a consequence primarily of high base elasticity rather than of graduated statutory rates.

Cyclical Behavior of State and Local Expenditures

Between 1946 and 1964 the gross national product in current dollars rose from $211 billion to $623 billion. The increase in state and local expenditures during the same period amounted to nearly 14 percent of the rise in the GNP. In this section the cyclical behavior of state and local expenditures is examined in as much detail as the available data permit. The discussion of the expenditure side need not be as extensive as the treatment of receipts, above, since the problem of distinguishing between automatic and discretionary behavior does not arise. All state and local expenditures, transfer payments as well as purchases of goods and services, are treated as autonomous in this study.

Results of the Marginal Ratio Analysis

The marginal ratios for each postwar expansion and contraction appear in Table 14 for total state and local expenditures and for a breakdown among seven categories of expenditures. A more detailed breakdown is not available in the national income accounts data, and the National Income Division does not attempt to separate the state from the local components of the quarterly estimates.

If the marginal ratio of expenditures to income is positive, be-

Table 14. Values of *M* for Postwar Expansions and Contractions: State and Local Expenditures

	EXPANSIONS			
Expenditure Categories	*1947-I to 1948-IV*	*1949-II to 1953-II*	*1954-II to 1957-III*	*1958-I to 1960-II*
Total State and Local Expenditures	0.170	0.041	0.097	0.070
Purchases of Goods and Services:	0.134	0.042	0.090	0.068
Compensation of Employees	0.063	0.023	0.050	0.038
New Construction	0.073	0.014	0.022	0.007
Other Purchases	−0.002	0.005	0.018	0.023
Transfer Payments to Persons	0.035	0.002	0.012	0.007
Net Interest Paid	−0.001	0	0.002	0.002
Current Surplus of Government Enterprises[a]	−0.002	0.003	0.007	0.007
	CONTRACTIONS			
Expenditure Categories	*1948-IV to 1949-II*	*1953-II to 1954-II*	*1957-III to 1958-I*	*1960-II to 1961-I*
Total State and Local Expenditures	−0.318	−0.170	−0.110	−0.259
Purchases of Goods and Services:	−0.292	−0.170	−0.095	−0.249
Compensation of Employees	−0.005	−0.045	−0.026	−0.063
New Construction	−0.169	−0.113	−0.027	−0.124
Other Purchases	−0.118	−0.012	−0.042	−0.062
Transfer Payments to Persons	−0.037	−0.004	−0.012	−0.030
Net Interest Paid	−0.001	−0.005	−0.001	−0.001
Current Surplus of Government Enterprises[b]	−0.012	−0.009	0.002	−0.021

Sources: National Income Division, U. S. Department of Commerce. U. S. Department of Commerce, *U. S. Income and Output* (1958), and *Survey of Current Business* (July 1962).

[a] Should be considered as a receipt rather than as an expenditure; thus, positive *M* is stabilizing, negative *M* is destabilizing.

[b] Should be considered as a receipt rather than as an expenditure; thus, negative *M* is stabilizing, positive *M* is destabilizing.

havior is fiscally perverse. Conversely, behavior is stabilizing if the marginal ratio is negative.[46]

The results that appear in Table 14 indicate that state and local expenditures were perverse during every postwar expansion and stabilizing during every contraction. These are, of course, merely the implications of a steadily increasing volume of expenditures. More interesting is the strong trend toward a lesser degree of perversity during expansions. The trend was broken only during the Korean War expansion, and, for reasons that are mentioned above in the second and third sections, the behavior of expenditures during that period can be explained by the special conditions that obtained. Most of the credit for the trend toward a milder degree of perversity is attributable to an improvement in the behavior of transfer payments and purchases of goods and services for new construction.

State and local expenditures were most stabilizing during the 1948-49 recession, though the behavior during the latest contraction was nearly as stabilizing as during the first. The experience of the 1960-61 recession reversed the trend toward less stabilizing behavior that developed during the first three postwar contractions.

Expenditures Adjusted for Secular Trend

When the marginal ratios for total state and local expenditures are recalculated using data for GNP and for expenditures that have been adjusted by removal of secular trend, the results that appear in Table 15 are obtained. Though these are not as striking as the results yielded by the same procedure in the third section, above, they are interesting at the very least because this procedure reveals that, abstracting from trend, state and local expenditures have been

[46] Note that Table 14 assumes that the values of M are additive for different categories of expenditures. If this assumption is questionable when dealing with receipts, it is even more suspect when it is invoked in an analysis of the expenditure side. While many studies (including the present one) do not distinguish among the income effects of alternative sources of receipts, the distinction between the effects of transfer payments and of purchases of goods and services is nearly always drawn (as it is in this study in this and the following section). Nevertheless, reliance on the additivity assumption in this section does not seem to be too unreasonable. The shifts in the transfers-purchases mix have not been very substantial in the postwar period, and, however substantial the shifts may have been, they are taken into account in the analysis in the next section.

a stabilizing factor in the economy during *every* postwar expansion and contraction. No significant tendency toward a greater or lesser degree of stabilizing influence appears, but the extraordinarily high marginal ratios that characterize the first expansion and the first contraction can be explained by the unique conditions that obtained during those two periods—the extremely rapid growth of expenditures in the immediate postwar years, and the slackening of expenditure growth during the Korean War. Coincidentally, during these periods the rates of growth of the GNP were, respectively, less and more rapid than the postwar average.

TABLE 15. Values of *M* for Postwar Expansions and Contractions: State and Local Expenditures

(Adjusted for secular trend)

Period	Total State and Local Expenditures
Expansions:	
1947-I to 1948-IV	−0.603
1949-II to 1953-II	−0.060
1954-II to 1957-III	−0.031
1958-I to 1960-II	−0.043
Contractions:	
1948-IV to 1949-II	−0.127
1953-II to 1954-II	−0.033
1957-III to 1958-I	−0.044
1960-II to 1961-I	−0.034

Sources: Same as for Table 14.

State and Local Fiscal Leverage

This section brings together the revenue and the expenditure aspects of budget policy in an attempt to define the net fiscal impact of the state and local sector on the economy during the postwar period. Up to this point, with the exception of the brief discussion of surpluses and deficits in the second section, expenditures and receipts have been treated separately. The state of budgetary balance is almost universally acknowledged to be an inferior measure of the impact of government budget policy on the economy.

Leverage Changes over the Cycle

The change in fiscal leverage during any period may be defined as the product of the multiplier and the change in the multiplicand. The multiplicand, or the net vertical shift in the aggregate demand curve, is the sum of positive leverage resulting from the expenditure side and negative leverage resulting from the tax side of the budget. Thus, the change in instantaneous fiscal leverage may be defined crudely as

$$\Delta IFL = \frac{1}{1-c}(\Delta G + a\Delta R - j\Delta T)$$

where G is government purchases of goods and services, a is the marginal propensity to consume of the recipients of transfer payments (R), j is the marginal propensity to consume of taxpayers, and c is the marginal propensity to consume of the average income recipient.[47] The chief weakness of ΔIFL as a measure of change in leverage is that in the real world the multiplier operates over time and changes in the multiplicand do not have their full effect instantaneously. To allow for this, we employ a second measure: the change in lagged fiscal leverage (ΔLFL). With this measure, changes in the multiplicand work through the multiplier process over time.[48]

Figure 10 presents estimates of the quarterly changes in lagged and instantaneous fiscal leverage of state and local governments during the period 1946-64. The cyclical turning points, as defined by the National Bureau of Economic Research, are indicated by the solid and broken vertical lines. The most obvious characteristic of the figure is the predominance of positive changes in fiscal leverage, indicated by the fact that nearly all the observations appear above the zero line. Infrequent though such cases are, every restrictive change in lagged or instantaneous leverage occurs during an expansion period. Increases in leverage clearly are larger during contractions than during expansions. State and local fiscal be-

[47] Following Professor Musgrave's testimony (*January 1962 Economic Report of the President,* Hearings before the Joint Economic Committee, 87 Cong. 2 sess. [1962], p. 461), we assume $c = 0.5$ (allowing for corporate saving and tax drain), $j = 0.5$, and $a = 0.7$.

[48] Leverage for any quarter is defined as $LFL_n=(G_n+aR_n-iT_n)+\frac{1}{2}(G_{n-1}+aR_{n-1}-iT_{n-1})+\cdots+\frac{1}{64}(G_{n-5}+aR_{n-5}-iT_{n-5})$.

FIGURE 10. Quarterly Changes in Instantaneous and Lagged Fiscal Leverage of State and Local Governments, 1946–1964[a]

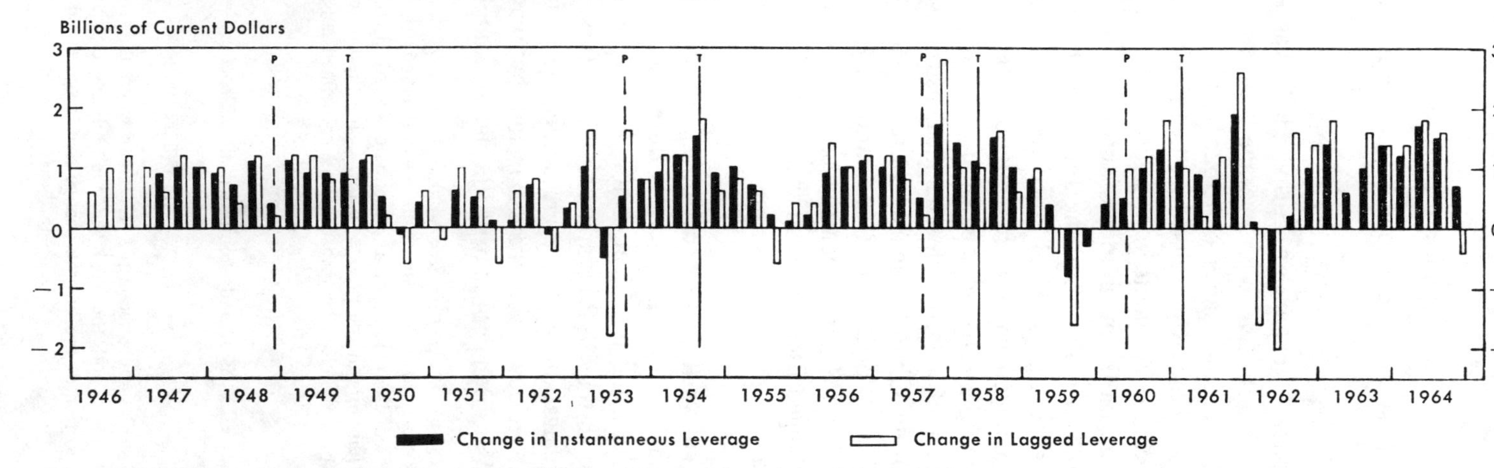

Sources: U. S. Department of Commerce, *U. S. Income and Output* (1958), and *Survey of Current Business* (February 1965)

[a] All data in current dollars.

havior appears to show some tendency to move in a countercyclical direction.

It is clear from Figure 10 that a major reason for the slowdown in the pace of expansion during 1962 was the precipitous swing to restriction in state-local leverage between the final quarter of 1961 and the second quarter of 1962. In fairness to the Council of Economic Advisers, which does not mention the fiscal behavior of state and local governments in its appraisal of the slowdown,[49] it should be noted that the magnitude of the swing in state-local leverage was not fully apparent until the July 1964 revisions of the national income accounts were published. However, this does not explain why the Council ignored the state-local sector in its most recent discussion of the 1961-64 expansion.[50]

The behavior of lagged state and local fiscal leverage *vis à vis* the behavior of the GNP during each of the expansion and contraction periods since World War II is summarized in Table 16. The fiscal policy effect (M_1), the measure used in this table, expresses the change in lagged fiscal leverage as a proportion of the change in the GNP that would have occurred had fiscal leverage not changed.[51]

Table 16 shows that the fiscal policy effect of state and local budgetary behavior has been perverse during every expansion. On the average, the state and local sector was responsible for accentuating the rise in the GNP by approximately 10 percent. This perversity was greatest during the years immediately after World War II. It was least serious during the expansion that was dominated by the Korean War. Behavior during the latest complete expansion,

[49] *Economic Report of the President, January 1963* (1963), pp. 13-22.

[50] *Economic Report of the President, January 1965* (1965), pp. 35-70.

[51] Let ΔI represent the amount of an autonomous vertical shift in the aggregate demand curve originating in the private sector. Using the instantaneous multiplier formulation (k) for simplicity, the measure may be defined conceptually as

$$M_1 = -\frac{k(\Delta G + a\Delta R - j\Delta T)}{k\Delta I}.$$

As the fiscal policy effect is actually computed in Table 16, it is defined as

$$M_1 = -\frac{\Delta LFL}{\Delta GNP - \Delta LFL},$$

where ΔGNP is the actual change in the GNP, and where the time periods involved are the trough-to-peak and the peak-to-trough phases of the cycle. Thus, M_1 measures the proportion of the income change that is prevented by fiscal behavior.

TABLE 16. Lagged Fiscal Leverage and the Gross National Product in the Postwar Cycles

	EXPANSIONS				
	1947-I to 1948-IV	*1949-II to 1953-II*	*1954-II to 1957-III*	*1958-I to 1960-II*	*1961-I to 1964-IV*
Change in Fiscal Leverage (billions of current dollars)	6.0	6.4	10.3	4.6	13.4
Change in the GNP (billions of current dollars)	39.9	112.4	89.4	71.2	133.2
Change in GNP minus Change in Leverage	33.9	106.0	79.1	66.6	119.8
Fiscal Policy Effect (percent) Expansions boosted by	17.7	6.0	13.0	6.9	11.2
	CONTRACTIONS				
	1948-IV to 1949-II	*1953-II to 1954-II*	*1957-III to 1958-I*	*1960-II to 1961-I*	
Change in Fiscal Leverage (billions of current dollars)	2.0	3.4	3.1	3.4	
Change in the GNP (billions of current dollars)	− 9.5	− 9.9	−15.4	− 2.7	
Change in GNP minus Change in Leverage	−11.5	−13.3	−18.5	− 6.1	
Fiscal Policy Effect (percent) Contractions checked by	17.4	25.6	16.8	55.7	

Sources: National Income Division, U. S. Department of Commerce; U. S. Department of Commerce, *U. S. Income and Output* (1958), and *Survey of Current Business* (July 1962, July 1964, February 1965).

largely because of a shift toward restriction in 1959, was almost as good as during the 1949-53 period. Between 1961 and 1964, with the exception mentioned earlier of the first half of 1962, state-local fiscal behavior again was a major factor accounting for the strength of the expansion.

State and local fiscal behavior has been highly stabilizing during every contraction. In the most recent recession, for example, the increase in fiscal leverage offset more than half of the decline that would have taken place had state-local leverage been constant.

In sum, the results of our first measure of net fiscal behavior show that although states and local governments have added to expansionary pressures during boom periods, they have made a very significant contribution by offsetting declines in the GNP during the recessions of the postwar period.

Fiscal Leverage at Full Employment Income

The preceding measure of the overall impact of budgetary changes over the cycle includes the total change in tax yield. As a consequence, M_1 reflects both built-in and discretionary changes. To isolate discretionary policy actions, and to appraise their adequacy in the context of a full employment policy, we now turn to a second indicator. This measure (M_2) expresses the net real shift in the total demand curve at the full employment level of income as a percentage of real full employment income. Following E. Cary Brown, the measure is defined as

$$M_2 = \frac{\dfrac{G}{P_g} - c\left[\dfrac{T_{FE}}{P_p} - \dfrac{R}{P_p}\right] + q\left[\dfrac{G}{P_p} - \dfrac{G}{P_g}\right]}{\dfrac{Y_{FE}}{P_y}}$$

where P_g, P_p, and P_y are, respectively, the implicit price deflators for government purchases, consumption expenditures, and the GNP; q is the private marginal propensity to spend national product; Y_{FE} is the full employment GNP; and where T_{FE} is the estimated total tax yield at full employment income. The third term in the numerator is a correction factor for the divergence between government and consumer prices. When the prices move identically, the correction term is zero. Fiscal policy is expansionary when $M_2 > 0$ and restrictive when $M_2 < 0$.[52]

[52] See Brown, "Fiscal Policy in the Thirties," pp. 857-80. For further discussion of the concepts and techniques involved in the analysis, see Council of Economic Advisers, *Economic Report of the President, January 1962* (1962), pp. 40-56; Arthur M. Okun, "Potential GNP: Its Measurement and Significance," *Proceedings of the Business and Economic Statistics Section of the American Statistical Association* (1962), pp. 98-104; Arthur F. Burns, "Examining the New 'Stagnation' Theory," *Morgan Guaranty Survey* (May 1961), pp. 3, 4; Council of Economic Advisers, "An Analysis of Professor Arthur F. Burns' Critique of the Council's Position," memo to Senator Paul H. Douglas, 10 June 1961, published as "The Council's View," *Morgan Guaranty Survey* (August 1961), pp. 3, 4; Arthur F. Burns, "A Second Look at the Council's Economic Theory," *Morgan Guaranty Survey* (August 1961), pp. 6-15. An excellent summary discussion, which appeared after this study was completed, is Michael E. Levy's *Fiscal Policy, Cycles and Growth* (Studies in Business Economics, No. 81, National Industrial Conference Board, 1963), pp. 59-81.

The estimating procedure used in this analysis will not be detailed here,[53] but the results are presented in Figure 11. The solid and broken vertical lines indicate the cyclical peaks and troughs as defined by the National Bureau of Economic Research. Figure 11 confirms the finding of every other stage of this study—that the astounding postwar expansion of the state and local sector overrides all other aspects of state-local fiscal behavior. Since 1947 the full employment state-local multiplicand has never amounted to less than 3 percent of the full employment GNP. A moderate upward trend has been operating throughout the period, and since 1955 the multiplicand has fluctuated moderately around the 4 percent level.

During every contraction but 1960-61, the full employment multiplicand increased as a fraction of full employment income. During two of the expansion periods the relative multiplicand actually declined. Such a decline during an expansion does not neces-

[53] The following points should, however, be noted:

(1) State and local expenditures, transfer payments as well as purchases of goods and services, are assumed to be autonomous. Thus all changes in expenditures are treated as shifts in the aggregate demand curve.

(2) Yield at full employment income is estimated by dividing receipts into seven classes and by estimating separately the yield of each class. The full employment level of receipts is $(T_0 + \Delta T)$, where

$$\Delta T = E_T \frac{\Delta Y}{Y_0} T_0.$$

The seven classes of receipts and the corresponding GNP elasticity assumptions are as follows: Personal Tax and Non-Tax Receipts (1.1); Corporate Profits Tax Accruals (2.5); Business Property Taxes (0.7); Taxes on Sales (0.9); Miscellaneous Indirect Business Taxes and Non-Taxes (0.7); Contributions for Social Insurance (1.1); and Federal Grants-in-Aid (0.0). The elasticity estimates are adapted from the results of this study and from the work of, among others, Netzer (in *Public Finances, Needs, Sources, and Utilization,* pp. 30, 39); Groves and Kahn ("Stability of Tax Yields," p. 90), and Lee Soltow ("The Historic Rise in the Number of Taxpayers in a State with Constant Tax Law," *National Tax Journal,* Vol. 8 [December 1955], p. 381).

(3) The marginal propensity to consume of taxpayers is assumed to be 0.5 and that of transfer recipients, 0.7.

(4) The full employment income series is an estimate of the gross national product that would be obtained if unemployment were 4 percent. The procedures used to derive the series are essentially those used by the Council of Economic Advisers. Estimates of full employment GNP in three quarters during the period —1947-II, 1955-III, and 1960-IV—serve as bench marks. The following formulas are used for interpolation between the bench marks:

For 1947-I to 1955-III: $GNP_t = \$280.6\, e^{0.0418\,(t-1947\cdot II)}$,
For 1955-III to 1964-IV: $GNP_t = \$396.0\, e^{0.0337(t-1955\cdot III)}$.

FIGURE 11. Effect of State and Local Fiscal Policy on Full Employment Demand, 1947–1964: The State-Local Full Employment Multiplicand as a Percentage of Full Employment Income[a]

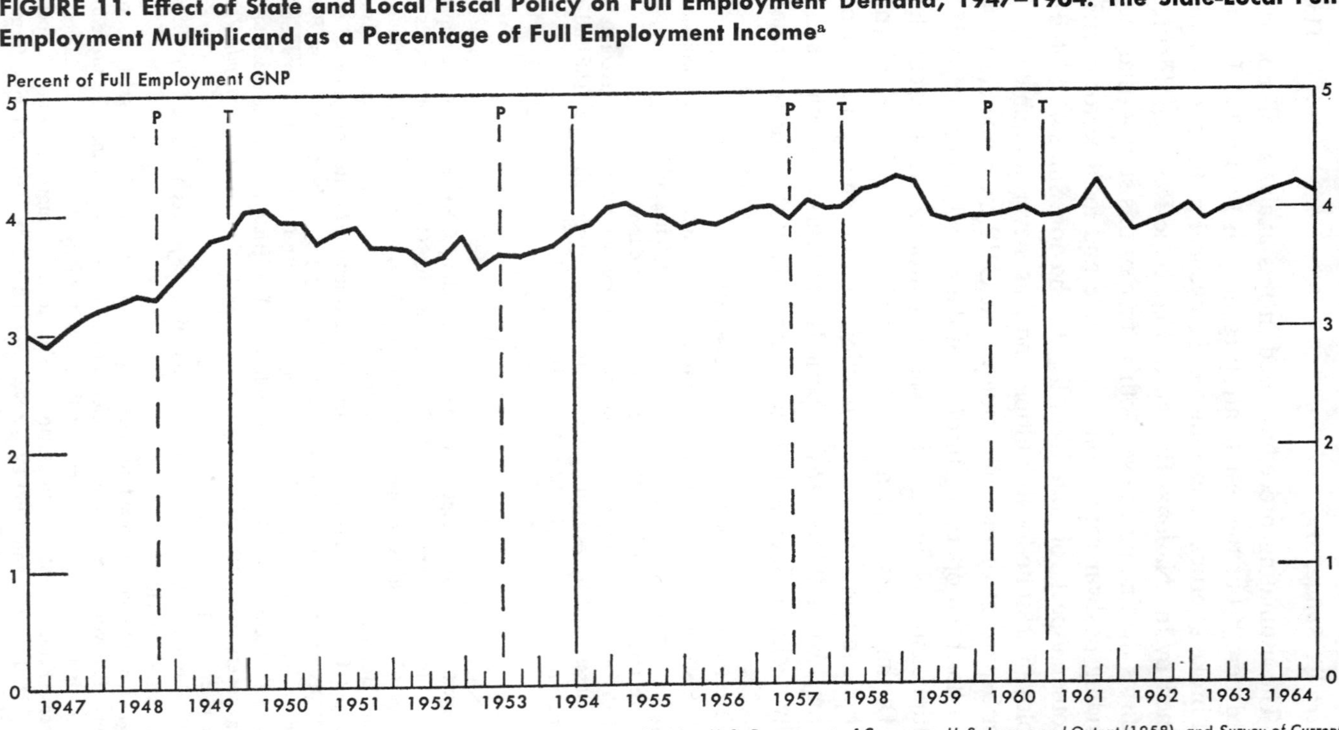

Sources: U. S. Department of Commerce, Office of Business Economics, National Income Division; U. S. Department of Commerce, *U. S. Income and Output* (1958); and *Survey of Current Business* (February 1965).

[a] All data in 1965 dollars.

sarily mean that fiscal behavior was stabilizing. It may mean no more than that the percentage increase in the absolute size of the multiplicand was less than the percentage increase in the bench mark income level. Perhaps the most interesting result shown by Figure 11 is the carryover, into two or three quarters of the following expansion, of the trend toward a higher ratio that occurs during all but one of the contractions. If the standard suggested by Wilfred Lewis were to be adopted, such a carry-over into the "recovery" stage of the cycle would be regarded as stabilizing.[54] In every case, the full employment multiplicand-GNP ratio declines between the recovery stage peak and the succeeding cyclical peak, and in two of the cases it falls substantially.

Summary and Conclusions

"In conclusion, it seems clear that state and local finances in prosperity and depression fall far short of achieving the objectives of a national fiscal program." Two decades have passed since Hansen and Perloff used these words to characterize the fiscal behavior of state and local governments over the cycle.[55] With the perspective granted by an additional twenty years, there are grounds for being considerably more optimistic.

Summary of Results

The fiscal behavior of state and local governments in the postwar period can be characterized by one word—growth. Between 1946 and 1964 the increase in state and local spending amounted to nearly 14 percent of the increase in the gross national product. By all indications, the expansion will continue; indeed, it may even accelerate in the years that lie ahead. Pressures in this direction on the demand side include the maturing fruits of the notorious "baby boom" and growing demands for "better" schools, "better" transportation, and "better" housing. Still other forces are at work on the supply side. In all likelihood the federal income tax cut of 1964-65 will lead to a substantial jump in the relative size of the

[54] *Federal Fiscal Policy,* p. 8. Lewis argues as well that changes in the unemployment rate over a period of years should logically be separated from short-term changes in unemployment caused by recessions or the cyclical instability of the economy.

[55] *State and Local Finance,* p. 69.

state and local sector in the next few years. Although it would be difficult to establish a direct connection between the federal tax cuts of 1954 and the wave of state and local increases that followed in 1955, it seems likely that they were related. There appears to be a consensus that state and local governments will take full advantage of another such opportunity to increase their share of the nation's tax bill. The common apprehension that increases in state and local taxes will cancel much of the expansionary effect of the federal tax cut, is of course, unwarranted. On the contrary, since the boom in state and local receipts will surely be used up in expenditure increases, the "balanced budget" increase in the state and local sector will in fact be more expansionary than if the full federal tax cut had ended up directly in the hands of consumers. Nonetheless, if a major objective of federal policy had been to encourage an expansion of the state and local sector, then a number of approaches other than an unconditional federal tax cut would have been more efficient per dollar of federal revenue foregone.[56]

Even leaving aside the question of compensating state and local rate increases, the federal tax cut will lead to an expansion of the relative size of the state-local sector. State income tax bases are in many cases inversely related to federal income tax payments. In nineteen of the income tax states taxpayers are permitted to deduct federal income taxes in whole or in part.[57] Federal tax reduction will broaden the income tax bases of these states; indeed, it probably will increase the income elasticity of these tax bases. This effect would be moderated if any states defined their income tax liability as a percentage of the federal liability, but the only states to have done so—Alaska and West Virginia—abandoned this provision in 1964.[58] Second, and of far greater importance, are the implications of the income effects of the federal tax cut. To the extent that the tax cut succeeds in reducing unemployment and stimulating economic growth, the increase in sales and income tax bases will be substantial. The crucial point is that to the extent that the GNP elasticity of state and local receipts exceeds unity, the state and

[56] See the recent discussion of some of these techniques by James A. Maxwell, *Tax Credits and Intergovernmental Fiscal Relations* (Brookings, 1962).

[57] Advisory Commission on Intergovernmental Relations, *Tax Overlapping*, pp. 122-26.

[58] *Ibid.*, p. 121.

local share of the increase in the GNP will exceed the present average share, and the sector will expand. Moreover, an increase in the GNP of the sort being considered here is likely to involve unusually high GNP elasticities of tax yields, especially for corporate profits taxes, but also for sales and income taxes.

Growth, then, has been and is likely to continue to be the essential characteristic of state and local fiscal behavior. But this study has determined that there is much more to the post-war record than expansion. Not only have the rates of increase of aggregate receipts and expenditures varied substantially since World War II, but underlying the aggregates even more significant patterns of behavior have been apparent.

Consider first the findings in this paper on the direction of changes in receipts and expenditures (see above, pages 67-82). The behavior of total state and local receipts was stabilizing during every expansion and perverse during every contraction. Expenditures, on the other hand, were stabilizing during all four contractions and destabilizing during every expansion. To note these conclusions is, of course, simply to spell out the stability implications of receipts and expenditures that continue to rise whatever the phase of the business cycle.

More important are the findings concerning the magnitude of the stabilizing or destabilizing behavior. In the third section it was determined that no clear trends are apparent in the values of M for total state and local receipts. Behind the totals, however, several important results deserve mention. State receipts have tended to become more stabilizing in each succeeding expansion since 1949, largely because of the behavior of sales taxes and personal tax and non-tax receipts. The unexciting results for local receipts are attributable to the behavior of property tax collections. Even though states and local governments share about equally in total revenues, state receipts consistently have been less destabilizing during contractions. For expansions the values of M for total state and local receipts have varied between $+0.07$ and $+0.14$. The values of M for contractions have varied between -0.01 and -0.18.

Even more interesting and important results were obtained by abstracting from the dominating secular trend. In the analysis above, the patterns of deviations from the trend for state and local receipts were found to have been more and more stabilizing with each succeeding cycle. An identical result was obtained when the behavior of receipts was related to the behavior of the GNP. It was further determined that when all data were adjusted to eliminate trend, the marginal yield-income ratio increased in every cycle.

On the expenditures side a strong trend toward a lesser degree of perversity during expansions was found. Generally, the behavior of expenditures during contractions does not appear to have been characterized by any significant trend. Expenditures were more stabilizing during contractions than they were perverse during expansions. Abstraction from the dominating upward trend revealed that the marginal expenditures-GNP ratio was stabilizing (negative) during every expansion and every contraction, a result that is decidedly inconsistent with the perversity hypothesis.

In the analysis above, an attempt was made to adjust tax yield data for changes in rates. Although only about 60 percent of total state and local receipts could be studied from this point of view, the results generally revealed even more stabilizing (or less perverse) behavior than did the unadjusted results. Where it was possible to compare the adjusted marginal ratios with the unadjusted, the trend toward more stabilizing behavior was even more apparent in the adjusted data. As a general rule the estimates in this study of the GNP elasticities of state and local receipts exceeded those found by other investigators, and, *ceteris paribus,* the higher the GNP elasticity the greater is the degree of built-in flexibility.

When receipts and expenditures were considered together, the findings were again dominated by the growth of the state and local sector. Leaving this question aside, the findings seem to support the following hypothesis regarding the fiscal behavior of state and local governments over the cycle. These governments have been a significant factor in moderating the seriousness of the postwar recessions and in promoting recovery. During each expansion period state and local government finances have been expansionary, but their strongest expansionary thrust has tended to fall in the early stages of the expansion, with a tapering-off appearing in the later stages of the boom.

This study has attempted to answer the following questions:

1. What have been the basic characteristics of the gross behavior of state and local receipts and expenditures during the postwar period?
2. Has there been any tendency for the behavior patterns to become more or less stabilizing during the period?
3. To what extent has state and local fiscal behavior been accounted for by the secular growth of the sector in the postwar period?
4. To what extent is the cyclical behavior of state and local finances a result of discretionary rather than automatic factors?

The first three questions have been answered satisfactorily, as the above summary of results should indicate. Because of serious limitations on the availability of data, however, little progress could be made toward a definitive answer to the fourth question. It is clear, nevertheless, that in those cases where analysis was feasible, the built-in response of state and local receipts to changes in the GNP is substantially more significant than most other investigators have supposed.

Some Policy Implications

Since the end of World War II stabilization policy in the United States has been riding the crest of an upward adjustment in the level of state and local expenditures. Through prosperity and recession alike, through periods of inflation and periods of relative price stability, and through all the phases of the cold war, the expenditures of the states and local governments have risen inexorably. It would appear that only an economic disaster of the magnitude of the Great Depression would be enough to stem the tide. Since receipts on the whole have kept pace with rising expenditures, the findings of this study seem to suggest that state and local governments in the aggregate have done a fairly balanced job of performing their allocation functions.

The chief limitation of a study such as this is the fact that it deals only with aggregates. Even though the behavior of all state and local governments taken together seems relatively satisfactory, it would be inappropriate to assume that individual governments do not, for this reason, face serious problems *vis á vis* the cycle. For policy purposes, individual governmental units are the factors with which we must be concerned. The aggregate figures might not be very different if all federal grants went to Mississippi, but the economic and political implications of such a program would be rather different from those of the present policy. The problems of regional differences in fiscal behavior and the impact of the business cycle deserve far more attention than they can be given here. Suffice it to say that the apparently satisfactory adaptation of state and local governments in the aggregate to the post-war cycles does not imply the absence of need for a selective federal program of regional grants.[59]

The most serious deficiency of state and local fiscal behavior from the point of view of stabilization policy is its tendency to continue to be expansionary when the economy nears full employment. If recoveries continue to be as anemic as those of the past nine years, this will not be a serious problem. But if the economy regains its buoyancy it may be worthwhile to consider such possibilities as reductions in federal grants-in-aid. Further, the evidence suggests that a tight money policy in a sustained boom will have a delayed but not inconsiderable effect on state and local construction.

Far more substantial federal policy measures would be essential in the event of a serious depression. The threat to state and local revenues posed by such a possibility, and the accompanying danger that state and local governments would resort to perverse rate increases and expenditure cuts, are probably more serious today than in 1929. The reason, of course, is that the income elasticity of the state and local revenue system has been gradually increasing. The yield of the relatively inelastic property tax, for example, accounted for 63 percent of total revenue in 1929, 42 percent in 1946, and only 38 percent in 1964.

Most students of state and local finance seem to agree on a number of proposals that would improve the ability of these governments to absorb temporary but severe losses of revenue. State and local governments would benefit if rigid debt limits were replaced by flexible administrative controls. Guaranteeing or marketing of local bond issues by state governments would make it possi-

[59] See Stanley Engerman's paper in this volume.

ble for these issues to find more buyers at reasonable costs during a depression. The federal government could help both levels of government by guaranteeing issues or even by direct investment, as was done by the RFC and the PWA during the 1930's.[60] Such "self-help" measures as stabilization reserves, which received a lot of attention until fairly recently, appear to be unrealistic, given the political environment in which state and local governments operate.[61]

A promising general approach to this problem has been suggested by Melvin I. White.[62] The "maintenance-of-standards" policy would call upon the states and localities not to raise their tax rates and at the same time to maintain their pre-depression or some secularly-rising level of real per capita services. The gap between expenditures and falling revenues would provide a specific goal for each government that would be met by borrowing and by special federal grants. Such a program, even if it were confined to construction expenditures, would represent an immense improvement over the record of the 1930's.

[60] See the discussion of these proposals by Mabel Newcomer, "State and Local Finnacing in Relation to Economic Fluctuations," *National Tax Journal,* Vol. 7 (June 1954), pp. 105, 106, 109.

[61] The most important experiments with stabilization reserves are the Revenue Deficiency Fund and the Tax Stabilization Reserve Funds, which were established in 1946 by California and New York, respectively. The experience of these states has not been especially promising, and no other states or local governments appear to have been favorably impressed by the experiment. For descriptions and evaluations of the California and New York reserves see David M. Blank, "Reform of State-Local Fiscal Relations in New York," *National Tax Journal,* Vol. 3 (December 1950), pp. 326-47, and Vol. 4 (March 1951), pp. 77-91; Mabel Newcomer, in *National Tax Journal,* pp. 106, 107; and Eugene A. Myers and Randall S. Stout, "The Role of the States and Local Governments in National Fiscal Policy," *National Tax Journal,* Vol. 10 (June 1957), pp. 174, 175. The theoretical aspects of reserve fund financing are considered in detail in Melvin and Ann White, "Impact of Economic Fluctuations on Municipal Finance," *National Tax Journal,* Vol. 7 (March 1954), pp. 29-35.

[62] "Comment" on "Stabilizing State and Local Finance," by Clarence Heer, in *Policies to Combat Depression* (A Conference of the Universities-National Bureau Committee for Economic Research, A Report of the National Bureau of Economic Research, Princeton, 1956), pp. 196-204.

W. IRWIN GILLESPIE*

Effect of Public Expenditures on the Distribution of Income

A NUMBER OF STUDIES have been carried out in recent years which estimate the distribution of the tax burden by income brackets,[1] but comparatively few have applied a similar approach to the expenditure side of the budget.[2] This study is designed to fill that gap by

* Carleton University, Ottawa. This paper is based upon the author's dissertation, "The Effects of Public Expenditures on the Distribution of Income: An Empirical Investigation" (Johns Hopkins, 1963).

[1] See the following selections from the extensive literature in this field: G. A. Bishop, "The Tax Burden by Income Class, 1958," *National Tax Journal*, Vol. 14 (March 1961), pp. 41-59; Richard A. Musgrave and others, "Distribution of Tax Payments by Income Groups: A Case Study for 1948," *National Tax Journal*, Vol. 4 (March 1951), pp. 1-53; Richard A. Musgrave, "Estimating the Distribution of the Tax Burden" (unpublished paper dated August 1961); Peter Newman, "An Empirical Study of the Distribution of the Tax Burden in the United States, 1955-1959" (unpublished paper dated September 1961); Helen Tarasov, "Who Pays the Taxes?" Monograph No. 3 of the Temporary National Economic Committee (1941), and "Who Does Pay the Taxes?" *Social Research, Supplement IV* (New School for Social Research, 1942), pp. 1-79; and Rufus S. Tucker, "Distribution of Tax Burdens in 1948," *National Tax Journal*, Vol. 4 (September 1951), pp. 269-85.

[2] Several previous attempts have been made to impute the benefits from government expenditures at the state level, and separately at the federal level. These

empirically analyzing the distributional impact of various expenditure policies. In addition, the study combines the expenditure analysis with a tax analysis in order to determine the redistributional impact of the entire budget structure.

It may well be argued that it is this redistributional result which matters in the end, and which must be considered in appraising the "progressive" or "regressive" value of fiscal operations at various levels of government. As will appear from the results, the "regressive" image of state-local finances, as against the "progressive" one of federal finances, based on allowance for the tax side of the picture only, undergoes considerable change when net effects are considered.

The Theory of Fiscal Incidence

The analysis by which the final results are obtained has two main aspects: (1) the theory of fiscal incidence, and (2) the estimation of fiscal incidence.[3] The theory and definition of fiscal incidence can be set forth in the following terms. Let us suppose that a private economy exists in which each individual owns a collection of assets (including the capitalized value of his labor), the income

---

attempts are limited in several respects: they do not separate federal from state and local benefits as rigorously as tax burden studies have done; they fail to provide a comprehensive or even a brief analysis of the actual effects of government expenditures in various fields; they do not analyze the probable incidence of such benefits. As examples, see John H. Adler and Eugene R. Schlesinger, "The Fiscal System, the Distribution of Income, and Public Welfare," and "Appendix," in Kenyon E. Poole (ed.), *Fiscal Policies and the American Economy* (Prentice Hall, 1951), pp. 359-421; Tibor Barna, *Redistribution of Incomes Through Public Finance in 1937* (Oxford, 1945); O. H. Brownlee, "Estimated Distribution of Minnesota Taxes and Public Expenditure Benefits," *Studies in Economics and Business,* No. 21 (University of Minnesota, 1960), pp. 2, 38; Alfred H. Conrad, "Redistribution Through Government Budgets in the United States," in Alan T. Peacock (ed.), *Income Redistribution and Social Policy* (London, Cape, 1954), pp. 178-268; Richard A. Musgrave and Darwin W. Daicoff, "The Incidence of Michigan Taxes," *Michigan Tax Studies: Staff Papers* (Michigan Secretary of Finances, 1958), pp. 131-84; and Rufus S. Tucker, "The Distribution of Government Burdens and Benefits," *American Economic Review,* Papers and Proceedings, Vol. 43 (May 1953), pp. 518-43.

[3] The analysis is set forth in somewhat more detail in my dissertation and in my paper, *The Incidence of Taxes and Public Expenditures in the Canadian Economy,* Report No. 6.1, A Study Prepared for the Royal Commission on Taxation (Ottawa, Queen's Printer, 1965), pp. 1-25.

flows from which define his "economic position" relative to any other individual. Prior to time *t* the individual had no method of satisfying his social wants—that is, those wants that can be satisfied only by goods consumed (or at least available for consumption) in equal amounts by all.[4]

At time *t* the individuals in this private economy decide to create a government to provide those goods necessary to satisfy their social wants. The function of this public sector is to divert resources from the private sector of the economy so as to provide goods which satisfy social wants. Various alternative methods may be used to effect the transfer of resources, and each may have a different impact on various aspects of an individual's "economic position." At some time, $t + 1$, the economy has made a complete adjustment to the introduction of the public sector. Each individual has experienced a change in his "economic position," because he now pays taxes and receives benefits from public services. It is this change in "economic position" which comes close to defining the term incidence.

It is necessary, however, to give operational content to the term "economic position." In the broadest sense it can be taken to include the collection of assets which an individual owns: that is, his wealth position. The lack of sufficiently detailed data on individual holdings of all assets, not to mention the dearth of theoretical analysis of taxes in terms of asset position, precludes any empirical investigation along this line. It is usual to rely on current income as a measure of an individual's relative position; and to the extent that current income is an accurate reflection of an individual's asset po-

[4] Richard A. Musgrave, *The Theory of Public Finance: A Study in Public Economy* (McGraw-Hill, 1959), Chaps. 1, 4; *Paul A. Samuelson,* "The Pure Theory of Public Expenditure," *Review of Economics and Statistics,* Vol. 36 (November 1954), pp. 387-89, and "Diagrammatic Exposition of a Theory of Public Expenditure," *Review of Economics and Statistics,* Vol. 37 (November 1955), pp. 350-56; and Charles M. Tiebout, "A Pure Theory of Local Expenditures," *Journal of Political Economy,* Vol. 64 (October 1956), pp. 416-24. Several recent attempts to extend the discussion to an examination of less than "pure" public expenditures have been made. See James M. Buchanan, "An Economic Theory of Clubs," *Economica,* Vol. 32 (February 1965), pp. 1-14; Albert Breton, "A Theory of Government Grants," *Canadian Journal of Economics and Political Science,* Vol. 31 (May 1965), pp. 175-87; and Burton A. Weisbrod, "Collective-Consumption Services of Individual-Consumption Goods," *Quarterly Journal of Economics,* Vol. 78 (August 1964), pp. 471-77.

sition, the measure of incidence will approach the measure of "economic position." In addition it is necessary to group individuals in some manner, and this is accomplished by grouping them (1) by "families and unattached individuals," and (2) by income classes.

In other words, when a public sector is introduced into a private economy, each family finds that its income position relative to others is altered both by the tax payments it makes and by the value of the benefits that it receives from government expenditures. It is in this sense that fiscal incidence can be defined as the changes in relative income positions of families due to the tax and expenditure policies of the public sector.

The next stage in the analysis is to erect on this theoretical foundation an operational structure that has an empirical content. That is, in order to measure fiscal incidence it is necessary (1) to derive an income base, (2) to estimate the distribution of tax payments by income class—tax incidence, and (3) to estimate the distribution of government expenditures by income class—expenditure incidence.

Estimation of Fiscal Incidence

The income base underlying this study is important because so long as income is used as a measure of "economic position," it is a significant determinant of incidence, whether tax, expenditure, or fiscal incidence. In addition, it has been found necessary to extend the notion of income beyond that which is found in the literature on tax burden studies. These studies derive an income concept that includes money income elements such as wages, salaries, rent, interest, and transfer payments, and they also include certain adjustments to render the income concept consistent with the analysis of tax incidence. For example, realized capital gains are added to income because they are a source of receipts for families and thus a part of families' taxable income base. Retained earnings of corporations can clearly be imputed to the shareholder as part of his income as can that portion of the corporation income tax which is unshifted; that is, which falls on profits. This income concept also includes certain items of nonmoney income, such as imputed rent of owner-occupied dwellings, food and fuel grown and consumed on the farm, services of financial intermediaries, net imputed interest paid, and room and board furnished to government employees.[5] This concept is designated in this study as gross money plus nonmoney income; the term gross refers to the fact that personal transfer payments are included in money income.[6]

This income base may be acceptable when one is solely concerned with the tax side of the budget, but it is not wholly satisfactory when one is examining both sides of the public sector. It does not include the benefits from government expenditures, but does include an amount used to pay taxes. In addition, the available statistical income distribution includes a certain portion of government expenditures—transfer payments to families. For the purpose of this analysis, the effect of taxation and government expenditures upon the distribution of income must be treated consistently. That is, (1) either the income base must exclude the entire public sector or it must include the entire public sector within its distribution;[7]

[5] One problem which arises in the use of this income concept is that certain income recipients—"bracket jumpers"—are forced into a higher bracket by the inclusion of nonmoney income. This effect is most noticeable in the lowest income bracket, but since the distribution of income recipients in this bracket cannot be ascertained, it is impossible to determine either the number of bracket jumpers or the proportion of income they carry with them when they are assigned to the next higher bracket. Such a determination is unnecessary, however, because bracket jumpers take with them their tax burden as well as their income. *If it is assumed that bracket jumpers carry with them an equal proportion of income and of taxes from the lowest bracket,* then the "effective" tax rate (as a percentage of income) will not change after allowance is made for bracket jumpers. Since this assumption is made here, bracket jumpers may be ignored, and "effective" tax rates treated as those which would result if the number of bracket jumpers were known. (It must be kept in mind, of course, that the amounts of income and taxes in the lowest bracket will both be overstated.)

[6] This income concept is $Y + R$, where R is transfer payments and Y is net money plus nonmoney income. It might be pointed out that the literature refers to this income concept, $Y + R$, as "broad" income. See, for example, Musgrave, "Estimating the Distribution of the Tax Burden," pp. 17-18.

[7] An income base that excludes the entire public sector is one which exists in the absence of the public sector; in other words, income without the public sector is money income plus some nonmoney elements. This income base is designated as Y, and is referred to as "broad" income. On the other hand, income with the existence of the public sector is money income plus some nonmoney elements, *less* tax payments *plus* government expenditures on goods and services and transfer payments. This income base is designated as $Y + B + R - T$, where Y and R are defined as in note 6, B is government expenditures on goods and services, and T is tax payments; this income base is referred to as "adjusted broad income."

and, in addition, (2) all government expenditures (expenditures on goods and services and transfer payments to families) must be treated identically in the income base.

Two views of the matter may be taken. One is to imagine the absence of a public sector in the economy, and to measure the distributive effect of taxes and expenditures as a percentage of income prior to the introduction of the public sector. In this case, benefits from public services would not be included in the income base, nor would taxes be excluded. An alternative is to imagine that the public sector is removed from the economy, and to measure the distributive effect of taxes and expenditures as a percentage of income prior to the removal. In this case the income base would include benefits from public expenditures and exclude taxes. The first experiment is represented by the equation, $(B + R - T)/Y$, where $- T/Y$ measures tax incidence, $(B + R)/Y$ measures expenditure incidence, and Y is "broad" income. The experiment with removal of the public sector is represented by the equation $(B + R - T)/(Y + B + R - T)$, where $- T/(Y + B + R - T)$ measures tax incidence, $(B + R)/(Y + B + R - T)$ measures expenditure incidence, and $(Y + B + R - T)$ is "adjusted broad income."

In the upper part of Table 1 these two situations are described by experiments 9 and 10 respectively. Table 1 also sets forth several other experiments which could be carried out either with taxes or expenditures, while the other budget component is assumed either not to exist, or held constant at a given level. Since the primary interest here is in the net distributional pattern of the budget, formulae 9 and 10 are estimated; there are no grounds for preferring one or the other and hence both are presented. The table also presents formulae 1 and 4 for taxes, and 5 and 8 for expenditures, primarily because they are the component shares of 9 and 10. Moreover, except for the fact that the definition used here excludes personal transfer payments, formula 1 represents the income concept used by most researchers.

Since the Survey Research Center data for family money income include "personal transfer payments received on a regular basis" these payments must be deducted in the interest of consistency with the preceding analysis and its summary in Table 1. The derivation of the two income bases, "broad" income (Y), and

TABLE 1. Hypothetical Budget Experiments

Introduce Taxes	*Introduce Expenditures*	*Introduce the Budget*
1. into a no-expenditure situation	5. into a no-tax situation	9. into a situation where no budget exists
2. into a situation where expenditures are given	6. into a situation where taxes are given	
Remove Taxes	*Remove Expenditures*	*Remove the Budget*
3. from a no-expenditure situation	7. from a no-tax situation	10. from a situation where the budget exists
4. from a situation where expenditures are given	8. from a situation where taxes are given	

Formulae for Effective Rates Under Different Budget Experiments

1. $\frac{T}{Y}$	5. $\frac{B+R}{Y}$	9. $\frac{B+R-T}{Y}$
2. $\frac{T}{Y+B+R}$	6. $\frac{B+R}{Y-T}$	
3. $\frac{T}{Y-T}$	7. $\frac{B+R}{Y+B+R}$	10. $\frac{B+R-T}{Y+B+R-T}$
4. $\frac{T}{Y+B+R-T}$	8. $\frac{B+R}{Y+B+R-T}$	

Note: Y = income; T = taxes; B = government expenditures on goods and services; R = transfer payments.

"adjusted broad income" $(Y + B + R - T)$, is to be found in Table 13.[8]

The empirical estimation of tax incidence is fairly straightforward, and has been dealt with at some length in the literature. The

[8] Note that throughout this investigation, *"broad" income* excludes transfer payments, whereas in other tax distribution studies, it includes transfers. Notwithstanding the fact that transfer payments are excluded from Y, the inclusive heading "broad" is retained because it includes, in addition to money receipts, various kinds of imputed income (capital gains, retained earnings, etc.), and nonmoney income (food grown and consumed on the farm, net rental value of owner-occupied farms, etc.).

estimation of the distribution of tax payments by income brackets involves two distinct steps: hypotheses are made about the incidence of various taxes by broad economic categories of factor shares and consumer outlays; these hypotheses are then translated into distributional changes by size brackets of income. The results obtained are a quantification of theoretical deductions, and to the extent that the hypotheses are valid one should get at least a close approximation of the distributional considerations of tax policy.

As an example consider the corporation profits tax. It is assumed that one-third of this tax is shifted forward, thus falling on consumers (short-run shifting is assumed to take the form of price increases); the remainder of the tax is assumed to fall on shareholders. The portion borne by consumers is allocated to taxpayers by a distribution of consumption expenditures by income class, and the portion borne by shareholders is allocated to taxpayers by a distribution of dividend earnings by income class. The final result is a distribution of tax payments (corporate tax payments) by income class.

Underlying this procedure is the assumption that the process of adding in or subtracting out changes in income which result from changes in taxes and/or expenditures leaves the "original" distribution of income unchanged. However, changes in tax policy do generate adjustments (other than those explicitly allowed for in the analysis) which could lead to a different distribution of income, and the impossibility of allowing for this aspect of the problem is an analytical weakness of the entire approach.[9]

Further difficulties may arise when the expenditure side of the budget is included.[10] The distribution of earnings in the absence of the budget will hardly be the same as that which prevails with the budget. But while this is granted as an analytical point, the objection does not seem sufficiently severe to rule out analysis of this type. For one thing, the size distribution of earnings is not a highly variable feature of economic life; for another, the distributional im-

[9] For a critical view of this point, see A. R. Prest, "Statistical Calculations of Tax Burdens," *Economica*, Vol. 22 (August 1955), pp. 234-45.

[10] The additional problem which results from the inclusion of expenditures may be less difficult than it first appears, because analysis of the tax side only (including the entire tax structure), must, strictly speaking, be framed in terms of differential incidence, thus requiring a corresponding estimate for an alternative tax structure.

plications of budget policy—including the total budget as well as marginal measures—are of major concern to the policy maker, and policy judgment based on some insight into the issue is better than one proceeding on uninformed hunches only.

The empirical estimation of expenditure incidence is much less precise than the tax incidence, primarily because any hypotheses about the distribution by income class of the benefits from government expenditures are less well developed. As a result it was necessary to construct a framework within which the analysis could be carried out.

In dealing with the expenditure side of the public sector, it is necessary to distinguish, first of all, between two types of expenditures—transfer payments and expenditures on goods and services. Transfer payments can be considered negative taxes (that is, negative lump-sum taxes, income taxes, and excises) and treated analogously. They may stay put or they may be shifted, and they are subject to the same level of argument as the analysis of tax incidence. In fact, in some cases, the incidence or distributional result is an important policy objective. Some transfer payments are conceived as instruments to effect income redistribution in just the same way as the progressive individual income tax is viewed.

Public expenditures on goods and services pose a different problem. Their effect upon the distribution of factor earnings will be disregarded under the assumption that money incomes before taxes are disregarded. But changes in the distribution of real income which arise because the government provides goods and services free of charge must be accounted for. These services are a part of the individual's real income, and their distribution may vary from that of money income.

In extending the type of analysis used with respect to the incidence of taxes to income in kind associated with public expenditures, one is faced with two alternative approaches. The first would consider the distribution by income class of the "costs incurred on behalf of" various individuals. For example, government expenditures for flood-control which benefit farmers could be allocated in a fashion similar to the allocation of corresponding transfer payments to farmers. The second approach would consider the distribution of "benefits" generated by public outlays. Since goods which satisfy social wants are not paid for through voluntary purchases in the market, there exists no automatic measure of consumer satisfaction in an observed market price. To estimate the benefits received by each individual one would have to know each individual's true valuation of services rendered; but since demand schedules for goods which satisfy social wants are not revealed, direct estimation is a difficult problem. This, of course, is one of the central difficulties in the theory of public economy; no attempt can be made here to estimate demand curves (based on preferences which may not be revealed) for each major group of consumers for services which will satisfy each social want. While this latter approach would be preferable, the former—estimation of "cost undertaken on behalf of"—is a more nearly manageable approach, and has proved useful as a first step.

It is evident, then, that the concern here is with the costs of providing services which satisfy social wants. These costs, incurred on behalf of certain individuals, are to be considered a component of those individuals' real income and additive to their money income. In pursuing this approach, the following must be determined: (1) those beneficiary groups on whose behalf expenditures are made, a determination which involves the problem of benefit shifting; (2) the average cost of providing the service to each group; (3) the distribution of the beneficiary group by size classes of income.

Most of this study is an examination of those government expenditures the costs of which are incurred on behalf of clearly delineated beneficiary groups, whether they are consumers or suppliers of factors. But this approach does not wholly neglect other expenditures, such as those for national defense, which are indivisible or unidentifiable by specific subgroups. These unallocable or "general" expenditures provide no clear basis on which costs (= benefits) may be distributed. Yet unless some basis of allocating such outlays is determined, a net distributional pattern cannot be established, because there is no way of knowing which taxes, corresponding to these "general" expenditures, to exclude.[11] The problem is dealt with by making several alternative assumptions about

[11] In the context of this investigation, the net distributional pattern of the budget refers specifically to a comparison of "taxes paid by" with "payments made on behalf of" (or "costs incurred on behalf of") for each income bracket.

the distribution of general expenditures. For example, it is assumed that these expenditures are distributed (a) equally per family, (b) similarly as income, (c) similarly as capital income, and (d) similarly as disposable income. All four alternatives give rise to extremely similar conclusions concerning the general pattern of expenditure incidence. While individual bracket estimates may differ, the relative patterns of the estimates by income class are remarkably alike.

Given these patterns of tax incidence and expenditure incidence, the final estimation of fiscal incidence follows quite directly. The distribution of tax payments is subtracted from the distribution of expenditure payments to effect a net pattern of fiscal incidence.

Some reconsideration of the meaning of "regression" and "progression" is needed once expenditures as well as taxes are included. Using the terms in parallel fashion, this study assumes that an expenditure schedule is regressive when the gain as a percentage of income declines as the level of income increases, and that it is progressive when the opposite occurs. It follows, however, that the implications for equality differ depending on whether the regressive schedule is applied to taxation or to expenditures. Whereas a "regressive" tax schedule is "against-the-poor" and "pro-rich," a regressive expenditure schedule is "pro-poor" and "against-the-rich."[12]

Distribution of the Tax Burden

In order to determine the redistributive effect of the budget on the distribution of income, the study of expenditure distribution requires a corresponding analysis on the tax side. The analysis in this paper does not attempt to add anything new to previous studies of this sort. Hypotheses set forth below about the incidence of various taxes are representative of those used by former investigators.[13]

With regard to federal taxes, it is assumed that: the individual

[12] A regressive pattern of fiscal incidence occurs either when a positive "effective" rate declines as income increases, or when a negative "effective" rate increases as income increases; in other words, a regressive pattern is also "pro-poor."

[13] As examples, see Newman, "Empirical Study of Distribution of the Tax Burden"; and Musgrave, "Estimating the Distribution of the Tax Burden," esp. pp. 10-15.

TABLE 2. Percentage Distribution of Federal, State and Local Tax Payments in the United States, 1960

Tax Payments	Family Money Income Brackets							
	Under $2,000	$2,000–$2,999	$3,000–$3,999	$4,000–$4,999	$5,000–$7,499	$7,500–$9,999	$10,000 and Over	Total
Federal Taxes:								
1. Individual income tax	0.6	1.7	3.1	4.7	17.4	15.2	57.3	100
2. Estate and gift taxes	—	—	—	—	—	—	100.0	100
3. Corporate profits tax	3.4	5.1	5.0	7.4	17.8	8.2	53.1	100
4. Federal excises and customs	4.6	7.6	8.8	16.1	38.9	11.7	12.3	100
5. Social security contributions	4.6	8.1	11.0	15.1	34.6	14.9	11.7	100
6. Total federal taxes	2.5	4.4	5.7	8.7	23.3	12.8	42.5	100
State and Local Taxes:								
7. Individual income tax	0.4	0.8	3.1	6.7	24.6	17.9	46.5	100
8. Estate and gift taxes	—	—	—	—	—	—	100.0	100
9. Corporate profits tax	3.4	5.1	5.0	7.4	17.8	8.2	53.1	100
10. Sales and excise taxes	4.4	7.3	8.7	16.0	38.8	11.9	12.9	100
11. Property taxes	5.0	6.8	7.2	12.5	33.7	15.3	19.4	100
12. Social security contributions	3.3	6.0	8.5	10.7	29.3	20.0	22.2	100
13. Total state and local taxes	4.2	6.4	7.4	13.2	33.9	14.0	20.7	100
14. Total taxes, federal, state, and local	3.0	5.0	6.2	10.0	26.5	13.2	36.1	100

Note: Details may not add to totals due to rounding.
Source: Table 14.

income tax is borne entirely by the individual; the estate and gift taxes fall entirely on those in the highest income bracket; two-thirds of the corporate profits tax is borne by the owners (and therefore is allocated by a distribution of dividends received), and one-third is shifted forward to consumers; excises and customs are shifted forward to consumers of the products taxed; social security contributions fall on wage earners (the employee's share and half the employer's share) and total consumption (half the employer's share).

State and local taxes, including the individual income tax, estate and gift taxes, and the corporate profits tax, are treated in the same way as their federal counterparts. In addition, it is assumed that: excise taxes are shifted to total consumption goods, while sales taxes are shifted to consumption goods less food product purchases;[14] property taxes are borne equally by homeowners (and renters) and consumers;[15] social security contributions are borne entirely by wage and salary earners.[16]

These assumptions result in the distribution of tax liability shown in Table 2. When these tax payments are expressed as a percentage of the income concepts described above, the result is the pattern of "effective" tax rates set forth in Table 3 and 4.

[14] It is recognized that not all states exempt food purchases from the sales tax. The true distribution will be bracketed by the total consumption expenditures distribution (Table 12, line 17) and the distribution of total consumption less food expenditures (Table 12, line 18). Since the difference between these series is slight, my preference for the latter will not affect the results significantly.

[15] This assumption is stated in an extremely simplified fashion. In his original paper, Musgrave used detailed aggregations for residential, business, and agricultural real estate which resulted in the application of very sketchy data to fourteen different categories. Census data indicate, however, that half of the property tax is paid by residential real estate, hence the assumption that this half is paid by homeowners (renters and homeowners are treated alike), and that the appropriate distribution series is "value of houses." The remaining half is paid by nonresidential real estate, and is assumed to be a general business cost; it is distributed proportionately to total consumption expenditures. Perhaps this treatment of the property tax could be improved, but it has served as the basis for the studies of Bishop, Musgrave, and Newman.

[16] The difference in treatment of federal and state social security contributions results from the nature of the state social security programs. On the state and local level, social security taxes consist of contributions by employers and employees to cash sickness benefit programs, and to employees' retirement pension plans. Following Newman ("Empirical Study of the Distribution of the Tax Burden," pp. 5-8), employees are assumed to pay all such taxes, which are distributed by the series "wages and salaries."

TABLE 3. Taxes as a Percentage of Income ("Broad" Income Concept),[a] 1960

Tax Sources	Family Money Income Brackets							
	Under $2,000	$2,000–$2,999	$3,000–$3,999	$4,000–$4,999	$5,000–$7,499	$7,500–$9,999	$10,000 and Over	*Total*
Federal Taxes:								
1. Individual income tax	3.9	7.0	7.9	6.6	6.7	8.1	15.6	10.4
2. Estate and gift taxes	—	—	—	—	—	—	1.2	0.4
3. Corporate profits tax	11.4	10.8	6.5	5.3	3.5	2.3	7.4	5.3
4. Federal excises and customs	9.6	9.9	7.1	7.2	4.8	2.0	1.1	3.3
5. Social security contributions	12.9	14.3	12.0	9.0	5.7	3.4	1.4	4.4
6. Total federal taxes	37.8	42.0	33.6	28.1	20.8	15.7	26.6	23.9
State and Local Taxes:								
7. Individual income tax	0.2	0.2	0.5	0.6	0.6	0.6	0.8	0.6
8. Estate and gift taxes	—	—	—	—	—	—	0.3	0.1
9. Corporate profits tax	0.6	0.6	0.4	0.3	0.2	0.1	0.4	0.3
10. Sales and excise taxes	11.2	11.7	8.6	8.7	5.8	2.5	1.4	4.0
11. Property taxes	12.7	10.8	7.0	6.7	5.0	3.1	2.0	4.0
12. Social security contributions	1.6	1.8	1.6	1.1	0.8	0.8	0.4	0.8
13. Total state and local taxes	26.2	25.1	18.0	17.4	12.4	7.1	5.3	9.8
14. Total taxes, federal, state, and local	64.1	67.2	51.6	45.5	33.2	22.8	31.9	33.7

Note: Details may not add to totals due to rounding.
Source: The distribution of tax payments, Table 14, expressed as a percentage of the distribution of "broad" income, Table 13, line 10.
[a] "Broad" income is defined in note 7 and its textual reference.

TABLE 4. Taxes as a Percentage of Income ("Adjusted Broad Income" Concept),[a] 1960

Tax Sources	*Family Money Income Brackets*							
	Under $2,000	*$2,000–$2,999*	*$3,000–$3,999*	*$4,000–$4,999*	*$5,000–$7,499*	*$7,500–$9,999*	*$10,000 and Over*	*Total*
Federal Taxes:								
1. Individual income tax	1.8	4.0	6.6	6.7	7.0	8.0	18.0	10.5
2. Estate and gift taxes	—	—	—	—	—	—	1.4	0.5
3. Corporate profits tax	5.4	6.2	5.4	5.4	3.6	2.2	8.5	5.4
4. Federal excises and customs	4.5	5.7	5.9	7.3	4.9	2.0	1.2	3.3
5. Social security contributions	6.1	8.2	10.0	9.3	5.9	3.4	1.6	4.5
6. Total federal taxes	17.8	24.1	27.9	28.7	21.5	15.6	30.6	24.2
State and Local Taxes:								
7. Individual income tax	0.1	0.1	0.4	0.6	0.6	0.6	0.9	0.6
8. Estate and gift taxes	—	—	—	—	—	—	0.3	0.1
9. Corporate profits tax	0.3	0.3	0.3	0.3	0.2	0.1	0.5	0.3
10. Sales and excise taxes	5.2	6.7	7.1	8.9	6.0	2.4	1.6	4.1
11. Property taxes	6.0	6.2	5.8	6.9	5.2	3.1	2.3	4.0
12. Social security contributions	0.8	1.0	1.3	1.1	0.9	0.8	0.5	0.8
13. Total state and local taxes	12.3	14.4	14.9	17.8	12.9	7.0	6.1	10.0
14. Total taxes, federal, state, and local	30.1	38.5	42.8	46.6	34.3	22.6	36.8	34.2

Note: Details may not add to tctals due to rounding.
Source: The distribution of tax payments, Table 14, expressed as a percentage of the distribution of "adjusted broad income," Table 13, line 13.
[a] "Adjusted broad income" is defined in the textual reference for note 7.

The tax burden, when measured against the "broad" income concept (which involves the S.R.C. concept of income net of transfers and corresponds to experiment 1 in Table 1), exhibits progressivity over the first two brackets, regressivity from $3,000 to $10,000, and progressivity beyond that. The "effective" tax rates for the first two income brackets are high both when compared with the remainder of the tax schedule and when compared with other tax burden studies. This can be explained by the exclusion from the "broad" income concept of personal transfer payments which are predominantly made to families in the lower income brackets. This exclusion reduces lower bracket incomes proportionately more than upper bracket incomes, and results in higher "effective" tax rates in these lower brackets. In fact, a more detailed breakdown of income classes under $2,000 would demonstrate, for some families living solely on transfer payments, that this "effective" tax rate would approach infinity.

The tax burden when measured against the "adjusted broad income" concept (which includes the distribution of expenditures and transfers, excludes the distribution of taxes paid, and corresponds to experiment 4 in Table 1), exhibits progressivity up to the $5,000 income level, regressivity from $5,000 to $10,000 and progressivity beyond $10,000. This "effective" rate schedule is progressive over the lower income range and more progressive (than in Table 3) beyond the $10,000 income level because taxes are excluded and expenditures included in the income concept. Over the lower income range, where expenditures exceed taxes, $(Y + B + R - T) > Y$, which reduces the regressivity of the tax structure; in the income bracket over $10,000, taxes exceed expenditures, thus, $(Y + B + R - T) < Y$, which causes the progressivity of the tax structure to increase in this income bracket.

Distribution of Public Expenditures

Estimates of effective expenditure rates by major categories are shown in Tables 5 and 6 for the "broad" income concept, and in Tables 7 and 8 for the "adjusted broad" income concept. The results are shown separately for the federal and state-local levels

TABLE 5. Federal Expenditures as a Percentage of Income ("Broad" Income Concept), 1960

Government Expenditure	Family Money Income Brackets							
	Under $2,000	$2,000–$2,999	$3,000–$3,999	$4,000–$4,999	$5,000–$7,499	$7,500–$9,999	$10,000 and Over	Total
Specific Expenditures:								
1. Highways[a]	—	—	—	—	—	—	—	—
2. Education	0.2	0.3	0.2	0.1	0.1	0.1	0.1	0.1
3. Social security	118.9	26.9	12.3	3.8	1.1	0.8	0.2	3.9
4. Veterans	21.5	5.6	3.8	2.1	1.4	0.7	0.3	1.4
5. Agriculture	3.6	2.5	1.0	0.3	0.2	0.3	0.3	0.4
6. Health	1.9	0.8	0.3	0.2	0.1	0.1	—[a]	0.2
7. Housing	1.0	0.5	0.2	0.1	—[a]	0.0	0.0	—[a]
8. Miscellaneous	10.9	4.4	2.5	1.9	1.1	0.6	0.4	1.1
General Expenditures:[b]								
9. Assumption A	112.0	45.2	28.0	18.8	13.2	9.8	4.7	12.7
10. Assumption B	12.8	12.8	12.7	12.7	12.6	12.5	12.6	12.7
11. Assumption C	36.8	28.6	14.3	7.2	4.9	5.5	20.7	12.7
12. Assumption D	12.0	17.1	13.4	11.8	13.6	15.5	10.4	12.7
13. Interest payments	3.9	2.6	1.6	0.8	0.5	0.6	1.4	1.1

Source: The distribution of Federal expenditures, Table 15, expressed as a percentage of "broad" income, Table 13, line 10.

[a] Less than 0.05 percent.

[b] Assumption A allocates general expenditures proportional to families; B, proportional to "broad" income; C, proportional to capital income; and D, proportional to disposable income.

TABLE 6. State and Local Expenditures as a Percentage of Income ("Broad" Income Concept), 1960

Government Expenditure	Family Money Income Brackets							
	Under $2,000	$2,000–$2,999	$3,000–$3,999	$4,000–$4,999	$5,000–$7,499	$7,500–$9,999	$10,000 and Over	Total
Specific Expenditures:								
1. Highways	7.0	6.8	4.4	4.4	2.5	1.8	0.8	2.1
2. Education	23.6	13.0	11.0	7.6	5.4	3.3	1.8	4.5
3. Social security	44.1	12.6	1.7	0.2	—[a]	0.0	0.0	1.1
4. Veterans	0.4	0.1	0.1	—[a]	—[a]	—[a]	—[a]	—[a]
5. Agriculture	0.7	0.7	0.4	0.2	0.1	0.1	0.1	0.1
6. Health	26.9	9.9	2.1	1.6	0.9	0.5	0.1	1.3
7. Housing	3.5	1.9	0.7	0.2	—[a]	0.0	0.0	0.2
8. Miscellaneous	17.1	5.6	3.1	2.0	1.2	0.7	0.4	1.3
General Expenditures:[b]								
9. Assumption A	17.2	7.0	4.3	2.9	2.0	1.5	0.7	2.0
10. Assumption B	2.1	2.0	2.0	2.0	2.0	2.0	2.0	2.0
11. Assumption C	5.7	4.4	2.2	1.1	0.7	0.8	3.2	2.0
12. Assumption D	1.8	2.6	2.1	1.8	2.1	2.4	1.6	2.0
13. Interest payments	0.7	0.3	0.2	0.1	0.1	0.1	0.2	0.2

Source: The distribution of State and Local expenditures, Table 16, expressed as a percentage of "broad" income, Table 13, line 10.
[a] Less than 0.05 percent.
[b] Assumption A allocates general expenditures proportional to families; B, proportional to "broad" income; C, proportional to capital income; and D, proportional to disposable income.

and derivations for the major categories are described in the following pages.

Highway Expenditures

At the outset it is necessary to delineate clearly those beneficiary groups on whose behalf highway expenditures are incurred. These include highway users and highway nonusers. Among highway users two main classes—passenger cars[17] and trucks—may be distinguished. Among passenger car users, there is little possibility of benefit shifting. When a road is improved, the concomitant cost reduction to the automobile owner accrues directly to him; he experiences a lower mileage cost of operating his automobile, and it is extremely unlikely that he will be forced to pass on this cost reduction to people other than his wife. In other words it is assumed that his family alone enjoys the cost reduction. The situation is different in the trucking industry. The provision of an improved road which leads to a per unit reduction in transportation costs may be considered to act as a negative sales tax which is passed on to the consumer of transported products. Consequently it can be assumed that the cost incurred by the government in providing roads capable of sustaining passenger vehicles and heavy trucks is incurred directly on behalf of "consumers of passenger travel" and "consumers of transported products," respectively.

Costs rendered on behalf of nonusers consist essentially in the basic cost of providing access to the sites of property owners. Most students of highway cost economics attach primary importance to determining this cost which is allocable to property owners. It is argued that

> . . . even in the absence of any sort of long-distance automobile travel owners of economically utilizable property would still want access to their sites. . . . A person desiring to live at an isolated country site should pay the cost for gaining access to his land; similarly, an industry

[17] Since buses provide the same service as passenger cars, and since they account for an insignificant portion of total vehicle miles traveled, they are included with cars in this discussion. In 1960, bus vehicle miles traveled were only 0.55 percent of total vehicle miles traveled. (U.S. Bureau of Public Roads, *Highway Statistics 1960* [1961], p. 80.) Bus passenger miles traveled are a slightly higher proportion—3.07 percent in 1958—of total passenger miles traveled (by motor vehicle). See Interstate Commerce Commission, *73d Annual Report* (1959), p. 43.

TABLE 7. Federal Expenditures as a Percentage of Income ("Adjusted Broad Income" Concept), 1960

Government Expenditure	Family Money Income Brackets							
	Under $2,000	$2,000–$2,999	$3,000–$3,999	$4,000–$4,999	$5,000 $7,499	$7,500–$9,999	$10,000 and Over	Total
Specific Expenditures:								
1. Highways[a]	—	—	—	—	—	—	—	—
2. Education	0.1	0.2	0.2	0.1	0.1	0.1	0.1	0.1
3. Social security	55.9	15.4	10.2	3.9	1.2	0.8	0.2	3.9
4. Veterans	10.1	3.2	3.1	2.1	1.5	0.7	0.3	1.4
5. Agriculture	1.7	1.4	0.9	0.3	0.2	0.3	0.3	0.4
6. Health	0.9	0.4	0.3	0.2	0.1	0.1	0.1	0.2
7. Housing	0.4	0.3	0.2	0.1	—[a]	0.0	0.0	—[a]
8. Miscellaneous	5.1	2.5	2.1	2.0	1.2	0.6	0.5	1.1
General Expenditures:[b]								
9. Assumption A	52.6	25.9	23.3	19.2	13.7	9.7	5.4	12.8
10. Assumption B	9.4	11.8	12.7	13.3	12.7	12.0	13.8	12.8
11. Assumption C	17.3	16.4	11.9	7.3	5.0	5.4	23.8	12.8
12. Assumption D	5.6	9.8	11.1	12.1	14.1	15.3	11.9	12.8
13. Interest payments	1.8	1.5	1.3	0.8	0.5	0.6	1.7	1.1

Source: The distribution of Federal expenditures, Table 15, expressed as a percentage of "adjusted broad income," Table 13, line 13.

[a] Less than 0.05 percent.

[b] Assumption A allocates general expenditures proportional to families; B, proportional to "broad" income; C, proportional to capital income; and D, proportional to disposable income.

TABLE 8. State and Local Expenditures as a Percentage of Income ("Adjusted Broad Income" Concept), 1960

Government Expenditure	*Family Money Income Brackets*							
	Under $2,000	*$2,000– $2,999*	*$3,000– $3,999*	*$4,000– $4,999*	*$5,000– $7,499*	*$7,500– $9,999*	*$10,000 and Over*	*Total*
Specific Expenditures:								
1. Highways	3.3	3.9	3.7	4.5	2.6	1.8	1.0	2.1
2. Education	11.1	7.5	9.1	7.7	5.6	3.3	2.1	4.5
3. Social security	20.7	7.2	1.4	0.2	—[a]	0.0	0.0	1.1
4. Veterans	0.2	0.1	0.1	—[a]	—[a]	—[a]	—[a]	—[a]
5. Agriculture	0.3	0.4	0.3	0.2	0.1	0.1	0.1	0.1
6. Health	12.6	5.7	1.8	1.6	0.9	0.5	0.1	1.3
7. Housing	1.7	1.1	0.6	0.2	—[a]	0.0	0.0	0.2
8. Miscellaneous	8.0	3.2	2.6	2.1	1.3	0.7	0.4	1.3
General Expenditures:[b]								
9. Assumption A	8.1	4.0	3.6	3.0	2.1	1.5	0.8	2.0
10. Assumption B	1.4	1.8	1.9	2.1	2.0	1.9	2.1	2.0
11. Assumption C	2.7	2.5	1.8	1.1	0.7	0.8	3.7	2.0
12. Assumption D	0.9	1.5	1.7	1.9	2.2	2.4	1.8	2.0
13. Interest payments	0.3	0.2	0.2	0.1	0.1	0.1	0.2	0.2

Source: The distribution of State and Local expenditures, Table 16, expressed as a percentage of "adjusted broad income," Table 13, line 13.

[a] Less than 0.05 percent.

[b] Assumption A allocates general expenditures proportional to families; B, proportional to "broad" income; C proportional to capital income; and D, proportional to disposable income.

desiring to locate a great distance from the city should pay the bill for creating the necessary road transportation facilities for this type of location.[18]

Conceptually, at least, it appears reasonable that in order to obtain an efficient allocation of resources to the transportation industry, the cost attributable to adjacent property owners should not be allocated to consumers of passenger travel or consumers of transported products. But it is difficult to determine empirically what portion of a road system exists solely for the purpose of providing access.

The first task, then, is to determine the division of cost responsibility between highway users and highway nonusers (property owners). This study relies on an estimate by William D. Ross that the highway nonuser share of an improvement program for all roads and streets in Louisiana was 25 percent.[19] This nonuser share of cost responsibility is herein allocated by the distribution of real property value, by income classes.[20] The remaining highway user share is divided between cars and trucks.

The so-called incremental cost analysis is applied to make these allocations. Two important assumptions which underlie this procedure are: (1) that even if all long distance travel were eliminated, access roads would be required by property owners, and (2) that even if truck travel were banned from highways, the American public would continue to demand the same quantity of road service as they do now, and conversely, if car travel were banned but truck travel permitted, the demand for highways would become negligible.[21] These assumptions lead to a distinction between "basic costs" and "specific costs."

The first component of "basic costs" is that cost necessary to provide an access road for property owners; without any through

[18] John R. Meyer and others, *The Economics of Competition in the Transportation Industries* (Harvard University Press, 1959), pp. 69-71.

[19] *Financing Highway Improvements in Louisiana* (Louisiana State University Press, 1955), pp. 212-13, Table 113; p. 218, Table 125. The methodology described by Ross as the basis of this estimate is discussed briefly in Chap. II of my dissertation.

[20] If it is assumed that the value of real estate is proportional to the value of houses, then the series, "value of houses," can be considered a proxy variable for the series on property value. Since property owners bear primary responsibility for the non-highway user share cost, it can reasonably be allocated according to the series on property value, and has been in this study.

[21] Meyer, *Economics of Competition in Transportation Industries*, p. 72.

traffic such a "basic road" would still be necessary and its cost is properly allocable to property owners. A second component is that additional cost entailed in providing (and maintaining) a surface adequate to withstand light vehicular traffic. "Basic costs" will vary with the number of light vehicles expected (daily or annually) to pass over a given road, and they are allocated entirely to passenger cars. "Specific costs" are those necessary to provide a highway adequate to meet the needs of various classes of heavier trucks and vehicles, usually taken to mean those of 6,000 to 10,000 pounds axle weight. Special features of road design and construction required by this group of vehicles are translated into cost estimates and allocated solely to this group. But this approach is not entirely satisfactory. Should the second increment of cost be allocated only to those vehicles in the 6,000 to 10,000 pound group when vehicles in the 10,000 to 18,000 pound group also require the design improvements which give rise to the second increment of cost? Logically, the heavier group should bear a portion of "specific costs." This entails distributing these costs to the second and to larger weight groups on some comparable basis, such as miles travelled on each road system.

This observation requires a re-examination of the treatment of "basic costs" (allocated entirely to cars), and the underlying assumption that public demand for roads would fall to zero if travel by car, but not by truck, were prohibited. This assumption may be accepted as true, but it does not necessarily mean that truck demand for roads will decrease to zero. Trucks alone would demand roads, under this assumption, and would incur the total costs of building them. Since in reality both cars and trucks use roads, it seems reasonable to allocate a portion of "basic costs" to each class of vehicles, again on some comparable basis, such as miles travelled on each road system.[22]

This reasoning underlies actual attempts to determine highway cost responsibility by the incremental cost approach; the results of

[22] Assume that for a given system of highways there are three vehicles (of increasing weight classes), v, each of which travels a certain number of miles, m, during a given period of time. The lightest vehicle incurs a first increment of road cost, c_1, which is a function of (axle and vehicle) weight. The second incremental cost, c_2, is the *additional* cost necessary to provide a road capable of sustaining the damage caused by the vehicle of the second weight class. To obtain the share

these studies (with adjustments) are used in Table 20 to estimate the respective cost shares (represented by S) for cars and trucks. If such studies were made for all states, each state could be weighted according to its highway expenditure (for 1960), and a total derived which would approximate the allocation of costs between cars and trucks for all roads and streets throughout the nation. Since such studies do not exist, this paper employs as an alternative an average of the results of the existing state studies.[23] The cost share allocated to trucks is distributed proportionately to "consumers of transported products," and the share allocated to cars is similarly distributed to "consumers of passenger travel."

When the distribution of expenditures for highways is expressed as a percentage of income, the results are "effective" expenditure schedules for highways, as shown in Tables 6 and 8. The schedule of rates associated with the "broad" income concept is regressive over the entire range, since the expenditure rate decreases as the level of income increases. The schedule of rates associated with the "adjusted broad income" concept is generally progressive up to $5,000 (except for a slight regressive dip over the second and third brackets), and regressive beyond $5,000.[24]

---

of each vehicle in total costs, certain adjustments must be made in the "incremental cost portion:"

$$S_1 = c_1 - \frac{m_2}{M_1} c_1 - \frac{m_3}{M_1} c_1$$

$$S_2 = c_2 + \frac{m_2}{M_1} c_1 - \frac{m_3}{M_2} c_2$$

$$S_3 = c_3 + \frac{m_3}{M_1} c_1 + \frac{m_3}{M_2} c_2 \cdot$$

Where S is the share of each vehicle in total costs, $M_1 = m_1 + m_2 + m_3$, and $M_2 = m_2 + m_3$. If $c_1 = \$60$, $c_2 = \$30$, and $c_3 = \$10$; and $m_1 = 100$, $m_2 = 40$, and $m_3 = 10$; then $S_1 = 40$, $S_2 = 40$, and $S_3 = 20$.

[23] In Table 20, line 8 was chosen over line 1 because it encompasses *all* roads and streets. The Highway Cost Allocation Study encompasses only the interstate highway system, and therefore is used in this paper only for federal expenditures.

[24] In Table 1 and its accompanying text, above, a series of income concepts was defined, and several experiments involving the introduction or removal of total

Expenditures on Education

In the case of public expenditures for education, allocation to beneficiary groups of the costs incurred by the government is quite straightforward. The government incurs these costs (including current and capital) on behalf of one beneficiary group—the students who receive the education. Since the focus here is on family money income, costs incurred on behalf of the students are conceived as being transferable to the parents—the family group to which students belong. This beneficiary group must be subdivided according to three distinct levels of education—elementary, secondary, and higher (college and adult)—because the cost per student differs at each level, and because not all students pass through all levels. To account for this, a "lifetime" concept is applied to education expenditures:[25] Total education expenditures are divided among expenditures undertaken on behalf of (1) those who complete elementary education only, (2) those who go through secondary education, and (3) those who complete higher education. By calculating the expenditure per student for the entire duration of his education, it is possible to derive the total cost of providing a public education which terminates at each of the three education levels as a given student body passes through the entire education system.

---

government expenditures were discussed. The problem at hand is analyzed by the introduction or removal of highway expenditures. This requires a new income concept, which can be derived by expanding several experiments in Table 1. Thus, experiments 5 and 7 should include (a) a situation in which neither taxes nor "other" (other than highway) expenditures exist, and (b) a situation in which no taxes are given, but which includes "other" expenditures. Experiments 6 and 8 are extended to include (a) a situation in which taxes are given, but in which "other" expenditures are absent, and (b) a situation in which both taxes and "other" expenditures are given. Since experiments 5 and 5(a) result in the same income concept, as do experiments 8 and 8(b), the income concepts defined by experiments 5(a) and 8(b), for which formulae are stated in Table 1, are used in this section of the paper.

[25] In 1960, state and local expenditures for the three levels of education amounted to $9,904 million (elementary), $4,533 million (secondary), and $3,394 million (higher), according to the *Survey of Current Business* (July 1961), pp. 18-19. Expenditures for elementary education comprised 68.6 percent of the state and local outlay for both elementary and secondary education, according to the U. S. Department of Health, Education and Welfare, *Biennial Survey of Education in the United States, 1954-56* (1959), p. 17.

The per-student expenditure figures (cost estimates) for 1960 are presented in Table 21, columns 3 and 4. Annual expenditure per student was derived by dividing the budget expenditure total for each level by the number of enrolled students for each level. It is assumed: (1) that these annual cost figures remain unchanged while a currently enrolled student body moves through the entire education process and (2) that those students who fail to achieve any given level nevertheless complete the penultimate year of that level. The expenditure per student per level was obtained by adding the annual costs per student for each year's attendance at each level.

The number of students is the second important variable. Analysis of actual enrollment figures for 1960 permitted a calculation of the total number of students who could be expected to complete a given level of education. This, in turn, permitted calculation of the total cost (the cost already embodied in the student, and cost expected to be embodied in him if he graduates according to expectations) of providing educational facilities at each level. The number of students expected to complete each level was multiplied by the expenditure per student per level, resulting in the total hypothetical expenditure per level for all students who pass through a given level in the educational process. The relative cost expended on students at each level, as shown in column 6, was 47.8 percent for those completing the elementary level only, 30.3 percent for those completing the secondary level, and 21.9 percent for those completing higher education.

After education expenditures were allocated among the student groups which completed the three levels of education, the expenditure for each group was distributed among income classes of parents of students in each group. Expressing the allocation of education expenditures thus obtained as a percentage of income, "effective" expenditure schedules, as set forth in Tables 5 through 8 were derived. With respect to the "broad" income concept, the schedule is regressive over the entire range of income since the expenditure rate decreases as the level of income increases. With respect to the "adjusted broad income" concept, while the general overall schedule is regressive, some progressiveness is evident over the second and third brackets.

Expenditures on Public Health and Housing

Public health expenditures include expenditures on public health services, government-operated public hospitals (hospitals providing services of a general nature and hospitals for the mentally ill), and sewage and sanitation at the state and local level.[26]

The public health services at all levels of the government share in common the objectives of treating communicable diseases, preventing their occurrence, and conducting research towards these goals. Additional services range from maternal and child health care to physical examinations, polio vaccinations for school age children, free services for handicapped children whose parents are unable to sustain the cost, free dental clinics, the detection of tuberculosis, and public health education. Most public health services and all public health research can be conceived as "pure social goods" which are consumed in equal amounts by all. All people equally consume (or at least have the opportunity of consuming) the services of "public health," either through a general reduction in the probability of contracting certain diseases, or, having contracted disease, through an increase in the probability of recovering.[27] This expenditure is here allocated by a family distribution series.

Expenditures on public hospitals include expenditures on general hospitals for the care of indigents and on institutions for the care of the mentally ill. As both classes of hospitals admit paying patients (some of whom may pay only a portion of the cost of providing services), it was thought unwise to allocate all public hospital expenditures to the lowest income bracket. Consequently, a distribution series for the patients of mental institutions had to be estimated on the basis of sketchy data.[28] Expenditures on general hospitals are distributed according to a series based upon information

[26] A small expenditure (1.8 percent of federal expenditures) is also incurred by the Food and Drug Administration. It was allocated to "consumption of food and drug products and meals eaten out."

[27] This point is argued in some detail by Burton Weisbrod in *The Economics of Public Health* (University of Pennsylvania Press, 1961), pp. 17-26.

[28] Methodology and reservations relevant to this series are discussed in Chap. IV of my dissertation.

about short-term hospital patients, and the expenditures on public mental institutions according to a series based upon data on mental patients.

Expenditures for sewage control and other sanitation services (street cleaning, snow removal, removal and disposal of garbage, ashes, and refuse, and cleaning of catch basins) are incurred on behalf of occupants (owners and renters) of housing units. A small portion of the cost of operating a sewage plant—that required for treatment of industrial waste—might more properly be allocable to industry, but since the relative cost shares of industrial and residential sewage treatment are not determinable, the industrial component has been ignored here,[29] and all these expenditures have been allocated according to a series which is a weighted average of owner-occupied and renter-occupied housing units.

When the distribution of all public health expenditures is expressed as a percentage of income, the result is "effective" expenditure schedules, as shown in Tables 5 through 8 for the various income concepts. In general the overall pattern is regressive, since the expenditure rate decreases as income increases.

Expenditures on public housing entail the provision of low-rent public housing for families of low incomes, defined either as those families in the lowest income group who cannot afford privately-built dwellings which are decent and safe, or, alternatively, those families whose yearly income (less allowable deductions for dependents) at the time of their admission to public housing does not exceed five times the annual rent in the low-rent public housing project. Each year, established occupants of low-rent projects and those beginning occupancy are examined by income brackets for eligibility. A distribution of the weighted average of these two groups has been used to allocate public housing expenditures. The "effective" expenditure rates are shown in Tables 5 through 8. As was to be anticipated, the public housing expenditure rate is regressive over the entire income range, and it terminates at $7,500 since no tenants of low-rent public housing projects have incomes above that level.

[29]Elsewhere, 20 percent of all sanitation expenditures were assumed to be allocable to industry, and, via reduced business costs, to consumers; there was no significant difference in the final distribution pattern. See Chap. X of my dissertation.

Expenditures on Social Security and Veterans

Expenditures on social security are mainly in the form of transfer payments since the only social security expenditure for goods and services is the cost of administration. Thus the cost incurred by the government on behalf of each person is essentially the actual monetary transfer paid out.

Social security transfer payments have several distinct effects on the economic system. The primary function of social security payments is to maintain a minimum level of income in the face of an interruption—either temporary or permanent—in the normal flow of this income. A second effect of the social security system is its redistribution of income by means of a reallocation of the economy's output among its citizens; this involves directing part of the output from those who work to those (the unemployed, aged, and disabled) who do not, and from those who do not experience insecurity to those who do. (An attempt at estimating this redistributive effect is described below.)

Public assistance payments, such as old age assistance, aid to dependent children, to the blind, and to the totally disabled, are based on the proven "need" of the recipient. No distribution of public assistance recipients by income brackets exists, but a distribution of public assistance recipients who reside in low-rent public housing projects is available, and this series is employed here to distribute public assistance payments.

Since the unemployment compensation benefit is a transfer paid directly to the unemployed, those in this category are the essential beneficiaries. Allocation of the payment first required a determination of that portion of total unemployed who were out of work for an entire year. It can be safely assumed that they fall into the lowest income bracket (under $2,000), and that their portion of unemployment benefits should be allocated to that bracket.[30] Census data include a distribution (by income class) of men who were unemployed for part of the year. This series is used to distribute the remaining portion of unemployment benefit payments.

Measured by benefits paid out, the largest component of the so-

[30] The average duration of benefit payments is twenty-five to thirty weeks. In order to receive benefit payments in excess of $2,000 during any one year, an unemployed worker would have to have had a former annual wage between $6,968 and $8,320; unemployment benefits, however, do not cover wages above $4,800.

cial security system is old age, survivors and disability insurance; within OASDI, the old age retirement benefit is the most significant component. Because it was felt necessary to provide some "floor" or minimum below which retirement income should not fall, the relationship between past earnings and retirement benefits is not strictly proportional; that is, the lower income brackets are more heavily weighted than higher brackets. This fact accounts for part of the redistributive effect of social insurance—though redistribution is principally a result of the fact that since the aged command a very limited amount of resources, they tend to be heavily concentrated in the lower income brackets.[31] The entire OASDI benefit payment has been allocated here by the series, OASDI beneficiaries. These were estimated from data provided by the Social Security Survey.

Budget expenditures on behalf of veterans or their dependents fall into three distinct groups: (1) expenditures on general health, welfare and education; (2) pensions (retirement and survivor benefits) for retired veterans; and (3) a program of disability payments.[32] All veterans are arranged into two subgroups: World War II veterans (including Korean veterans), for which a distributive series exists; and World War I veterans (including "other" veterans) who are assumed to be distributed similarly to the aged population. In addition *it is assumed that disabled veterans are randomly distributed throughout the veteran populations of the two subgroups,* and that therefore they are distributed among income classes in the same proportions as the entire group.[33] Non-pension expenditures are divided between World War I and World War II veterans, and distributed according to the distributive series. All pension payments are allocated to World War I veterans.[34]

[31] See, for example, "Income of Old-Age and Survivors Insurance Beneficiaries: Highlights from Preliminary Data, 1957 Survey," *Social Security Bulletin,* Vol. 21 (August 1958), pp. 17-23; hereafter referred to as the Social Security Survey.

[32] At the federal level these expenditures amounted to $2,263 million, $911 million, and $2,438 million, respectively, according to the *Social Security Bulletin: Statistical Supplement* (1960), p. 6, Table 7. The ratio of the retirement benefit to the disability benefit (27.2 to 72.8) was applied to the item in the national accounts.

[33] With respect to veterans of World War II, it is probable that some disabilities shifted certain disabled veterans from a higher to a lower income class. As a consequence, this approach may understate the portion of disability payments allocated to the lower income brackets.

[34] World War II veterans comprise 77.3 percent of all veterans, according to U. S. Bureau of the Census, *U. S. Census of Population, 1960: United States Summary,* PC(1), IC (1962), p. 1-209, Table 77.

The distribution of social security payments and veterans' payments, expressed as a percentage of income, results in "effective" expenditure rates as shown in Tables 5 through 8. With respect to both income concepts, the "effective" expenditure schedules are regressive over the entire range, since the rates decrease as the level of income increases. The sizeable rate in the lowest income bracket reflects the combined influence of public assistance, unemployment compensation and OASDI.

Expenditures on Agriculture

The most interesting and important component of the farm program consists of the support payments to farmers which maintain prices of farm products at a higher level than would obtain in a free market system.[35] The distributive effects of these payments extend beyond farmers to other individuals—to the general consumer, for example. Within the context of a simple model, an attempt has been made to allow for these broader effects in order to estimate the total impact of the farm price-support program.

It is assumed that one farm crop is representative of the mixed output of the farm community and that the demand and supply curves are linear in logarithms.[36] The demand and supply structure is shown in Figure 1. Prior to the imposition of the price support program the demand and supply curves for the farm crop are *DD* and *SS,* respectively, with the equilibrium output at *E*. Introduction of the government price-support program maintains the price for the farm crop at P_1; the demand curve has now become *DFD′* and is perfectly elastic beyond point *F*. The new equilibrium output is at *G*, where amount AQ_1 is purchased at price AP_1. Consumers purchase *AL* at this price and the government purchases the surplus LQ_1.

[35] There are also farm service expenditures, including the financing of farm ownership, and expenditures on research and marketing. The former are allocated directly to farmers on the basis of a per capita distribution of the farm population. The prevalence of farm prices determined at a fixed level by the farm price-support program led to the assumption that a cost reduction attributable to research and marketing programs would be translated into increased production (and ultimately into increased farm income). Thus, this expenditure was allocated in proportion to a distribution of farm income.

[36] This assumption is used to ensure both a positive value for the equilibrium price and output, and a constant elasticity of demand and supply schedules.

FIGURE 1. The Total Impact of the Farm Price-Support Program

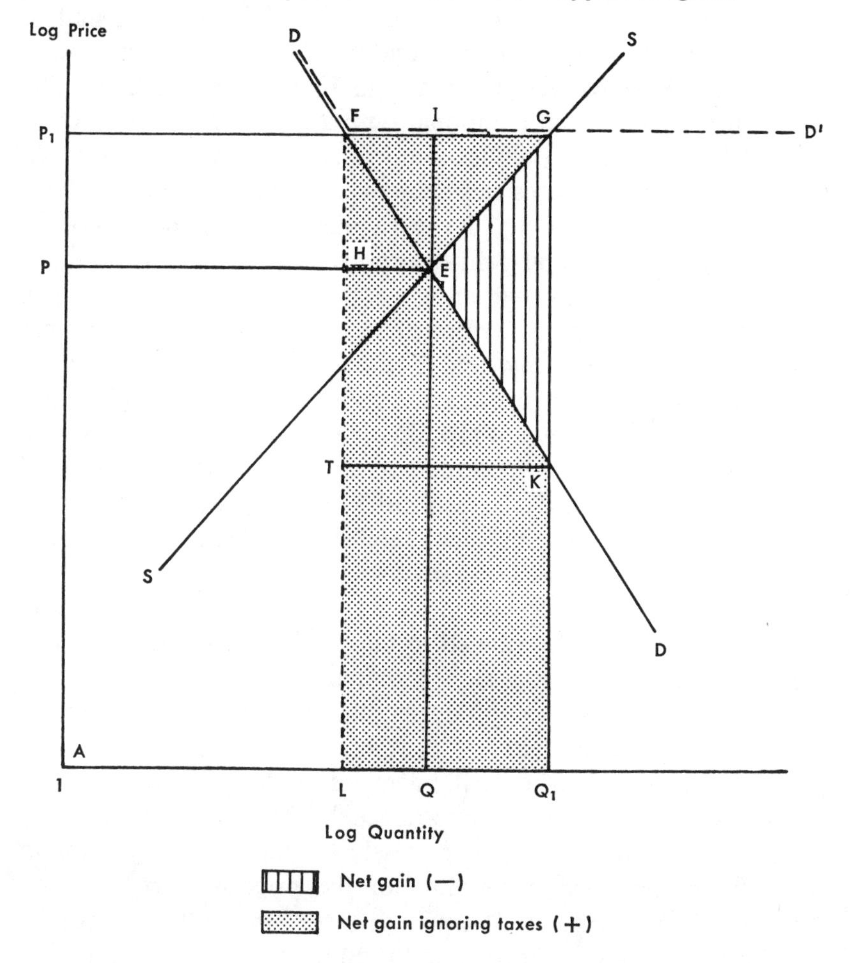

There are several gains (a loss is called a negative gain) which various groups experience as a result of this new price-support situation. Consumers pay a higher price, P_1, and experience a negative gain of $PEFP_1$. First, those consumers who purchased the quantity *HE* at the lower price, *P*, are now priced out of the market; they experience a loss of consumers' surplus which can be approximated by the triangle *HEF*. Second, those consumers who continue to buy *AL* at P_1 experience an income loss ($PHFP_1$); in effect they pay an excise tax to the farmers. The total effect on consumers is the negative gain, $PEFP_1$.

The gain to farm factors is $PEGP_1$. As a first result, the farm community receives a higher per unit price, PP_1, for each unit of the farm crop produced under conditions of perfect competition (that is, AQ), which results in a gain in income of $PEIP_1$. The higher price induces an additional output, QQ_1, in the farm community. This additional output requires farm resources of QQ_1GE; the government purchases this subsequent output, paying the farm community QQ_1GI for it. The extra income from the additional output is EGI. The total gain to farm factors is $PEGP_1$.

The price-support program results in a surplus, LQ_1, for which it is difficult to establish a value. The surplus is a gain to the nation or the total economy, and in the first instance it is assumed that it can be valued at the increase in revenue which would occur if sold on the market by a discriminating monopolist. This assumption results in valuing the surplus as the area under the demand curve, LQ_1KF. For several reasons this results in an overstatement of the value of the surplus: first, spoilage will reduce the quantity of the surplus available for resale; second, there already exists a stock of the surplus crop which would have to be sold first before a true value could be attributed to the surplus added in 1960. Under Alternative A, it is assumed that the existing stock and the added stock are disposed of during the current year, the former being sold before the latter.[37] In other words, LQ_1 is valued at a point farther to the right on the demand curve.

Taxpayers are the last group affected. They experience a negative gain of LQ_1GF, which is precisely the amount of the support payment to the farm community of the price-support program. After the total impact is determined, taxes are subtracted out, as they have already been accounted for on the tax side of this investigation.

The total impact of the price-support program can be summarized as follows:

1. Gain to consumers equals $-PEFP_1$.
2. Gain to farmers equals $PEFP_1 + FEG$.
3. Gain to nation due to surplus equals LQ_1KF.

[37] Alternative A is used to obtain the empirical results of this section. Two other approaches were tested: valuing the surplus at zero, and assuming that the existing crop could be sold in 1960 with the additional surplus sold in the following year. Neither method affected the final result, which is shown in Table 11.

4. Gain to taxpayers equals — *EGK* — LQ_1KF — *EGF*.
5. Net gain equals —*EGK*.
6. Net gain ignoring taxes equals LQ_1KEGF.

The (negative) net gain, item 5, is an important aspect of the farm price-support program. To determine its distribution (by income classes) one must consider the distribution of gains in items 1 through 4. The gain to consumers is distributed in proportion to food consumption and the gain to farmers in proportion to farm income. The gain to the nation is distributed on a basis of total federal taxes paid, on the assumption that if the surplus were disposed of in the manner described above, the main benefit would accrue to taxpayers in the form of lower surplus payments. In a sense, then, the value of the surplus can be considered a potential gain to taxpayers. The negative gain to taxpayers is distributed proportionately to total federal taxes paid. The net gain (—*EGK*), thus reflects not only the level but also the distribution (by income classes) of the total impact of the farm price-support program.

For present purposes, the distribution of the "net gain ignoring taxes," or item 6, is the required estimate. Since taxes have already been considered in the distribution of the tax burden, deduction of the tax distribution from the distribution of the net gain results in the distribution of the positive gain experienced by families in various income brackets. This gain, like other "payments made on behalf of," may then be expressed as an "effective" expenditure rate.

The empirical estimation was carried out in two steps: first, "gains" associated with the total impact of four major price-support crops (wheat, corn, cotton, and grain sorghum) were estimated; second, this information was used to estimate the level and distribution of "gains" for the entire farm price-support program.[38] When the distribution of public expenditures on research, marketing, financ-

[38] See Chap. IV of my dissertation for more on the detailed procedure. During 1960, the estimated *levels* of the gains for taxpayers were $1,946 million, according to the statement of total farm-related expenditures in the *Survey of Current Business*, Vol. 41 (July 1961), pp. 18-19; 68 percent of this total is attributed to the price-support program in *Annual Report of the Secretary of the Treasury on the State of the Finances* (1961), p. 34, Table 4; the price-support payment is a (negative) "gain" for taxpayers. Other estimated levels of the gains were $1,487 million for consumers, $1,915 million for farm factors, and $224 million for the nation (Alternative A). The *distribution* of the net gain, ignoring taxes, was (in ascending income classes): $71 million, $103 million, $65 million, $ — 9 million, $160 million, $110 million, and $308 million, for a total of $652 million.

ing farm ownership, and administration is added to the distribution of the total impact of the price-support program, the result is a distribution of all farm-related public expenditures, as shown in Table 15.[39]

The "effective" expenditure schedules for farm-related public expenditures are set forth in Tables 5 and 6. For both income concepts the schedules are regressive over the entire income range, although above the fourth bracket the rates are almost proportional and extremely small.

Miscellaneous Expenditures

Table 9 contains those expenditures which have not yet been considered, and which are capable of being allocated to specific beneficiary groups within the economy. For the sake of convenience they have been grouped together and called miscellaneous expenditures.

TABLE 9. Miscellaneous Expenditures, 1960

(Millions of dollars)

Expenditure on	*Federal*	*State and Local*
1. Labor and manpower	106	331
2. Civilian safety; fire protection	0	989
3. Natural resources	1,473	1,482
4. Postal services	716	0
5. Commerical regulation	62	538
6. Public utilities	0	235
7. Commerce and business subsidies	1,140	83
8. Transfer payments: civil servant pensions	936	1,468
9. Total	4,433	5,126

Source: *Survey of Current Business*, Vol. 41 (July 1961), pp. 18–19.

The following list of assumptions underlies the allocation of these expenditures.[40] Expenditures on labor and manpower are allocated by a distribution of wages and salaries. Expenditures on civilian safety, fire protection, and public utilities (electricity, water, and

[39] The total, $1,568 million, falls short of the corresponding item in the national income accounts, for which the total is $2,862 million, owing to the way in which the price-support program is treated in this study.

[40] These assumptions are discussed in greater detail in Chap. VIII of my dissertation.

gas) are incurred on behalf of property, and thus are allocated to business and residential property, the former being distributed proportionately to total consumption, the latter distributed proportionately to a weighted average of homeowners and renters. Expenditures on natural resources, postal services, commercial regulation and subsidies to businesses other than the transportation industry are allocated by a distribution of total consumption. Expenditures on public utilities (transit facilities) and subsidies to the transportation industry are allocated by the series, "expenditures on transportation." Civil service pensions are allocated by a distribution of OASDI payments.

Interest Payments

Tables 5 through 8 include estimates of the distribution of interest payments on the public debt. As stated, the purpose of this investigation is to examine the public budget as a means of redistributing real income during the process of providing goods and services to satisfy public wants. Taxes, on one side of the budget, are collected partly in order to pay the interest on the public debt. Since these payments are part of the expenditure side of the budget, they contribute to a redistribution of real income among families (except in the situation in which the distribution of interest payments by income class is exactly the same as the distribution of tax payments by income class). This fact requires an examination of the distribution of interest payments to those families and individuals who actually receive interest as holders of the public debt.[41]

The estimating procedure entails two distinct steps: determination of the amount of interest paid to each class of owner of the public debt, and exploration of the possibility of shifting such interest receipts to persons other than owners. The public debt is held by individuals, commercial banks, special government investment accounts, Federal Reserve banks, corporations, other financial institutions, such as savings banks, and nonresidents. Given this ownership of the public debt, the portfolio mix (of public debt instruments), and the average interest paid on each instrument, it is possible to compute the interest paid to each owner.

The interest payments which accrue on that part of the public

[41] A complete discussion of the methodology employed and of alternative methods of treating interest payments is to be found in Chap. VII of my dissertation.

debt held by the government itself—or various agencies whose net revenues accrue to the government—are eliminated. For example, the net income of the Federal Reserve banks is paid to the Treasury department, and becomes, in effect, an alternative source of revenue which effects a reduction in the tax needs of the government. This allows the federal tax burden to be lower than it would ordinarily have been. These payments have already been accounted for on the tax side of the analysis, where they contributed to a smaller total tax burden. In addition, interest payments made on that part of the public debt held by nonresidents of the United States are excluded since they do not accrue to American families.

It was not possible in this study to determine conclusively whether interest paid to some institutional investors, such as commercial banks, accrues to the owners through increased dividend payments, or via retained earnings, or whether it ultimately accrues to the customers of the institution via improved quality or reduced cost of financial services. It is assumed here that such interest payments do accrue to the owners of the debt.[42] The interest payment attributable to each major class of owner is allocated by the distributive series for each owner; that is, interest payments on the debt held by commercial banks are allocated to the owners and distributed by "dividends received," while interest payments on savings bonds held by individuals are allocated to individuals and distributed by the "value of savings bonds held." The sum of all such allocations is the total distribution of interest payments on the public debt, and it appears in the relevant tables.

Existence of a Deficit or Surplus

This investigation has been carried out with the express purpose of obtaining the net distributional effect of the budget, where government expenditures are taken to reflect a positive addition to, and taxes are considered to reflect a negative subtraction from, income. The form of the analysis implies a balanced budget, but the real existence of an imbalance requires a consideration of alternative methods of treating it.

[42] The assumption that all interest payments are shifted to customers alters the magnitudes but not the general pattern of total interest payments by income class, shown in Tables 5 through 8.

If during the year in question taxes exceeded expenditures, as Table 10 shows was the case in 1960 for all levels of government, the general level of the net distributive schedule would be lower than it would have been had the excess taxes been spent, and thus been accounted for in the analysis. If the benefits from the additional expenditures had been allocated proportionately to the underlying distribution of income, then the net schedule would simply have shifted upward proportionately. There is no reason to assume, however, that this occurred, and therefore the existence of the surplus may have affected not only the level but also the shape of the net distributive schedule. A corresponding argument can be made in the case of an excess of expenditures over taxes.

TABLE 10. Total Taxes and Expenditures Accounted for, 1960

(Millions of dollars)

Level of Government	*Expenditures*	*Taxes*	*Deficit*
Federal	82,928	95,075	(+) 12,147
State and local	50,667	39,072	(−) 11,595
Total, all levels	133,595	134,147	(+) 552

Source: See Appendix. The surplus does not correspond exactly with the surplus given in the national income accounts for several reasons: non-taxes were omitted from governmental revenue; special treatment of the agricultural surplus problem reduced total expenditures on agriculture; and treatment of interest payments excluded a portion of these payments (see Chap. VIII of my dissertation).

The purely mechanical basis of the discussion up to this point does not settle the matter; the implications of the existence of a surplus would have to be accounted for by a more complete analysis. But such an accounting would be most difficult since these implications depend upon which of several models of income determination one chooses to assume. Let us suppose that in the context of a "classical or full employment" setting, the pre-tax incomes of A and B are $100 each. The government collects taxes of $10 from A and holds these taxes as a surplus. As a result, private expenditures decrease by 5 percent (from $200 to $190). A's disposable income is now $90, while B's is still $100. However, the deflationary impact of declining expenditures drives the price level down by 5 percent. Thus A's disposable real income (in initial prices) becomes $94.7, whereas B's disposable real income rises to $103.3. In other words, there has been a redistribution of real income via a tax of 5.3 percent on the income of A, and a transfer of the same amount to B. In the analysis used, a loss of $10 has been recorded for A, thus overstating his true burden and disregarding the gain to B altogether.

If the "classical" rules of the game were really applicable, such an adjustment in the results would be justifiable. But alternative models of income determination call for different reasoning. If one were to assume a model allowing for unemployment, for example, then the existence of a surplus would not only impose a differential burden on taxpayers, but also, via the multipler, a lower output would be created which would impose burdens well in excess of tax collections. For purposes of this analysis, it was not feasible to enter into such complications. Therefore it is assumed, for all practical purposes, that the budget is balanced. Table 10 indicates that this assumption is reasonably well justified for all levels of government combined, and that even for the two subgroups it is not a gross distortion of reality.

"General" Expenditures

As mentioned previously, there is a further class of expenditures for which there is no clear basis for allocation to subgroups within the economy. In fact, these expenditures (for national defense, international affairs, etc.) nearly fulfil a true "social want," because equal amounts of them are consumed (or are available for consumption) by all. This class of expenditures is here termed "general."[43] If they were not accounted for, it would be impossible to determine the net distributive pattern of the budget, because the relevant taxes to be excluded on the tax side of the analysis would remain unknown. Consequently, alternative assumptions about the distributive effects of "general" expenditures were used.

[43] "General" expenditures are those for (1) national defense, (2) general government control, (3) international affairs, and (4) civilian safety, police, and prisons. At the federal level, during the year 1960, expenditures for each of these categories amounted to $46,731 million, $1,421 million, $2,213 million, and $48 million, respectively; state and local expenditures during 1960 amounted to $268 million, $4,931 million, zero, and $2,566 million, respectively (see Tables 15 and 16).

As a first approach, hereafter assumption A, these expenditures may be allocated equally to all families in correspondence with the idea, mentioned above, that "social wants" are satisfied by goods and services which must be consumed (or at least are available for consumption) in equal amounts by all. Although a per capita distribution would differ little from a per family distribution, the latter was chosen since the family has been the unit of reference throughout this investigation.

One might postulate, secondly, that benefits from "general" expenditures relate to the earning of income. Under a broad interpretation, hereafter assumption B, "general" expenditures are allocated by a distribution of total income, using the "broad income" concept. If the postulate is interpreted more narrowly, under assumption C, "general" expenditures are allocated by a distribution of capital income, thereby reflecting the "protectionist" version of the benefit doctrine common in the nineteenth century. The series used for capital income is the weighted average of dividends received and interest received.

It might also be argued that the benefits from "general" expenditures complement the income-using aspect of economic activity. Disposable income is the broadest measure of income, since it includes consumption and savings. In this view, assumption D, "general" expenditures are allocated according to disposable income (family money income minus tax payments).

When assumption A (families) is used, the distribution of the "general" expenditure schedule is regressive over the entire income range. With assumption B (total income) the distribution is proportional. Assumption C (capital income) results in a distribution which is regressive up to an income of $7,499, and progressive beyond $10,000, while assumption D (disposable income) results in a distribution which is progressive up to an income of $10,000 and regressive beyond that level.

Net Benefits and Burdens

The final task of this study is the integration of the analyses of tax burdens and expenditure benefits in order to derive the pattern of fiscal incidence for the total budget structure.

TABLE 11. "Effective" Rate Schedules for Taxes, Expenditures and Fiscal Incidence, 1960[a]

(Percent)

Item	Family Money Income Brackets							
	Under $2,000	$2,000–$2,999	$3,000–$3,999	$4,000–$4,999	$5,000 $7,499	$7,500–$9,999	$10,000 and Over	Total
1. Families	14	9	9	11	28	15	14	100
2. Family money income	2	4	5	8	28	20	33	100
"Effective" Rate Schedules								
Tax Payments:								
3. Federal	17.8	24.1	27.9	28.7	21.5	15.6	30.6	24.2
4. State and local	12.3	14.4	14.9	17.8	12.9	7.0	6.1	10.0
5. Total, all levels	30.1	38.5	42.8	46.6	34.3	22.6	36.8	34.2
Expenditures:								
6. Federal	41.8	43.8	37.3	26.0	18.9	16.0	17.3	21.1
7. State and local	43.4	39.1	24.0	19.2	12.6	8.3	6.2	12.9
8. Total, all levels	85.2	82.9	61.3	45.2	31.5	24.3	23.5	34.0
Fiscal Incidence:								
9. Federal	24.0	19.7	9.4	−2.7	−2.6	0.4	−13.3	−3.1
10. State and local	31.1	24.7	9.1	1.4	−0.3	1.3	0.1	2.9
11. Total, all levels	55.1	44.4	18.5	−1.3	−2.9	1.7	−13.2	−0.2

Source: Tables 12, 14, and 18.
Note: Details may not add to totals due to rounding.
[a] For the standard case.

The Standard Case

Rather than detailing the results for both income concepts and all four assumptions about general expenditures, that situation in which "adjusted broad income" is the base and general expenditures are assumed proportional to income (assumption B) has been selected for detailed treatment. This situation is designated the *Standard Case*.

Table 11 sets forth the relevant schedules for taxes, expenditures, and for fiscal incidence. Lines 6, 7, and 8 describe the "effective" expenditure schedules for all government expenditures; these are subdivided according to the level of government at which the expenditures are made. At the federal level, the expenditure schedule is generally regressive, but exhibits some progressiveness over the first and second and the sixth and seventh brackets. The schedule at the state and local level is regressive over the entire income range.[44] When all levels of government are combined, the pattern is again regressive over the entire range of incomes. In general, the degree of regression decreases in all income brackets from $2,000 to $9,999. Closer analysis shows that federal expenditure regression is greater than state and local expenditure regression except over brackets two and five and two and six, where state and local regression is greater than federal regression.[45]

The "effective" pattern of fiscal incidence for the entire government budget by level of government is set forth in lines 9, 10, and 11. This pattern is obtained by subtracting the distribution of taxes from the distribution of expenditures; a positive sign indicates that an income bracket has gained through budgetary redistribution, and a negative sign that an income bracket has lost. The same approach is used in Figures 2 and 3 for the separate levels of government, and in Figure 4 for combined levels.

[44] The *general pattern* of the Standard Case is not altered either by imputing intergovernmental transfer to the federal level, by the effect of the "general" expenditure assumption (with the exception of assumption C, which results in a net pattern of losses over the middle income range and almost no redistribution in the highest income range), or by the effect of the income base. See Chap. IX of my dissertation.

[45] These observations on the *degree* of regressiveness or progressiveness are based on the coefficients of "average rate progression" as shown in Table 19 for the income range $2,000 to $9,999.

FIGURE 2. Federal Taxes, Expenditures, and the Net Budget Pattern, 1960

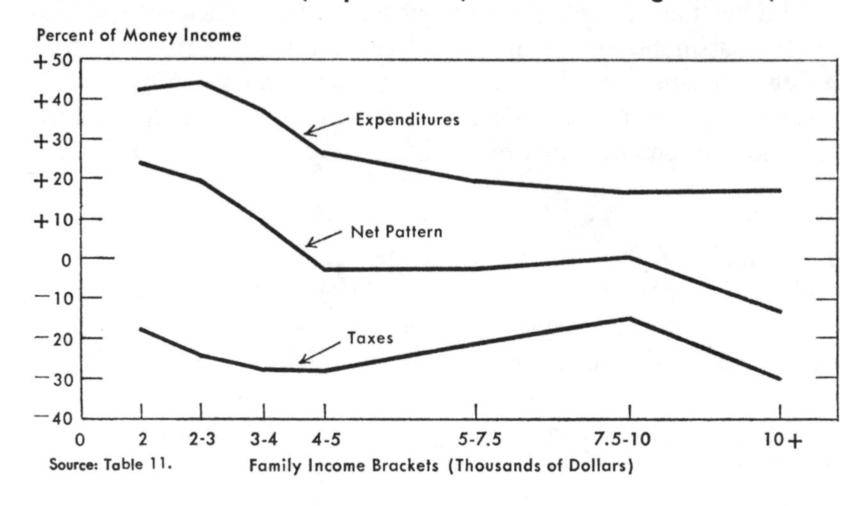

FIGURE 3. State-Local Taxes, Expenditures, and the Net Budget Pattern, 1960

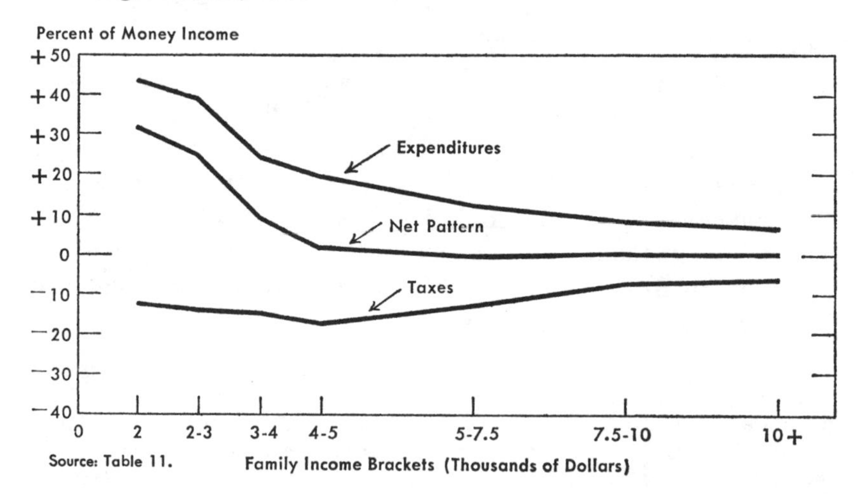

The federal pattern of fiscal incidence generally favors low incomes, burdens high incomes, and is mainly neutral over a wide middle income range. The state and local pattern also favors low incomes, but it is essentially neutral over both the middle and upper income ranges.[46] A comparison of the two patterns controverts the conventional view that the state-local tax structure is regressive and the federal tax structure progressive; indeed, just the reverse is true,

FIGURE 4. Taxes, Expenditures, and the Net Budget Pattern, Federal and State-Local Combined, 1960

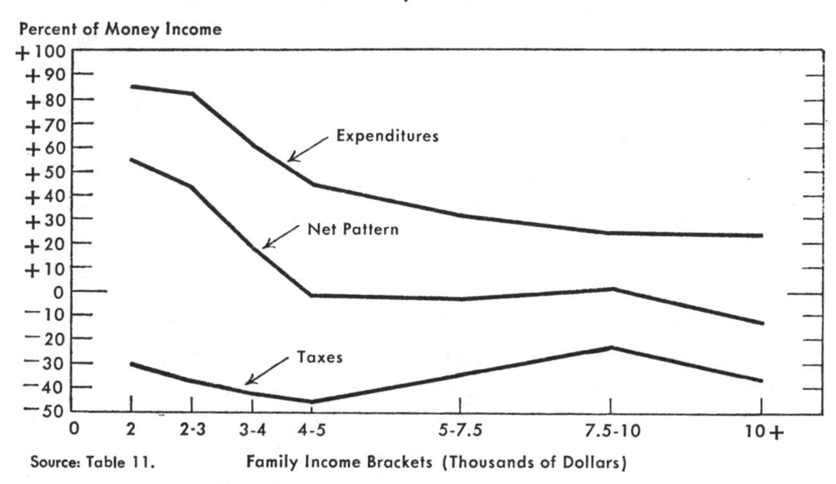

Source: Table 11.

for in net terms, the state-local structure grants larger benefits to the lower income range than does the federal. At the state-local level, a sharply "pro-poor" expenditure schedule outweighs a "pro-rich" tax schedule, resulting in a net pattern which is "pro-poor" over the lower income ranges. Moreover, it appears that at the state-local

[46] The apparent disparity between the neutral effect of the state-local net pattern on middle and high incomes, and its favorable effect on low incomes, is resolved by reference to the treatment in this paper of intergovernmental transfers (grants-in-aid); that is, the taxes from which these transfers arise are collected by the federal government but expended by state and local governments. If those state and local expenditures which are financed out of intergovernmental transfers are allocated to the federal level, the income ranges from $4,000 to $4,999 and from $5,000 to $7,499 both show a net burden. But the levels of these net burdens are relatively small (—0.6 percent and —1.5 percent, respectively), thus the overall state and local net pattern is essentially unchanged. See Tables IX.A-3 and IX.A-7 in Chap. IX in my dissertation.

level there is little or no redistribution above $5,000. The presumed regressive nature of the state-local fiscal structure (based only upon an analysis of taxes) is greatly mitigated if the total picture is considered.

The pattern of fiscal incidence for all levels of government, shown in Figure 4, is mainly regressive with a proportional range over the middle income brackets. Here, too, there is practically no redistribution over the middle income ranges ($4,000-$9,999); losses are concentrated in the upper income brackets and gains in the lower income brackets. In the broadest terms: (1) the middle income brackets pay the cost of providing themselves with government services; (2) redistribution occurs from the upper income brackets to the lower income brackets, but not in the middle income brackets.

Some policy implications of these findings may be suggested briefly. While the pattern of the tax burden is regressive over the middle income range (hereafter, $4,000-$9,999), the pattern of fiscal incidence changes only slightly over this same range. Although this pattern is not the only important distributional aspect of budget policy, it serves significantly to mitigate the "burdensome" regressive character of the tax structure when that structure is considered by itself, and it thus raises the question whether suggested reforms of the tax structure to render it less regressive are relevant. In the context of total fiscal incidence—at least over the middle income range—the allocation of benefits and costs seems to be optimal. More basically, the question arises whether equity—particularly vertical equity (the redistributive aspect of budget policy)—should be considered only with reference to tax burden distribution, or whether the relevant criterion should be defined in terms of net benefit (or burden) distribution. If the latter view is taken, tax reform and expenditure reform can no longer be considered independent problems.

It seems pertinent to ask whether mere chance or intentional fiscal policy cause the budget to operate over the middle income range so as to pose a regressive or "pro-poor" pattern of expenditures against a regressive or "pro-rich" distribution of the tax burden, resulting in a net proportional change of almost zero. Chance seems the more probable answer, for while it is a part of fiscal policy to redistribute income (especially by means of transfer payments) to the very lowest income brackets, it appears that this intention does not extend to the middle range of incomes.

The pattern which emerges from this analysis also offers an interesting distributional perspective on the future course of fiscal federalism in the United States. If past patterns are repeated, growth in the state-local sector will continue on the whole to favor low income groups, and to have an essentially neutral effect upon the middle and higher income ranges. Growth in the federal sector, if past patterns continue, will remain generally unfavorable for upper income groups, neutral in the middle, and favorable (if less strikingly so) at the lower end. Reorientation toward a larger state-local share in the budget picture will probably result in increased aid to the low income ranges, increased withdrawals from high income ranges, and no notable effect on the middle ranges. This conclusion may have to be altered, however, if reliance on grants or shared-tax devices is increased.

Limitations

In conclusion, some of the major limitations inherent in this analysis should be recalled. Among these, perhaps the most basic is the assumption that the distribution of earnings before tax is unaffected by the fiscal process. The second is the necessity to hypothesize about the shifting of various tax burdens and expenditure benefits. The third is the fact that in some cases the distribution of particular tax or expenditure items has to be based on data which are not altogether satisfactory. Since it is impossible to determine actual benefits derived from public expenditures, "expenditures undertaken on behalf of" various income groups had to be adopted as a less satisfactory, but workable, alternative. Finally, there was the difficulty of dealing with "general" expenditures; these cannot be imputed readily to any particular group, but their exclusion would make it impossible to obtain a net benefit series.

Apart from these difficulties, one additional problem remains to be noted. This analysis addresses itself to the distribution of net benefits among size groups of income only, and although such an approach is an interesting aspect of the distribution problem, it is not the only one. Other distributional categories, based, for example, upon sex, age, or family status, are also of interest. A study of redistribution by size groups alone may conceal important shifts among such categories within any one income group. This shortcoming, which has been noted with respect to studies of tax incidence, may be more serious when the pattern of fiscal incidence is being considered.

Appendix

The basic tables upon which the analysis is based, and brief notes explaining their derivation, are presented in this Appendix.

TABLE 12:

Lines 1 through 6: U.S. Treasury Department, Internal Revenue Service, *Statistics of Income 1960: Individual Income Tax Returns* (1962), p. 4, Table C, p. 76, Table 15, p. 5, Table D, and p. 34, Table 3. The series for capital gains includes 100 percent of long-term gains. Adjustments were made to render the "adjusted gross income" bracket concept closer to our "family money income concept," according to Newman, "Empirical Study of Distribution of the Tax Burden," pars. 4.9-4.14.

Lines 7 and 8: George Katona and others, *1961 Survey of Consumer Finances,* Monograph No. 24, Survey Research Center, Institute for Social Research (University of Michigan, 1962), p. 9, Tables 1 and 2.

Line 9: During 1960, dividends received and interest received were $9,914 million and $5,057 million, respectively (*Statistics of Income,* p. 5, Table D, p. 34, Table 3). These weights were used with the two distributive series given in this Table, lines 4 and 5, in order to obtain line 9.

Line 10: The distribution of disposable income is obtained by subtracting the distribution of tax payments (Table 14, line 14) from the distribution of family money income (Table 13, line 1).

Line 11: The "value of homes" occupied is the result of applying the extrapolating procedure to the Newman series for 1958 ("Empirical Study of Distribution of the Tax Burden," pars. 3.4-3.5) which was in turn calculated from data provided by Brazer. The 1958 series is (in ascending income brackets): 10.5, 7.2, 7.3, 9.6, 26.1, 18.0 and 21.3. The extrapolating procedure is a method of updating a series. If during 1956, X percent of item A was located in the first bracket; and if this amount of A is Y percent of first bracket income during 1956, then by multiplying Y times the 1960 first bracket income, the amount of item A assumed to be in the first bracket during 1960 is obtained.

Line 12: The series on the federal individual income tax liability is taken from Newman, "Empirical Study of Distribution of the Tax Burden," pars. 4.1-4.2. He, in turn, relied on the tax liability of "consumer units" by personal income class given in M. Liebenberg and others, "Size Distribution of Personal Income, 1957-60," *Survey of Current Business* (May 1961), pp. 11-21. The consumer unit is very similar to the family unit, and an adjustment factor is available (Newman, par. 4.1), which allows one to calculate the distribution by money income classes. The resulting distribution is given in line 12.

TABLE 12. Distributive Series, 1960

(Percent)

Series	Family Money Income Brackets							
	Under $2,000	*$2,000–$2,999*	*$3,000–$3,999*	*$4,000–$4,999*	*$5,000–$7,499*	*$7,500–$9,999*	*$10,000 and Over*	*Total*
1. Wages and salaries	3.3	6.0	8.5	10.7	29.3	20.0	22.2	100
2. "Covered" wages and salaries, net	4.6	8.3	11.8	14.7	33.0	16.1	11.5	100
3. Net gains from the sale of capital assets	5.2	4.9	3.6	3.2	7.4	6.8	68.9	100
4. Dividends received	2.8	3.9	3.1	3.0	7.2	6.5	73.5	100
5. Interest received	7.8	9.2	7.6	6.5	16.3	12.2	40.4	100
6. Net rental income	10.5	11.3	8.5	7.0	14.4	10.4	37.9	100
7. Families	14	9	9	11	28	15	14	100
8. Family money income, total	2	4	5	8	28	20	33	100
9. Capital income	4.6	5.7	4.6	4.2	10.3	8.4	62.2	100
10. Disposable income	1.5	3.4	4.3	6.9	28.9	23.8	31.2	100
11. Value of houses	5.5	6.1	5.5	9.0	28.6	18.9	26.3	100
12. Individual income tax liability	0.6	1.7	3.1	4.7	17.4	15.2	57.3	100
13. State and local individual income tax liability	0.4	0.8	3.1	6.7	24.6	17.9	46.5	100
14. Expenditures on transportation fares	5.5	7.3	7.3	11.9	23.2	17.4	27.4	100
15. Expenditures on gasoline and oil	5.3	9.3	9.6	17.8	32.5	15.2	10.3	100
16. Expenditures on goods capable of								

18. Consumption less food expenditures	4.3	7.2	8.6	16.0	38.7	12.0	13.2	100
19. Total food expenditures	5.8	8.8	9.5	16.7	37.9	10.9	10.4	100
20. Farm operator families	26.5	20.1	12.3	11.0	18.9	6.3	4.9	100
21. Farm operator family income	7.9	11.7	10.1	11.5	27.0	12.7	19.2	100
22. Value of liquid assets[a]	10.2	7.6	8.3	9.1	20.0	16.4	28.3	100
23. Value of U. S. Savings bonds	8.9	9.8	10.4	8.3	17.1	16.8	28.7	100
24. Value of savings accounts[b]	11.2	8.4	9.6	8.5	20.9	18.4	23.0	100
25. Value of life insurance	5.6	3.7	5.5	7.9	24.7	16.3	36.3	100
26. Elementary students	9.1	6.7	11.4	14.3	35.3	12.8	10.4	100
27. Secondary students	10.8	8.0	8.5	10.7	33.3	13.2	15.5	100
28. College students	3.2	7.8	8.9	11.1	24.8	19.0	25.2	100
29. Food, drug and eating-out expenditures	5.6	8.5	9.2	16.4	37.2	11.7	11.4	100
30. Short-stay general hospital patients	32.5	14.0	13.9	7.5	17.2	0	0	85.1
31. Mental hospital patients	45.9	29.4	2.3	7.0	9.6	3.0	2.8	100
32. Occupancy of all housing	19.0	8.9	9.6	10.7	24.8	13.9	13.1	100
33. All low-rent housing families	36.7	30.6	18.7	9.5	4.5	—	—	100
34. Public assistance payments	63.4	28.8	6.4	1.3	0.1	—	—	100
35. Unemployment compensation	19.8	12.0	14.1	13.9	25.2	9.9	5.1	100
36. OASDI benefit payments	55.5	18.9	12.7	5.8	3.6	2.5	1.0	100
37. World War II veterans	7.0	5.1	9.9	13.7	39.3	14.1	10.9	100

Note: Details may not add to totals due to rounding.

[a] Liquid assets, for the purpose of this series, include U. S. savings bonds, checking accounts and savings accounts in banks and shares in savings and loan associations; currency is excluded.

[b] Savings accounts, for the purpose of this series, encompass savings accounts in banks and shares in savings and loan associations.

Line 13: The series on the state individual income tax liability is a distribution for the state of Wisconsin (following Newman rather than Bishop, who used the *Wisconsin 1957 Report;* see Newman's discussion of this point, pars. 5.1-5.3), obtained from: University of Wisconsin Study Committee, *Wisconsin's State and Local Tax Burden* (University of Wisconsin, 1959), p. 49, Table 4A, and p. 57, Table 9. The series for 1956 is: 0.8, 2.0, 4.5, 8.6, 24.3, 14.8, and 45.0 (in ascending income classes). The extrapolating procedure outlined by Newman (pars. 4.22 to 4.25) was used to obtain the series for 1960.

Lines 14 through 19: *Life Study of Consumer Expenditures* (Time, 1957), Vol. 1, p. 17 and Vol. 7, p. 148, for the year 1955-56. Newman's extrapolating procedure was used to obtain the series for the year 1960.

Lines 20 and 21: The farm-related series are from M. Liebenberg and others, *Survey of Current Business* (April 1962), p. 11, Table 4; they are adjusted from personal income classes to money income classes.

Lines 22 through 24: "1959 Survey of Consumer Finances: The Financial Position of Consumers," *Federal Reserve Bulletin,* Vol. 45 (1959), pp. 700-23, esp. Table 5 and Suppl. Table 7. The survey data include the number of spending units in each income class and the percentage distribution of spending units by value of assets held within each income class. The value of assets is given by bracket value (that is, zero, $1-$199, $200-$499, etc.) in order to reduce the underestimation that results in survey data on liquid assets. First the number of spending units by asset value was computed within each income class. On the assumption that the mean asset value can be used to represent the bracketed asset value, the distribution by asset value of the value of assets within each income class was computed. Third, simple addition resulted in the total value of assets held within each income class, the distribution of which appears in line 22 (similar steps were applied to lines 23 and 24). Survey data reveal that families and spending units are distributed very similarly. It was assumed, therefore, that this distribution, which is actually for the value of assets held by spending units, can be used for the value of assets held by families.

Line 25: The distribution of the "value of life insurance" by income class is estimated from data in the *1960 Survey of Consumer Finances,* p. 92, Table 5–6, which provide a distribution of the percentage of spending units insured in each income bracket. Given the distribution of all spending units (same source, Tables 1-1 and 1-2) it is possible to estimate the distribution of the number of insured spending units by income bracket. Table 5-6 also gives the mean annual premium payment; simple multiplication results in the distribution of the total annual premium payment by income class. The distribution of the value of premium payments is a close proxy variable for the value of the life insurance policy, and the distribution of spending units is almost identical with the distribution of family units.

Lines 26, 27, and 28: The distributions of elementary, secondary, and college students are derived in my dissertation, pp. 128, 133-34, Table III.A-5, lines 7, 8, and 10, from data provided in John B. Lansing, Thomas Lorimer, and Chikashi Moriguchi, *How People Pay for College* (Survey Research Center, September 1960), p. 108, Table 41.

Lines 29, 30, and 31: See my dissertation, pp. 163, 168-70, Table IV.A-6, lines 1, 3, and 4, respectively.

Line 32: The distribution of families in all housing units is the weighted average of the distributions of families (by income) in owner-occupied housing units and renter-occupied housing units. See U.S. Bureau of the Census, *U.S. Census of Housing 1960; United States: Metropolitan Housing,* Final Report, HC(2)-1 (1961), p. 1-5, Table A-3. Of the total housing units, 61.9 percent are owner-occupied and 38.1 percent renter-occupied.

Line 33: The distribution of all low-rent housing families is the weighted average of the distributions of families already in low-rent public housing and families moving into low-rent public housing. See Housing and Home Finance Agency, "Statistics on PHA Operations," in *Families in Low-Rent Projects, 1960,* Item 225.1 (August 1961), p. 47, Table I; and in *Families Moving into Low-Rent Housing, 1960,* Item 226.1 (October 1961), p. 43, Table 3. During 1960 there were 390,151 families already in, and 115,704 families admitted into, low-rent public housing.

Lines 34, 35, and 36: See my dissertation, Chap. V. Line 34 is from data provided in *Families in Low-Rent Projects, 1960,* p. 54. Table 8; line 35 is partially from: U.S. Bureau of the Census, *Current Population Reports 1960; Consumer Income,* Series P-60, No. 37 (1961), p. 33; and line 36 is estimated from data provided in the *Social Security Survey,* p. 17, Table 1.

Line 37: The distribution of World War II veterans is the weighted average of veterans, aged 25 to 34, and 35 to 44, given in *Current Population Reports 1960; Consumer Income,* p. 40, Table 23.

TABLE 13:

Lines 1 and 8: The total for family money income ($372,319 million) is obtained by subtracting from family personal income ($383,719 million given in Liebenberg and others, *Survey of Current Business* [April 1962], p. 11, Table 4) the net non-money items which comprise the difference between family money, and family personal income. This total is distributed by line 8, Table 12. The distributions of the individual non-money income items, such as food and fuel grown and consumed on farms, the net rental value of owner-occupied homes, imputed services of financial intermediaries, etc., are found in my dissertation, Table A-2.

Line 2: The capital gains total includes long-term gains at 100 percent from *Income Statistics, 1960: Individual Income Tax Returns,* p. 76, Table 15. The distributive series is given in Table 12, line 3.

Line 3: Total retained earnings are obtained from *Survey of Current Business* (April 1962), p. 6, Table 2, line 23; in 1960 they amounted to $8,569 million. Retained earnings are distributed according to Table 12, line 4.

Line 4: The 1960 corporate profits tax in the *Survey of Current Business* (April 1962), p. 16, Table 20 is given at $21,186 million. It is assumed that one-third of the tax is shifted to the consumer, the remainder falling on profits. The amount ($14,124 million) which falls on profits must be imputed to income by line 4, Table 12.

Line 5: It is assumed that one-half of the employers' contribution for social security on the federal level, and all of the employers' contribution on the state and local level are shifted to wage earners. This portion must therefore be added to income. See *Survey of Current Business* (July 1961), p. 17, Table 21, and p. 20, Table 25, which show federal employer share of $9,680 million and state employer share of $1,807 million. A total of $6,647 million is added to money

TABLE 13. Estimation of the Various Income Concepts, 1960

(Millions of dollars)

Item	Family Money Income Brackets							
	Under $2,000	$2,000–$2,999	$3,000–$3,999	$4,000–$4,999	$5,000–$7,499	$7,500–$9,999	$10,000–and Over	Total
1. Family Money Income	7,446	14,893	18,616	29,786	104,249	74,464	122,865	372,319
Adjustments								
2. Capital gains	616	571	428	380	873	800	8,078	11,747
3. Retained earnings	240	334	266	257	617	557	6,298	8,569
4. Unshifted portion of the corporation profits tax	395	551	438	424	1,017	918	10,381	14,124
5. Backward shifted portion of the employer's social security contribution	282	510	725	904	2,126	1,140	958	6,647
6. Total adjustments	1,533	1,966	1,857	1,965	4,633	3,415	25,715	41,087
7. Family Money Income, Adjusted (1+6)	8,979	16,859	20,473	31,751	108,882	77,879	148,580	413,403
8. Net addition of nonmoney items	1,589	685	497	647	1,970	1,466	4,538	11,400
9. Subtraction of personal transfer payments	4,266	7,510	4,783	2,905	4,053	1,870	1,418	26,805
10. "BROAD" INCOME CONCEPT (7+8−9)	6,302	10,034	16,187	29,493	106,799	77,475	151,700	397,998
11. Government expenditures	11,158	14,234	11,670	12,753	31,874	18,523	28,468	128,679
12. Tax payments	4,040	6,743	8,353	13,419	35,449	17,684	48,457	134,147
13. "ADJUSTED BROAD INCOME" CONCEPT (10+11−12)	13,420	17,525	19,504	28,827	103,224	78,314	131,711	392,530

Note: Details may not add to totals due to rounding.

income. The federal share of $4,840 million is distributed by "covered" wages, Table 12, line 2; the state share is distributed by all wages and salaries, Table 12, line 1.

Line 9: Personal transfer payments, which include social security benefits, civil servant pensions, veterans payments and agricultural payments have been subtracted. The detailed distributions behind line 9 are given in my dissertation, Table I.A-3, along with a description of the adjustment process to allow for excessive transfers in the lower income bracket.

Line 11: The distribution of government expenditures (net of interest payments) is from Tables 15 and 16 for assumption B (where general expenditures are distributed proportionately to income), and it includes personal transfer payments.

Line 12: The distribution of taxes is from Table 14, line 14.

TABLE 14:

The aggregate totals for all taxes are taken from the *Survey of Current Business* (July 1961), pp. 16-17, Tables 20 and 21. The total for federal taxes, $95,075 million, falls short of the national income accounts total by $962 million, the amount of non-taxes which were excluded. In the state and local tax receipts section, $4,011 million in non-taxes and $6,128 million in federal grants were excluded. This accounts for the difference between the state and local total tax payment of $39,072 million and the national accounts receipts of $49,211 million.

Lines 1 and 7: The federal individual income tax liability is distributed by line 12, Table 12; the state income tax liability by line 13.

Lines 2 and 8: It is assumed that estate and gift taxes are all borne by the highest income bracket.

Line 3: Of a total corporate profits tax of $21,186 million, it is assumed that one-third ($7,062 million) is shifted forward to consumers—and therefore is allocated by total consumption expenditures, Table 12, line 17—and two-thirds falls on profits; this amount, $14,124 million, is allocated by the distribution of dividends given in Table 12, line 4. Line 9 is treated similarly.

Line 4: It is assumed that excises and customs are shifted forward to consumers on a basis of total consumption, Table 12, line 17. Actually a more detailed study would distribute each excise tax by the product consumed; when this method has been used (by Musgrave, "Estimating the Distribution of the Tax Burden," and Newman, "Empirical Study of Distribution of the Tax Burden"), the overall results are not significantly different from a distribution of total consumption expenditures.

Line 5: On the federal level, employee social security contributions amount to $8,015 million, while employer contributions are $9,680 million. It is assumed that all the employees' and half the employers' contributions fall on wage earners; this amount, $12,855 million, is distributed by "covered" wages and salaries, Table 12, line 2. The remaining $4,840 million is assumed to be shifted forward to consumption goods.

Line 10: On the state and local level, excises amount to $5,299 million, and sales taxes to $10,693 million. Since most state sales taxes exempt food products, the latter item was distributed by a consumption series which excludes food

TABLE 14. Distribution of Tax Payments, 1960

(Millions of dollars)

Tax Payment	*Family Money Income Brackets*							
	Under $2,000	*$2,000–$2,999*	*$3,000–$3,999*	*$4,000–$4,999*	*$5,000–$7,499*	*$7,500–$9,999*	*$10,000 and Over*	*Total*
Federal Taxes:								
1. Individual income tax	248	703	1,282	1,942	7,184	6,279	23,669	41,307
2. Estate and gift taxes	—	—	—	—	—	—	1,781	1,781
3. Corporate profits tax	720	1,088	1,059	1,561	3,764	1,744	11,250	21,186
4. Federal excises and customs	603	996	1,153	2,110	5,098	1,533	1,612	13,106
5. Social security contributions	814	1,435	1,943	2,669	6,125	2,636	2,073	17,695
6. *Total federal taxes*	2,385	4,222	5,437	8,282	22,171	12,192	40,385	95,075
State and Local Taxes:								
7. Individual income tax	10	20	79	172	630	458	1,190	2,560
8. Estate and gift taxes	—	—	—	—	—	—	460	460
9. Corporate profits tax	39	59	58	86	206	95	614	1,156
10. Sales and excise taxes	704	1,173	1,386	2,564	6,199	1,903	2,063	15,992
11. Property taxes	801	1,086	1,134	1,989	5,350	2,426	3,068	15,855
12. Social security contributions	101	183	259	326	893	610	677	3,049
13. Total state and local taxes	1,655	2,521	2,916	5,137	13,278	5,492	8,072	39,072
14. Total taxes, federal, state and local	4,040	6,743	8,353	13,419	35,449	17,684	48,457	134,147

Note: Details may not add to totals due to rounding.

purchases given in Table 12, line 18. The excises were allocated by general consumption, Table 12, line 17.

Line 11: It is assumed that half of the property tax is borne by homeowners and renters, the remainder by consumers (following Musgrave, Bishop, and Newman). The portion borne by consumers (shifted via non-residential and agricultural taxes) is distributed by total consumption given in Table 12, line 17. That portion falling on residential real estate (homeowners and renters alike) is distributed by Newman's series on the "value of houses occupied," given in Table 12, line 11.

Line 12: State and local social security contributions are assumed to fall entirely on the wage-earner, and therefore are distributed by the series of "wages and salaries" given in Table 12, line 1.

TABLE 15:

Line 1: Federal expenditures on highways of $54 million are allocated to highway users, 68.1 percent being distributed by line 15, and 31.9 percent by line 16, both of Table 12. The non-user expenditure is distributed by Table 12, line 11.

Line 2: The distribution of federal expenditures on education is proportional to the series, "college students," given in Table 12, line 28.

Lines 3 and 4: Federal social security payments include unemployment compensation of $2,939 million, and OASDI benefit payments of $12,461 million, which are distributed by Table 12, lines 35 and 36. Federal veterans' payments of $2,263 million on health, education and welfare, and $2,438 million on disability payments are divided between World War I and II veterans (in a ratio of 22.7 to 77.3), the former share being distributed by Table 12, line 36; the latter by line 37. Pension payments of $911 million are allocated entirely by Table 12, line 36.

Line 5: Public expenditures associated with the farm price-support program are allocated as follows: the consumer "gain" of $–1,487 million by food consumption, Table 12, line 19; farm factor "gain" of $1,915 million by farm operator family income, Table 12, line 21; and value of the surplus ($224 million) to the nation (Alternative A) by total federal taxes, Table 14, line 6. Expenditures on financing farm ownership ($444 million) and research and marketing services ($472 million) are allocated by Table 12, lines 20 and 21, respectively.

Line 6: Federal public health expenditures for public health services, F.D.A. and public hospitals of $499 million, $11 million, and $109 million, respectively, are allocated by Table 12, lines 7, 29, and 31. See *Survey of Current Business* (July 1961), pp. 18-19; and *Annual Report of the Secretary of the Treasury*, Table 4.

Line 7: Expenditures on public housing are distributed by Table 12, line 33.

Line 8: The distribution of miscellaneous expenditures (by the text assumptions) is found in my dissertation, p. 283, Table VIII.A-1, line 5.

Lines 9 and 10: Line 9 is the sum of lines 1 through 8. Line 10 adjusts total specific (allocable) expenditures to allow for excessive transfer payments in the first bracket, noted above. (Also see my dissertation, pp. 42-43, Table I.A-3, and pp. 320-21, Table IX.A-1.

TABLE 15. Distribution of All Federal Expenditures, 1960

(Millions of dollars)

Expenditure	Family Money Income Brackets							
	Under $2,000	$2,000–$2,999	$3,000–$3,999	$4,000–$4,999	$5,000–$7,499	$7,500–$9,999	$10,000 and Over	Total
Specific Expenditures:								
1. Highways	3	4	6	11	19	9	7	59
2. Education	12	30	34	42	95	73	96	382
3. Social security	7,496	2,702	1,993	1,127	1,197	598	287	15,400
4. Veterans	1,352	559	611	613	1,499	561	417	5,612
5. Agriculture	226	247	168	94	216	198	421	1,568
6. Public health	121	78	49	65	154	79	74	619
7. Public housing	60	50	31	16	7	0	0	164
8. Miscellaneous	688	437	409	565	1,214	502	615	4,433
9. Total	9,958	4,107	3,301	2,533	4,401	2,020	1,917	28,237
10. Specific expenditures adjusted[a]	4,108	5,345	4,553	3,424	5,768	2,640	2,400	28,237
General Expenditures:[b]								
11. Assumption A	7,058	4,537	4,537	5,545	14,116	7,562	7,058	50,413
12. Assumption B	1,260	2,067	2,470	3,831	13,158	9,427	18,199	50,413
13. Assumption C	2,319	2,874	2,319	2,117	5,193	4,235	31,357	50,413
14. Assumption D	756	1,714	2,168	3,478	14,569	11,998	15,729	50,413
15. Interest payments	245	257	257	242	553	488	2,239	4,278
Total Expenditures:								
16. Assumption A	11,411	10,139	9,347	9,211	20,440	10,690	11,697	82,928
17. Assumption B	5,613	7,699	7,280	7,497	19,479	12,555	22,838	82,928
18. Assumption C	6,672	8,476	7,129	5,783	11,514	7,363	35,996	82,928
19. Assumption D	5,109	7,316	6,978	7,144	20,890	15,126	20,368	82,928

Note: Details may not add to totals due to rounding.

[a] Adjusted to allow for excessive personal transfer payments in the first income bracket.

[b] Assumption A allocates general expenditures in proportion to families; B, to "broad" income; C, to capital income; and D ,to disposable income

Lines 11 through 14: The distribution of general expenditures for the four assumptions is by: Table 12, line 7, for families; Table 13, line 10, for "broad" income; Table 12, lines 9 and 10, for capital and disposable income, respectively.

Line 15: The distribution of interest payments is found in my dissertation, pp. 251-52, Table VII.A-4, line 13.

TABLE 16:

Line 1: State and local highway expenditures of $6,326 million (75 percent), are allocated to highway users, 56.4 percent being distributed by line 15, and 43.6 percent by line 16, both of Table 12. The non-user expenditure ($2,109 million) is distributed by Table 12, line 11.

Line 2: State and local expenditures on education are divided among education levels on the basis of the percentage breakdown in Table 21, column 6; $8,523 million is distributed by line 26, $5,403 million by line 27, and $3,905 million by line 28, all of Table 12. The sum is shown in line 2.

Lines 3 and 4: State and local social security payments include public assistance of $4,385 million, which is allocated by Table 12, line 34. State and local veterans' payments of $106 million are treated in the same way as on the federal level.

Line 5: The distribution of agricultural expenditures of $567 million on research and marketing is by Table 12, line 21.

Line 6: State and local public health expenditures for public health services, all public hospitals and sewage and sanitation of $573 million, $2,853 million (this is 86.1 percent of the total cost of public hospitals; the remainder is designated as the paying patient share, and it is netted out), and $1,782 million, respectively, are allocated by Table 12, line 7, and weighted average of lines 30, 31, and 32. See *Survey of Current Business* (July 1961), pp. 18-19, and U.S. Bureau of the Census, *Government Finances in 1960,* G-GF60-No. 2 (September 19, 1961), p. 19, Table 4.

Line 7: See Table 15.

Line 8: The distribution of miscellaneous expenditures is found in my dissertation, pp. 283-84, Table VIII.A-1, line 12.

Lines 9 through 14: See Table 15.

Line 15: The distribution of interest payments is found in my dissertation, pp. 253-54, Table VII.A-5, line 9.

TABLE 17:

Lines 1, 4, 7, and 10: Lines 16 through 19 of Table 15 are expressed as percentages of the "broad" income concept, Table 13, line 10.

Lines 2, 5, 8, and 11: Lines 16 through 19 of Table 16 are expressed as percentages of "broad" income, Table 13, line 10.

TABLE 18:

Lines 1, 4, 7, and 10: Lines 16 through 19 of Table 15 are expressed as percentages of "adjusted broad income," Table 13, line 13.

Lines 2, 5, 8, and 11: Line 16 through 19 of Table 16 are expressed as percentages of "adjusted broad income," Table 13, line 13.

TABLE 16. Distribution of All State and Local Expenditures, 1960

(Millions of dollars)

Expenditure	Family Money Income Brackets							
	Under $2,000	$2,000–$2,999	$3,000–$3,999	$4,000–$4,999	$5,000–$7,499	$7,500–$9,999	$10,000 and Over	Total
Specific Expenditures:								
1. Highways	440	682	718	1,286	2,644	1,385	1,279	8,435
2. Education	1,485	1,308	1,779	2,230	5,776	2,546	2,707	17,831
3. Social security	2,780	1,263	281	57	4	0	0	4,385
4. Veterans	28	11	12	11	26	10	7	106
5. Agriculture	45	66	57	65	153	72	109	567
6. Public health	1,696	994	348	460	921	406	382	5,207
7. Public housing	223	186	114	58	27	0	0	607
8. Miscellaneous	1,079	557	507	595	1,291	539	558	5,126
9. Total	7,776	5,067	3,816	4,762	10,842	4,958	5,042	42,264
10. Specific Expenditures Adjusted[a]	5,596	6,504	4,267	4,908	10,921	5,004	5,065	42,264
General Expenditures:[b]								
11. Assumption A	1,087	699	699	854	2,174	1,165	1,087	7,765
12. Assumption B	194	318	380	590	2,027	1,452	2,803	7,765
13. Assumption C	357	443	357	326	800	652	4,830	7,765
14. Assumption D	116	264	334	536	2,244	1,848	2,423	7,765
15. Interest payments	41	35	36	40	95	76	314	638
Total Expenditures:								
16. Assumption A	6,724	7,238	5,002	5,802	13,193	6,245	6,466	50,667
17. Assumption B	5,831	6,857	4,683	5,538	13,043	6,532	8,183	50,667
18. Assumption C	5,994	6,982	4,660	5,274	11,816	5,732	10,209	50,667
19. Assumption D	5,753	6,803	4,637	5,484	13,260	6,928	7,802	50,667

Note: Details may not add to totals due to rounding.
[a] Adjusted to allow for excessive personal transfer payments in the first income bracket.
[b] Assumption A allocates general expenditures in proportion to families; B, in proportion to broad" income; C ,in proportion to capital income; and D ,in proportion to disposable income.

TABLE 17. "Effective" Expenditure Schedule for All Government Expenditures ("Broad" Income Concept), 1960

(Percent)

Level of Government[a]	Family Money Income Brackets							
	Under $2,000	$2,000–$2,999	$3,000–$3,999	$4,000–$4,999	$5,000–$7,499	$7,500–$9,999	$10,000 and Over	Total
Assumption A:								
1. Federal	181.1	101.0	57.7	31.2	19.1	13.8	7.7	20.8
2. State and local	106.7	72.1	30.9	19.7	12.4	8.1	4.3	12.7
3. Total, all levels	287.8	173.1	88.6	50.9	31.5	21.9	12.0	33.5
Assumption B:								
4. Federal	89.1	76.4	45.0	25.4	18.2	16.2	15.1	20.8
5. State and local	92.5	68.3	28.9	18.8	12.2	8.4	5.4	12.7
6. Total, all levels	181.6	144.7	73.9	44.2	30.4	24.6	20.5	33.5
Assumption C:								
7. Federal	105.9	84.5	44.0	19.6	10.8	9.5	23.7	20.8
8. State and local	95.1	69.6	28.8	17.9	11.1	7.4	6.7	12.7
9. Total, all levels	201.0	154.1	72.8	37.5	21.9	16.9	30.4	33.5
Assumption D:								
10. Federal	81.1	72.9	43.1	24.2	19.6	19.6	13.4	20.8
11. State and local	91.3	67.8	28.6	18.6	12.4	8.9	5.1	12.7
12. Total, all levels	172.4	140.7	71.7	42.8	32.0	28.5	18.5	33.5

[a] Assumption A allocates general expenditures proportional to families; B proportional to the "broad" income concept; C, proportional to capital income; and D, proportiona to disposable income.

TABLE 18. "Effective" Expenditure Schedule for All Government Expenditures ("Adjusted Broad Income" Concept), 1960

(Percent)

Level of Government[a]	Family Money Income Brackets							
	Under $2,000	$2,000–$2,999	$3,000–$3,999	$4,000–$4,999	$5,000–$7,499	$7,500–$9,999	$10,000 and Over	Total
Assumption A:								
1. Federal	85.0	57.9	47.9	32.0	19.8	13.7	8.9	21.1
2. State and local	50.1	41.3	25.6	20.1	12.8	8.0	5.9	12.9
3. Total, all levels	135.1	99.2	73.5	52.1	32.6	21.7	14.8	34.0
Assumption B:[b]								
4. Federal	41.8	43.8	37.3	26.0	18.9	16.0	17.3	21.1
5. State and local	43.4	39.1	24.0	19.2	12.6	8.3	6.2	12.9
6. Total, all levels	85.2	82.9	61.3	45.2	31.5	24.3	23.5	34.0
Assumption C:								
7. Federal	49.7	48.4	36.6	20.1	11.1	9.4	27.3	21.1
8. State and local	44.7	39.8	23.9	18.3	11.4	7.3	7.8	12.9
9. Total, all levels	94.4	88.2	60.5	38.4	22.5	16.7	35.1	34.0
Assumption D:								
10. Federal	38.1	41.7	35.8	24.8	20.2	19.3	15.5	21.1
11. State and local	42.9	38.8	23.8	19.0	12.8	8.8	5.9	12.9
12. Total, all levels	81.0	80.5	59.6	43.8	33.0	28.1	21.4	34.0

[a] Assumption A allocates general expenditures in proportion to families; B, in proportion to the "broad" income concept; C, in proportion to capital income;andD, in proportion to disposable income.

[b] The standard case.

TABLE 19. Coefficients of Average Rate Progression for Selected Income Ranges

Item	Family Money Income Bracket Changes						
	$2,000–$2,999 to $3,000–$3,999	$3,000–$3,999 to $4,000–$4,999	$4,000–$4,999 to $5,000–$7,499	$5,000–$7,499 to $7,500–$10,000	$2,000–$2,999 to $4,000–$4,999	$2,000–$2,999 to $5,000–$7,499	$2,000–$2,999 to $7,500–$10,000
"Adjusted Broad Income"							
1. Taxes	.888	.381	−.524	−.346	.546	−.110	−.231
2. Federal expenditures	−1.343	−1.132	−.303	−.086	−1.201	−.650	−.386
3. State and local expenditures	−3.120	−.481	−.281	−.127	−1.343	−.692	−.427
4. Total expenditures[a]	−4.463	−1.613	−.584	−.213	−2.543	−1.343	−.813
5. Federal net pattern	−2.128	−1.212	.004	.089	−1.511	−.583	−.268
6. State and local net pattern	−3.223	−.771	−.072	.047	−1.572	−.653	−.325
7. Total net pattern[a]	−5.351	−1.984	−.068	.136	−3.084	−1.235	−.593
Expenditures, Total:							
8. Assumption A	−5.310	−2.144	−.831	−.323	−3.178	−1.740	−1.076
9. Assumption C	−5.723	−2.214	−.678	−.172	−3.360	−1.716	−.992
10. Assumption D	−4.318	−1.583	−.460	−.441	−2.476	−1.241	−.727
Net Pattern, Total:							
11. Assumption A	−6.198	−2.515	−.315	.027	−3.717	−1.633	−.855
12. Assumption C	−6.612	−2.585	−.162	.178	−3.900	−1.609	−.772
13. Assumption D	−5.207	−1.954	+.064	.198	−3.016	−1.144	.507

[a] The standard case.

TABLE 19:

This table provides one of the measures which may be used to determine the degree of regression or progression over a given income range. Average rate progression measures the rate of change of the average rate of tax, and it is described by the formula:

$$\frac{\frac{T_1}{Y_1} - \frac{T_0}{Y_0}}{Y_1 - Y_0},$$

where T_1 is the tax payment associated with the income Y_1, and T_0 is the tax payment associated with income Y_0, with $Y_1 > Y_0$. Average rate progression is equal to zero when the tax system is proportional, positive when the tax system is progressive, and negative when the tax system is regressive. When this measure is applied to expenditures and net distributed income (as in Table 19), this observation is in no way altered. When a negative coefficient becomes smaller it indicates that the particular rate is becoming less regressive over the stated income range. The very lowest and highest income bracket rates were excluded from this table.

TABLE 20. The Incremental Allocation of Cost to Consumers of Passenger Travel and Consumers of Transported Products

(Percent)

	Consumer of Passenger Travel (Automobiles)	*Consumer of Transported Products (Trucks)*	*Total*
1. Highway Cost Allocation Study	68.1	31.9	100
2. Louisiana	57.2	42.8	100
3. Kentucky	59.3	40.7	100
4. Montana	49.9	50.1	100
5. North Dakota	47.1	52.9	100
6. Ohio	59.8	40.2	100
7. Minnesota	65.1	34.9	100
8. States studied (average)	56.4	43.6	100

TABLE 20:

Most incremental cost allocation studies present their findings in cost responsibility estimates *per vehicle.* These were converted here into cost responsibility estimates for all vehicles of one classification; the sum of cars and buses results in the car cost portion, and the sum of all trucks and transport trailers in the truck cost portion.

Line 1: "A Preliminary Allocation of Cost Responsibility by the Incremental Method," *Hearings on the President's Proposals for Financing the Federal-Aid Highway,* 87 Cong. 1 sess. (1961), pp. 114-30, esp. Table IV-B-2.

Line 2: William D. Ross, *Financing Highway Improvements in Louisiana* (Louisiana State University, 1955), p. 226, Table 133.

Line 3: James W. Martin, *Financing Kentucky's Roads and Streets* (Bureau of Business Research, University of Kentucky, 1956), p. 57, Table 2.

Line 4: William L. Hall, *Financing Modern Highways for Montana,* A report on Highway Finances to the Montana Fact Finding Committee on Highways, Streets and Bridges (1956), p. 44, Table 5-9.

Line 5: William E. Koenker and Arlyn J. Larson, *Equitable Highway Cost Allocation in North Dakota* (Bureau of Business and Economic Research, University of North Dakota, 1956), p. 60, Table XIV, which gives "adjusted" cost responsibility estimates.

Line 6: D. F. Pancoast, *Allocation of Highway Cost in Ohio by the Incremental Method* (Ohio Department of Highways, December 1953), p. 70, Table 10.

Line 7: *An Incremental Analysis Based Upon the Ten-Year A.S.F. Proposed Highway Program (Minnesota)* (Public Administration Service, 1954), Table 6, column 8.

Line 8: The average of lines 2 through 7.

TABLE 21:

Column 2: Students expected to complete each level of education: The student enrollment estimates for 1960 are from U.S. Department of Health, Education, and Welfare, *Annual Report 1960* (1961), pp. 207, 228, for public school students; at the higher education level 59 percent of college students are in tax-supported colleges and universities. The proportion of students continuing from one grade to the next, and from one level of education to the next, for 1955-56 (the latest data available), are found in U.S. Department of Health, Education, and Welfare, *Biennial Survey of Education in the United States, 1954-56* (1959), p. 13, Table 6, col. 14.

Elementary Education: Of 27,980,000 public school students enrolled in 1960, 7.1 percent, or 1,917,000, will not finish the eighth grade. The students presently enrolled in secondary school and higher education (10,703,000) have also completed eight years of elementary school. In total, 36,766,000 students have (or will have) completed the first eight years; 7.1 percent of these students will not continue to secondary school.

Secondary Education: 34,916,000 students will eventually be enrolled in high school (8,490,000 students actually enrolled in 1960, and 24,213,000 who will enter from elementary school); 32.7 percent (10,694,000) will not complete high school and they are assumed to have reached the level of less than four years. In addition, the 2,213,000 students enrolled in higher education have completed four years of secondary schooling. 48.2 percent of the graduating students will discontinue their education after high school.

Higher Education: 22,099,000 students graduate from high school; but only 11,401,000 enter colleges or universities (48.2 percent having terminated their education after high school). Of these students, 6,727,000 (59 percent) are in

TABLE 21. An Estimation of the Cost Incurred in Providing Education to that Portion of the Student Body Expected to Complete each Level of Education, 1960

Level of Education (Years)	*Students Expected to Complete each Level (000)*	*Annual Expenditure per Student*	*Expenditure per Student per Level*	*Total Expenditures per Level*	
				Millions of Dollars	*Percentage*
(1)	(2)	(3)	(4)	(5)	(6)
Elementary:					
Under 8 years	1,917		$2,478	$ 4,750	
8 years	36,766		2,832	104,121	
Total	38,683	$ 354		108,871	47.8
Secondary:					
1 to 3 years	10,694		1,602	17,132	
4 years	24,222		2,136	51,738	
Total	34,916	534		68,870	30.3
Higher:					
1 to 3 years	3,254		4,602	14,975	
4 years	5,686		6,136	34,889	
Total	8,940	1,534		49,864	21.9
Grand Total				227,605	100.0

publicly-supported colleges and universities. In addition, 2,213,000 students were enrolled in these colleges during 1960. Of the total public college student body of 8,940,000, 36.4 percent (3,254,000) can be expected to leave college before they obtain a degree. 5,686,000 students will graduate from college.

Column 3: The annual expenditure per student is obtained by dividing the budget expenditure at each level of education by the 1960 enrollment at each level.

Column 4: The expenditure per student per level is obtained by multiplying column 3 times the number of years of completed schooling in column 1. (It is assumed that those students not completing a level advance to the penultimate year.)

Column 5: Column 2 multiplied by column 4.

BENJAMIN BRIDGES, JR.*

Allowances for State and Local Nonbusiness Taxes

IN RECENT YEARS, many writers have proposed a variety of drastic changes in the treatment of state-local nonbusiness taxes as deductions under the federal individual income tax. Some criticize the present deductions as inequitable, while others believe that tax allowances should be used more actively to influence state tax policy or to transfer revenue from higher to lower levels of government. A brief examination of these underlying issues, especially the question of equity, will precede a quantitative appraisal of various deduction and credit plans. Results of the appraisal and a discussion of the implications of my findings for tax policy conclude the essay.

* Social Security Administration, Office of Research and Statistics. This paper is based upon the author's dissertation, "Treatment of State and Local Nonbusiness Taxes Under the Federal Individual Income Tax: Tax Deductions and Tax Credits" (Johns Hopkins, 1962).

Tax Allowances and Equity

Equity is a normative concept. Rational men can and do disagree in defining what constitutes perfect equity,[1] though the bases of argument about horizontal equity (the principle that equal units should be taxed equally) differ from those relevant to vertical equity (the principle that unequal units should be taxed according to some definite pattern).

In either case, before the principles of vertical and horizontal equity can be discussed or utilized, it is necessary to select an index of equality. Income is the most widely accepted index of equality, and, among various concepts of income suggested for this purpose, the idea of accretion advanced by Simons has gained greatest support.[2] Income, according to Simons, equals consumption plus the increase in net worth. It includes the net imputed income produced by owner-used consumer durables, where net imputed income is equal to gross imputed income minus all costs of earning that income.

The question under consideration here is how state-local nonbusiness taxes should be treated under the federal individual income tax so as to comply with this index of equality. More specifically, the problem at hand is to determine under what conditions allowances for state-local taxes will be helpful, and what form they should take—in particular, whether they should be deducted from income taxable under the federal tax, or credited against this tax.

Proposed Principles

Two definitions of conditions under which allowances are appropriate seem useful tests of the "equitableness" of the treatment of nonbusiness taxes under the federal individual income tax provisions:

(a) A deduction is appropriate if the state-local tax is a cost in-

[1] See Richard A. Musgrave, *The Theory of Public Finance: A Study in Public Economy* (McGraw-Hill, 1959), Chap. 8.

[2] Henry C. Simons, *Personal Income Taxation* (University of Chicago, 1938) and *Federal Tax Reform* (University of Chicago, 1950).

curred in earning income. This follows from the concept of taxable income as *net* income.

(b) An allowance—deduction or credit—may be appropriate where the federal government wishes to counteract the redistributive effects of a particular state or local nonbenefit tax. The more closely the tax is tied to voluntary payment, the smaller the redistributive effects are likely to be, and hence the weaker the case for an allowance.

From these two tests certain principles emerge:[3]

1. No allowance should be permitted for benefit taxes which are not costs of earning income. Such taxes pass the test neither of (a) nor (b). They can be considered payments for government services; they are similar in principle to payments for nongovernment services, and therefore should be treated in the same manner as are private expenditures for final products.
2. Ordinarily, at least, no allowance should be made for nonbenefit taxes which are not a cost of earning income. They do not pass test (a), nor can they be considered to pass test (b) unless there is explicit evidence that they impose an arbitrary burden. Such allowances should be permitted only for those taxes which seem excessively high in a horizontal sense (that is, relative to the average tax for equal income units), or a vertical sense (that is, relative to the average tax for unequal units). Moreover, such allowances should be granted only for those taxes which exceed

[3] For further discussion of such principles, see Joseph A. Pechman, "What Would a Comprehensive Income Tax Yield?" *Tax Revision Compendium: Compendium of Papers on Broadening the Tax Base,* House Committee on Ways and Means (1959), pp. 251-81; Melvin I. White, "Proper Income Tax Treatment of Deductions for Personal Expense," *Tax Revision Compendium,* pp. 365-74; C. Harry Kahn, "Personal Deductions in the Individual Income Tax," *Tax Revision Compendium,* pp. 391-406; Harvey E. Brazer, "Tax Deductibility of State and Local Taxes under the Individual Income Tax," *Tax Revision Compendium,* pp. 407-18; Walter W. Heller, "Deductions and Credits for State Income Taxes," *Tax Revision Compendium,* pp. 419-33; Melvin I. White, "Deductions for Nonbusiness Expenses and an Economic Concept of Income," *Federal Tax Policy for Economic Growth and Stability,* Joint Committee on the Economic Report (1956), pp. 353-66; C. Harry Kahn, *Personal Deductions in the Federal Income Tax* (National Bureau of Economic Research, 1960), Chap. 5; James A. Maxwell, *Tax Credits and Intergovernmental Fiscal Relations* (Brookings, 1962), Chap. 5; Dan Throop Smith, *Federal Tax Reform: The Issues and a Program* (McGraw-Hill, 1961), Chap. 4; and William Vickrey, *Agenda for Progressive Taxation,* (Ronald, 1947), Chap. 4.

certain limits; a floor principle, like the one now applied to medical expenses, should be used.

3. Deductions should be permitted for (benefit or nonbenefit) taxes which are costs of earning income. Although this principle seems explicit in test (a), a qualified caution is in order. Test (a) assumes that except for inclusion of these taxes, income is properly defined. This will tend to be true if income is in money alone, but need not hold if income is imputed. If imputed income is not included in gross income, allowances for taxes incurred in earning gross income would exaggerate rather than diminish the distortion which results from exclusion of imputed income. Therefore, deduction of taxes incurred in the earning of imputed income should be permitted only if gross income includes imputed income.

4. No allowances should be permitted for regulatory taxes which, by definition, are designed to treat equals unequally.

5. Allowances for state-local taxes may produce an additional form of inequity—geographical discrimination. Such discrimination results when allowances are granted for taxes which are not costs of earning income and/or for taxes which are costs of earning income which is not included in gross income. For example, in Community A, benefit taxes are levied upon consumer durables. These taxes are costs of earning income. In Community B the services which are financed in Community A by benefit taxes are financed by private expenditures and/or user charges. These private expenditures and/or user charges are also costs of earning income. Allowance for Community A's taxes but not for Community B's corresponding private expenditures and/or user charges would cause geographical discrimination.[4] As another example, in Community C, nonbenefit taxes are levied upon consumers. In Community D, nonbenefit taxes are levied upon firms which shift them partly to consumers. In Community D it is not administratively feasible to permit consumers allowances for such taxes, but this means that allowance for Community C's taxes would cause geographical discrimination. In addition, geographical discrimination results when allowances are granted for *some,* but not *all* taxes which are not costs

[4] Brazer, in *Tax Revision Compendium,* pp. 414-15.

of earning income, and/or for taxes which are costs of earning income which is not included in gross income.

Evaluation of Current Law

The list of deductible state-local nonbusiness taxes now includes real and personal property taxes, motor fuel taxes, general retail sales taxes, and individual income taxes. Alcohol taxes, tobacco taxes, motor vehicle license fees, and motor vehicle operators' license fees were deductible until passage of the Revenue Act of 1964, but are now excluded. User charges and special assessments are not deductible. Each deductible tax is subjected, below, to a test of its conformity with the principles of appropriateness just outlined.

PROPERTY TAXES. Imputed net rental income from owner-occupied houses (calculated by deducting from imputed gross rental income all costs of earning income, including property taxes) should be included in accretion income, while interest and taxes should be deductible. Since under federal law imputed rental income of owner-occupied houses is not included in income, and interest is deducted, no allowance should be permitted for property taxes on owner-occupied houses (principle 3). Deductibility of such taxes discriminates in favor of home owners (both with and without mortgages) and against renters. This discrimination is the more severe since real property is not available to all on equal terms. Finally, deductibility of property taxes is undesirable because it leads to geographic discrimination (principle 5).

If it is undesirable on equity grounds, can the current policy of deductibility nevertheless be defended as a form of subsidy to homeowners? Probably not, because even if the desirability of such subsidy was accepted, deduction of property taxes is hardly an efficient form of subsidy. The objective of this subsidy is presumably to encourage low-income families to purchase adequate homes, but the value of the subsidy (via deductibility) would increase with the value of the home and vary directly with the size of income, not inversely, as it should in order to benefit low-income families. Furthermore, many people cannot take advantage of the subsidy. Many low-income families cannot or do not itemize their personal deductions. A direct subsidy or a properly devised credit plan would better serve to encourage purchase of adequate homes by low-income families. Finally, deductibility of property taxes discourages the use of user charge and special assessment financing—sources of public revenue which Brazer feels have many merits.[5]

SELECTIVE SALES TAXES AND LICENSE FEES. Under federal law the imputed income from owner-operated motor vehicles is not included in gross income. Moreover, such inclusion would not be administratively feasible. Motor fuel taxes and motor vehicle license fees can be considered benefit taxes. Peter Newman estimates that about 75 percent of private automobile license fees are levied on the weight of the automobile, and the remaining 25 percent on the basis of a flat rate.[6] Automobile weight, like motor fuel consumption, is a crude indicator of the benefit received from use of public streets and roads. Moreover, highway user charges, or tolls, cannot be deducted. Under these circumstances there is a clear case against deduction of these benefit taxes. Allowances for them would cause geographical discrimination (principle 5) and increase discrimination in favor of owner-operators of vehicles as against passengers of taxis and buses, and renters of motor vehicles (principle 3).

No allowances should be granted for sumptuary taxes, such as those on tobacco products and alcoholic beverages, which were deductible until 1964. Such allowance is basically unjustified (principle 4), and undesirable because it results in geographical discrimination (principle 5). The disallowance of such deductions under the Revenue Act of 1964 is welcome.

GENERAL RETAIL SALES TAXES. The permissible deduction of retail sales taxes seems undesirable for a number of reasons. To begin with, such an allowance can be justified according to principle 2 only with difficulty. Second, it should be noted that sales or gross receipts taxes levied on the manufacturer or wholesaler are not deductible, nor are various other business taxes which, like retail sales taxes, are at least partly shifted to consumers. Thus, allowance for general retail sales taxes causes personal as well as geographical discrimination (principle 5). Third, allowances for

[5] *Ibid.*, p. 415.

[6] Peter Newman, "An Empirical Study of the Distribution of the Tax Burden in the United States" (unpublished paper, 1961), Chap. 5, Sec. 11.

general retail sales taxes as well as for selective sales taxes result in serious problems of tax error, tax evasion, and tax enforcement.

INDIVIDUAL INCOME TAXES. Deduction of income taxes passes neither test (a) nor (b). They do not constitute a cost of earning income, which, for purposes of this argument, is necessarily defined as income *before* tax, nor can they be considered arbitrary burdens imposed upon the taxpayer. Indeed, income taxes appear to me only slightly more compulsory than general sales taxes. Finally if allowances were granted for income taxes but not for other currently deductible state-local taxes, the result would be personal as well as geographic discrimination (principle 5).

Although some still justify the deduction of income taxes on grounds of equity,[7] most supporters of this allowance now use other arguments. Thus, allowances are recommended in order to avoid confiscatory rates, as a means of moderating interstate income tax differentials,[8] or as a device to induce states to place greater reliance on the income tax. Tax allowance has also been justified as a means of transferring revenue from the federal to the state-local level. This argument may assume considerable importance when state-local finances promise to become increasingly strained,[9] while

[7] Deduction of income taxes is supported partly on grounds of equity by Melvin White and James A. Maxwell. White favors deductibility for income taxes but not for sales taxes, on the hypothesis—which seems unrealistic to me—that general sales taxes are largely voluntary payments which have many of the aspects of prices, but income taxes are compulsory payments which have minimal price aspects. See White, in *Federal Tax Policy,* p. 367, and in *Tax Revision Compendium,* p. 368. Maxwell favors deductibility for general taxes (income, property, and general sales taxes), but no allowances for selective sales taxes and license fees. He argues that not only income, but also property and general sales taxes should be deducted because they all are general nonbenefit taxes. To permit deductibility for income taxes only would be inequitable, since there are numerous similarities between income taxes and these other general taxes. Furthermore, Maxwell holds that the element of compulsion associated with income taxes does not differ significantly from that associated with general sales taxes. Finally, he considers allowance for income taxes (but not for other general taxes) undesirable because it would discriminate against states not having income taxes. See Maxwell, *Tax Credits,* pp. 97-106.

[8] As examples, see Pechman, in *Tax Revision Compendium,* pp. 269-74; and Vickrey, *Progressive Taxation,* Chap. 4.

[9] See Otto Eckstein, *Trends in Public Expenditures in the Next Decade* (Committee for Economic Development, 1959); National Planning Association, *Long-Range Projections for Economic Growth: The American Economy in 1970* (The Association, 1959); Gerhard Colm and Manuel Helzner, "Financial Needs and

at the same time the federal revenue outlook requires repeated tax reductions. This argument frequently implies the allowance of state income taxes as credit against the federal income tax.[10] The allowance of state income tax as deduction and as credit is examined below.

Analysis of Deduction Plans

In this section, four plans for partial or complete removal of federal deductibility of state-local nonbusiness taxes are analyzed. Plan 1 calls for removal of deductibility without any change in federal-bracket tax rates. Plan 2 requires removal of deductibility, accompanied by an equiproportionate reduction in all federal-bracket tax rates just sufficient to leave 1958 federal tax liability unchanged. Plan 3 specifies removal of deductibility of state-local taxes, other than income taxes, without any change in federal-bracket tax rates. Plan 4 calls for removal of deductibility of taxes which do not exceed 3 percent of adjusted gross income (AGI), without any reduction in federal-bracket tax rates. The effects of these four plans upon tax revenues and tax progression are discussed below; their

Resources over the Next Decade: At All Levels of Government," in *Public Finances: Needs, Sources, and Utilization* (National Bureau of Economic Research, 1961), pp. 3-21; Dick Netzer, "Financial Needs and Resources over the Next Decade: State and Local Governments," in *Public Finances: Needs, Sources, and Utilization,* pp. 23-65; and Robert J. Lampman, "How Much Government Spending in the 1960's?" *Quarterly Review of Economics and Business,* Vol. 1 (February 1961), pp. 7-17.

[10] Among recent proposals of this sort see: Robert R. Nathan and Edward D. Hollander, "The Role of Individual Income Taxes in Federal-State-Local Fiscal Relations," *Tax Revision Compendium,* pp. 219-29; Walter W. Heller, in *Tax Revision Compendium,* pp. 419-33; Orville L. Freeman, "Strengthening the States' Tax Base," a statement presented at the 51st Annual Meeting, Governors' Conference, 1959; and Orville L. Freeman, report given at the 51st Annual Meeting, Governors' Conference, 1959, *Proceedings of the Governors' Conference: 1959,* pp. 54-56. Also, see Morton Grodzins, "The Federal System," *Goals for Americans,* Report of the President's Commission on National Goals and Chapters Submitted for the Consideration of the Commission (1960), pp. 278-79; John W. Gardner, "National Goals in Education," *Goals for Americans,* p. 99; and George Meany, statement in *Goals for Americans,* p. 29; Senator Barry Goldwater, *Washington Post,* Jan. 29, 1961; and Robert Heller, "A Proposal for Financing Tax Supported Education," *Harvard Educational Review,* Vol. 28 (Summer 1958), pp. 214-31.

effects upon interstate income tax differentials are considered later. The estimates presented in this section do not take account of the changes in the deductibility provisions which were introduced by the Revenue Act of 1964.

Effects on Tax Revenues

Effects (gains or losses) of each plan are estimated for the federal government, state-local governments, and taxpayers as a whole.

Plan 1. First, the revenue effects of plan 1 for 1958: Adoption of plan 1 would increase total federal individual income tax liability by $1,920 million, as shown in Table 8, column 1.[11] In other words, the cost to the federal government of allowing deductibility of state-local nonbusiness taxes would be $1,920 million. Since adoption of plan 1 would cause only a slight decrease in state-local tax collections, there would be a sizable increase in combined federal-state-local revenue.

In 1958, estimated deductible taxes amounted to $12,420 million.[12] Tax deductions totaled $7,480 million or 60 percent of deductible taxes. Tax deductions on taxable and nontaxable returns were $7,080 million and $400 million respectively. Deductible taxes of $4,940 million, or 40 percent of deductible taxes, did not appear as tax deductions. The estimated cost of deductibility ($1,920 million) was 15.5 percent of total deductible taxes and 25.7 percent of total taxes deducted. In other words, 15.5 percent of deductible state-local taxes and 25.7 percent of deducted state-local taxes were, in effect, paid by the federal government.

The revenue effects of plan 1 for 1948-58 follow. Over this period, tax deductions on taxable returns as shown in Table 1, column 1, increased steadily from $1,500 million in 1948 to $7,081 million in 1958. Such deductions increased from 0.8 percent of adjusted gross income in 1948 to 2.3 percent in 1958, as shown in Table 1, column 2; they increased from 2.0 percent of taxable income before tax deductions in 1948 to 4.5 percent in 1958, as shown in Table 1, column 3.

Several factors help to explain the rise in tax deductions relative to total AGI. First, over the period 1948-58 estimated deductible

[11] For a brief description of the method of estimation, see App. A, item 1.

[12] For a brief description of the method of estimation, see App. A, item 2.

TABLE 1. Tax Deductions and Deductible Taxes, 1948–58

Year	Deductions on Taxable Returns (Millions of dollars)	Deductions on Taxable Returns ÷ AGI (Percent)	Deductions on Taxable Returns ÷ Before-Tax-Deduction Taxable Income on Taxable Returns (Percent)	Deductible Tax (Millions of dollars)	Deductible Tax ÷ AGI (Percent)	Tax Deductions on Taxable Returns ÷ Deductible Tax (Percent)
	(1)	(2)	(3)	(4)	(5)	(6)
1948	$1,500	0.81	2.0	$ 4,783	2.6	31.4
1949	1,812	0.98	2.5	5,451	2.9	33.2
1950	2,068	1.02	2.4	6,036	3.0	34.3
1951	n.a.	n.a.	n.a.	6,926	3.0	n.a.
1952	3,034	1.25	2.7	7,756	3.2	39.1
1953	3,453	1.35	2.9	8,380	3.3	41.2
1954	3,826	1.50	3.2	8,997	3.5	42.5
1955	n.a.	n.a.	n.a.	9,859	3.6	n.a.
1956	5,543	1.86	3.8	10,806	3.6	51.3
1957	n.a.	n.a.	n.a.	11,739	3.8	n.a.
1958	7,081	2.29	4.5	12,420	4.0	57.0

Note: n.a. denotes not available.

Sources: Column 4, Deductible Taxes were estimated by use of the method described in Kahn, *Personal Deductions*, pp. 231–33, Appendix H. The Kahn-method estimates were then reduced by 8.5 percent to correct for overstatement.

taxes increased relative to total AGI. As shown in Table 1, columns 4 and 5, deductible taxes increased from $4,783 million, or 2.6 percent of AGI in 1948, to $12,420 million, or 4.0 percent of AGI in 1958. This rise in the ratio of deductible taxes to AGI was largely due to increases in effective tax rates for income taxes and for sales and gross receipts taxes. The GNP elasticity of deductible state-local taxes as a group probably was close to 1.[13] In other words, for given effective tax rates for deductible taxes, the ratio of deductible taxes to AGI (or GNP) would have remained virtually unchanged.

Second, over the period 1948-58, tax deductions on taxable returns increased relative to estimated deductible taxes. Those deductions included in Table 1, column 6, increased from 31.4 percent of deductible taxes in 1948, to 57.0 percent of deductible taxes in 1958. This rise in the ratio of tax deductions to deductible taxes resulted largely from decreasing use of the standard deduction. For taxable returns, the ratio of amount of standard deductions to amount of total (standard plus itemized) deductions decreased from 57.9 percent in 1948 to 37.2 percent in 1956.[14] Most federal taxpayers pay some deductible state-local taxes. Hence the declining use of the standard deduction implies concomitant increases in tax deductions. In 1958, deductions for taxes appeared on 98 percent of taxable returns with itemized deductions.

Over the period 1954-58 the cost of tax deductions on taxable returns increased from $1,043 million in 1954, to $1,507 million in 1956, to $1,904 million in 1958. In addition, the cost of such deductions increased from 0.41 percent of AGI in 1954 to 0.51 percent of AGI in 1956 to 0.62 percent of AGI in 1958. The ratio of cost of such tax deductions to the deductions themselves was 27.3 percent in 1954, 27.2 percent in 1956, and 26.9 percent in 1958.

Plan 2 calls for removal of deductibility accompanied by an equiproportionate reduction in all federal statutory bracket rates just sufficient to leave 1958 federal tax liability unchanged. A proportionate reduction of 5.3 percent would be required. Bracket rates would range from 18.94 percent to 86.18 percent instead of from 20 percent to 91 percent.

Adoption of plan 2 would cause a very slight decrease in state-

[13] Netzer, in *Public Finances*, pp. 29-30, Tables 2-4.

[14] Kahn, in *Personal Deductions*, p. 165, Table 58.

local tax collections—a smaller decrease than that which would be caused by adoption of plan 1. Hence there would be a very slight decrease in the combined federal-state-local tax burden.

Plan 3 calls for removal of deductibility of state-local taxes other than income taxes without any change in federal bracket rates. As shown in Table 8, column 3, the combined 1958 cost of deductibility of property and sales-license taxes is $1,460 million, or $460 million below the plan 1 figure.[15] In other words, adoption of plan 3 would increase federal individual income tax liability by $1,460 million. The decrease in state-local tax collections would again be small relative to the increase in federal tax collections. A sizable increase in the combined federal-state-local tax revenue would again result.

Plan 4 calls for removal of deductibility of taxes which do not exceed 3 percent of AGI, without any reduction in federal bracket rates.

As shown in Table 8, columns 3 and 4, adoption of plan 4 would cause an increase of $1,070 million in federal revenue, or $390 million less than for plan 3.[16] Adoption of plan 4 would cause a slight decrease in state-local tax collections. However, this decrease would be quite small relative to the increase in federal tax collections. Thus there would be a sizable increase in the combined federal-state-local tax burden even for plan 4.

Effects on Progression

In the literature, tax progression has been defined with respect to several different income concepts. In this essay, progression is defined in relation to adjusted gross income. Various measures of the degree of progression have been applied to each concept of income.[17] Here the degree of progression is defined as the rate of change with respect to income of the average rate of tax.[18] This

[15] For a brief description of the method of estimation, see App. A, item 3.

[16] For a brief description of the method of estimation, see App. A, item 4.

[17] For a discussion of the various measures of the degree of progression see Richard A. Musgrave and Tun Thin, "Income Tax Progression, 1929–1948," *Journal of Political Economy*, Vol. 56 (December 1948), pp. 498–514.

[18] Let Y_1 and Y_0 be adjusted gross incomes (where $Y_1 > Y_0$), A_1 and A_0 be the effective average tax rates for Y_1 and Y_0, T_1 and T_0 be the tax liabilities for Y_1 and Y_0, and P be

measure, which has been referred to as "average rate progression," depends only upon the structure of tax rates and is independent of the distribution of income. It may be applied to points of income or to specific income ranges, but it does not measure the degree of progression of the rate structure as a whole. For a decrease (increase) in yield, progressivity increases (decreases) or decreases (increases) as average tax rates are decreased (increased) by a larger or smaller number of percentage points for lower incomes than for higher incomes.[19]

Certain conclusions about direction of change in progression due to removal of deductibility can be reached quickly by general reasoning. If the ratio of tax deductions to income is the same for all incomes, the necessary and sufficient condition for progression (average rate progression) to remain unchanged following removal of deductibility, is that all effective marginal tax rates be equal. If the deduction-income ratio and the effective marginal tax rate both decrease (increase) as income increases, then removal of deductibility would decrease (increase) progression. If the deduction-income ratio and the marginal tax rate move in opposite directions as in-

---

the degree of progression. We have the following relations:

$$A_1 = T_1/Y_1;\; A_0 = T_0/Y_0,$$

$$P = \frac{A_1 - A_0}{Y_1 - Y_0} = \frac{T_1/Y_1 - T_0/Y_0}{Y_1 - Y_0}.$$

[19] Let ΔT_1 and ΔT_0 be the changes in tax liability for Y_1 and Y_0 due to a change in tax yield, and ΔP be the change in the degree of progression due to the change in tax yield. A tax is said to increase, remain unchanged, or decrease in progressivity as ΔP is positive, zero, or negative.

$$\Delta P = \frac{\Delta T_1/Y_1 - \Delta T_0/Y_0}{Y_1 - Y_0},$$

$$\Delta P \gtrless 0 \text{ as } \frac{\Delta T_1/Y_1 - \Delta T_0/Y_0}{Y_1 - Y_0} \gtrless 0,$$

$$\text{or as } \Delta T_1/Y_1 \gtrless \Delta T_0/Y_0.$$

come increases, removal of deductibility may increase or decrease progression.[20]

The data show that as a fraction of AGI, tax deductions increase slightly at successively higher levels of income. Since effective marginal tax rates also increase with AGI, adoption of plan 1 would cause progression to increase.

An empirical estimation of the effects of progression follows.

Plan 1. Over practically the entire income scale, removal of deductibility would increase average federal tax rates by a smaller number of percentage points for lower income classes than for higher income classes. This may be seen in Table 2, column 1. Hence, federal income tax progression would increase over practically the entire range of incomes. But the increase in the average federal tax rate for the class of income at and above $1,000,000 would be only 3.1 percentage points, while the increases for the $150,000-$200,000, $200,000-$500,000, and $500,000-$1,000,000 classes would be 3.4, 3.5, and 3.5 percentage points, respectively.

Progression would increase for three reasons. First, the ratio of number of taxable returns to number of returns increases from .42 to more than .99 as AGI increases. Second, the ratio of number of taxable returns with tax deductions to number of all taxable returns increases from .04 to .99 as AGI increases. Third, the relevant marginal tax rates increase from 20.0 percent to 90.2 percent as AGI increases. However, the ratio of tax deductions to AGI on taxable returns with tax deductions decreases from .065 to .036 as AGI rises. Tax deductions per taxable return with tax deduction increase from $59 to $73,000 as AGI rises.

Plan 2. Adoption of plan 2 would cause a slight increase in progression, as shown in Table 2, column 2. For each income class below $15,000 there would be a small tax decrease; each above $15,000 would experience a small tax increase. However, in no

[20] Let Y_1 and Y_0 be incomes (where $Y_1 > Y_0$), M_1 and M_0 be the effective marginal tax rates for Y_1 and Y_0, A_1 and A_0 be the effective average tax rates for Y_1 and Y_0 before removal of deductibility, T_1 and T_0 be the tax liabilities for Y_1 and Y_0 before removal of deductibility, Z be the ratio of tax deductions to income for Y_1 and Y_0, and P be the degree of progression. Then

$$\Delta P \gtreqless 0 \text{ as } M_1 Z Y_1 / Y_1 \gtreqless M_0 Z Y_0 / Y_0 \text{ or as } M_1 \gtreqless M_0.$$

TABLE 2. Change in Average Federal Tax Rates Due to Adoption of Plans 1–4, by AGI Classes, 1958

(Percent)

AGI Class ($000)	Plan 1 (1)	Plan 2 (2)	Plan 3 (3)	Plan 4 (4)
.6– 1	.03	−.1	.02	.01
1– 2	.1	−.1	.1	.04
2– 3	.2	−.1	.2	.1
3– 4	.3	−.1	.3	.2
4– 5	.4	−.1	.4	.2
5– 6	.5	−.003	.5	.3
6– 7	.6	−.01	.5	.3
7– 8	.6	−.05	.5	.3
8– 9	.6	−.05	.6	.3
9– 10	.6	−.1	.5	.3
10– 15	.7	−.1	.6	.4
15– 20	1.1	.1	.8	.6
20– 25	1.4	.3	.9	.8
25– 50	1.9	.4	1.1	1.1
50–100	2.7	.7	1.5	1.6
100–150	3.0	.6	1.4	1.9
150–200	3.4	.9	1.5	2.1
200–500	3.5	.9	1.3	2.2
500–1,000	3.5	.7	1.2	2.4
1,000 and over	3.1	.4	.9	2.4
.6 and over	.7	—	.5	.4

class would the tax decrease exceed 0.1 percent and in no class would the increase exceed 0.9 percent of AGI. The changes in average tax rates would be rather small because the ratio of cost of deductibility to federal tax before tax deductions rose only slowly and irregularly with rising AGI.

Plan 3. Over the interval from $600 to $100,000, adoption of plan 3 would increase average tax rates by a smaller number of percentage points for lower income classes than for higher income classes. As shown in Table 2, column 3, tax progression would increase over this interval. However, for the range of incomes above $100,000, tax progression would generally decrease.

Plan 4. Over practically the entire income scale, adoption of plan 4 would increase average federal tax rates by a smaller number of percentage points for lower income classes than for higher income classes. As shown in Table 2, column 4, tax progression would increase over practically the entire range of incomes.

State-by-State Effects

The granting of deductibility can be viewed as an indirect federal subsidy to states, amounting to $1,920 million in 1958. One can think of this subsidy as being fully financed by an equiproportionate increase in all federal-bracket tax rates. Thus one can think of plan 2 as calling for the removal both of this subsidy and of the tax increase which finances it.

It is often considered desirable that such subsidy-tax systems aid states with low fiscal capcity and/or high fiscal effort at the expense of states with high fiscal capacity and/or low fiscal effort. A state is said to be aided if its federal subsidy exceeds its accompanying federal tax increase, that is, if its net federal tax is decreased. Per capita personal income can be taken as a crude measure of fiscal capacity. The ratio of general revenue of state-local governments (from own sources) to personal income can be taken as a crude measure of fiscal effort.

Plan 2 did not associate the net federal tax decrease as a percentage of federal tax and per capita personal income (Spearman r^2 of —.01; not significant at the 5 percent level).[21] The net federal tax decrease would equal the decrease in federal tax resulting from a 5.3 percent reduction in all federal bracket rates minus the increase in federal tax resulting from the removal of deductibility. In other words, adoption of plan 2 would not appreciably affect the existing interstate inequalities in per capita personal income.

In addition, there was no association between the net federal tax decrease as a percentage of federal tax and fiscal effort (Spearman r^2 of .05; not significant at the 5 percent level). There was little association between fiscal capacity (per capita personal income) and fiscal effort (Spearman r^2 of —.13; significant at the 5 percent level). Moreover, there was only a loose positive association between cost of deductibility per capita and personal income per capita (Spearman r^2 of .57; significant at the 1 percent level).

[21] For a brief description of the method of estimation, see App. A, item 5.

Analysis of Credit Plans

This section is a corresponding analysis of three credit plans, based again upon 1958 data. Plan 5 calls for the replacement of deductibility with a sliding-scale credit for state income taxes. Plan 6 requires the replacement of deductibility with a constant-percentage credit for state income taxes. Under plans 5 and 6 each taxpayer would receive a credit for 100 percent of his state income tax up to a stated percentage of his pre-credit federal tax. Under terms of the sliding-scale credit, the higher a taxpayer's federal tax the lower is this stated percentage. For the constant-percentage credit, this stated percentage is the same for all taxpayers. The specific credit levels were chosen so that if the maximum potential credit were fully utilized, adoption of plans 5 or 6 would leave federal revenue for 1958 unchanged. Plan 7 calls for the replacement of deductibility with a credit for a stated percentage of deductible state-local taxes, the percentage again being chosen so as to leave federal revenue for 1958 unchanged. This equalization of costs (cost of credit equals cost of deductibility) facilitates evaluation of credit-deductibility substitutions such as those called for by plans 5, 6, and 7.

The effects of these three plans upon tax revenues and tax progression are discussed below; consideration of their effects upon interstate income tax differentials is taken up in the following section. Like the estimates in the preceding section, those in this section do not take account of the changes in the deductibility provisions introduced by the Revenue Act of 1964.

Some general reflections provide a useful preface to empirical estimates of the effects upon revenue of various credit plans.

Nature of Revenue Credits

This discussion logically begins with the properties of credits (including sliding-scale, constant-percent, or flat-amount)[22] for 100 percent of state income tax up to a stated percentage of federal in-

[22] Under a flat-amount credit, each taxpayer's maximum credit equals the same dollar amount, or 100 percent of his pre-credit federal income tax, whichever is smaller.

come tax. Under such plans, state income taxes do not have to exceed certain minimum limits before they may be used as credits against the federal tax; federal credits equal 100 percent of state income taxes not in excess of the maximum limit. Since credits are allowed for 100 percent of eligible state income taxes, increases in state income taxes are free of cost to state taxpayers so long as such increases continue to be eligible for federal credits. Thus, where such full credits are available, state governments are provided with a very strong incentive to introduce state income taxes, and to increase rates. This incentive, to be sure, extends only up to the maximum limit, but such a limit is necessary to prevent excessive federal revenue losses.

The effect of the credit-deductibility substitution upon federal, state, and combined revenue depends upon how state governments react to such a substitution. Certain definitions must be made before this process can be understood.

The term "offset tax," as used here, refers to that amount of state income tax liability which would become eligible for credit against federal tax, assuming the state law remains unchanged. In other words, offset tax is equal to that amount of the maximum potential federal credit which would be absorbed by existing state income taxes. The term "free revenue" refers to that amount of the maximum potential federal credit which would *not* be absorbed by existing state income taxes.[23] Free revenue is so called because it could be captured by a state government, after the credit is introduced, free of cost to the state's taxpayers. That is to say, state income taxes could be increased by the amount of free revenue while leaving combined federal-state tax liability unchanged. The increase in state tax would be fully offset by a reduction in federal tax. For example, the existing state income tax liabilities of taxpayers Adams, Baker, and Carter are $0, $20, and $200 respectively. Each is allowed a maximum potential credit of $100. Offset tax would be $0, $20, and $100 for Adams, Baker, and Carter respectively, while

[23] For states with income taxes which grant deductibility of federal income tax, the credit-deduction substitution may cause state income tax liability to change even in the absence of change in state income tax laws. However, since such changes are likely to be rather small, in defining offset tax and free revenue it is not necessary to specify whether existing state income tax refers to tax before or after the credit-deduction substitution.

free revenue would be $100, $80, and $0 respectively. The sum of free revenue and offset tax equals the maximum cost of the credit to the federal government.

State governments may react in various ways. Reaction A produces no change in state income tax laws. Reaction B is a change in state income tax laws which affects persons whose state tax is less than the maximum potential credit in such a way that the state tax is increased just sufficiently to capture all free revenue. For all other persons the state tax is not changed.[24] Reaction C is an increase in the state tax for every federal taxpayer, by the full amount of the maximum credit.

Of course these disparate reactions are not the only possible ones. The most likely short-run reaction would be neither A, B, nor C alone, but some combination of them. Given sufficient time, state governments would probably capture most of the free revenue.[25] Moreover, state-local governments would probably capture some, but not most, of the offset tax. A large proportion of the offset tax might become gains for taxpayers (via reduction in liability) rather than revenue gains for state-local governments (via increased state-local rates). A federal tax reduction which merely permits, rather than strongly encourages, state-local governments to raise their tax rates is likely to lead to a relatively large net tax reduction. Hence the actual overall state-local government reaction would probably resemble reaction B more closely than A or C.

If one of the chief purposes of the credit is to subsidize state-local governments, then it is desirable, *ceteris paribus,* that free revenue largely exceed the offset tax. Because personal exemptions granted by state governments tend to be more generous than those granted by the federal government, state income tax liability relative to federal income tax liability tends to be smaller for low-income taxpayers than for other taxpayers. Of the three equal-cost credits mentioned above, the flat-amount credit would provide the largest allowances for low-income taxpayers. The sliding-scale credit would provide larger allowances for such taxpayers than

[24] See note 23.

[25] See Glenn D. Morrow, "State Constitutional Limitations on the Taxing Authority of State Legislatures," *National Tax Journal,* Vol. 9 (June 1956), pp. 126-33. This article is somewhat out of date.

would the constant-percent credit. Therefore free revenue would be largest for the flat-amount credit, next largest for the sliding-scale credit, and smallest for the constant-percentage credit.

Credits for stated percentages (less than 100 percent) of all currently deductible taxes have quite different properties. There are neither minimum nor maximum credit limits, and no revenue could be captured by state-local governments wholly free of cost to their taxpayers. The incentive to introduce or raise state income taxes would thus be less, but not subject to an upper limit.

Plan 5. Under the selected sliding-scale credit each federal taxpayer would be permitted a credit of 100 percent of state income tax up to 12 percent of the first $200 of pre-credit federal tax, 6 percent of the next $300 of federal tax, and 2 percent of federal tax in excess of $500.[26] For example, a taxpayer with $900 of pre-credit federal tax would be permitted a maximum credit of $50 (12 percent of $200, plus 6 percent of $300, plus 2 percent of $400). If such a taxpayer had a state income tax liability of $40, he would receive a $40 federal credit. If he had a state liability of $60, he would receive a $50 federal credit.

In addition, taxpayers in income-tax states which do not grant full deduction for federal income tax would be permitted to deduct from federal gross income that part of their tax which results from the excess of combined federal-state marginal rates above 94 percent. If $10,000 is subject to a combined marginal rate of 97 percent (for example, a federal rate of 87 percent plus state rate of 10 percent), then $300 of state tax (97 percent minus 94 percent times $10,000) is deductible from federal gross income. Such partial deductibility combined with the credit would prevent combined marginal rates from exceeding 93 percent.

For 1958 the maximum potential credit would have been approximately $1,920 million. Free revenue as defined above would have been $1,150-$1,160 million, and offset tax would have been

[26] A husband and wife filing a joint return are regarded as one taxpayer. For a husband or wife filing a separate federal return, the credit probably should be limited to 12 percent of the first $100 of federal tax, 6 percent of the next $150 of federal tax, and 2 percent of federal tax in excess of $250. This halving of the width of the credit brackets would prevent the credit from inducing married couples to file separately rather than jointly (and thus avoid an increase in federal government administrative costs).

$770-$760 million. This is shown in Table 10, columns 1 and 2.[27]

If state tax laws remain unchanged (reaction A as defined above), the adoption of plan 5 would cause a $1,150 million increase in federal revenue, no change in state-local revenue, and a $1,150 million increase in combined revenue. If state taxes were increased just sufficiently to capture all free revenue (reaction B), the substitution would cause no change in federal revenue, but a $1,150 million increase in state-local revenue. If state taxes were increased by the full amount of the maximum credit (reaction C), the substitution would again leave federal revenue unchanged, but raise the state-local gain to $1,920 million.

It was argued above that overall state reaction would probably resemble reaction B more closely than A or C. If this were true, federal revenue would remain virtually unchanged while state revenue would increase considerably. This would not be the case, however, should state governments reduce the rates of state taxes other than income taxes.

Sixty percent of the maximum potential credit would be free revenue. Hence, given reaction A, only 40 percent of the potential credit would be absorbed. Reaction B or C would result in absorption of 100 percent of the potential credit. With state income tax collections of $1,570 million in fiscal 1958, about half of the existing state income tax would be offset by the credit.

Plan 6 calls for replacing deductibility with a constant-percentage credit for state income tax. The maximum potential credit was chosen to equal approximately the 1958 increase in federal revenue resulting from the removal of deductibility. A credit rate of 5.3 percent is called for.

The maximum credit would be $1,920 million. Free revenue would be $1,000-$1,100 million and existing state tax offset by the credit would be $800-$900 million.

Given reaction A, adoption of plan 6 would cause a $1,000-$1,100 million increase in federal revenue, no change in state-local revenue, and a $1,000-$1,100 million increase in combined tax revenue. Given reaction B, adoption of plan 6 would cause no change in federal revenue, a $1,000-$1,100 million increase in state-local revenue, and a $1,000-$1,100 million increase in com-

[27] For a brief description of the method of estimation, see App. A, item 6.

bined revenue. Given reaction C, adoption of plan 6 would cause no change in federal revenue, a $1,920 million increase in state-local tax revenue, and a $1,920 million increase in combined revenue.

Fifty to 60 percent of the maximum credit would be free revenue. Hence, for reaction A, only 40 to 50 percent of the potential credit would be absorbed. For reaction B or C, 100 percent of the potential credit would be absorbed. About half of the existing state income tax would be offset by the credit.

Plan 7 calls for replacing deductibility with a credit for a stated percentage of currently deductible state-local taxes. The credit rate of 17.5 percent was chosen because substitution at that rate of the credit for deductibility would leave federal revenue approximately unchanged. Little change in total state-local tax collections would be likely to occur as a result of the adoption of plan 7. Hence, total federal-state-local tax collections would show little change.

Effects on Progression

The effects of these plans upon the progression of the combined federal-state tax system are discussed below.

Plan 5. Adoption of plan 5 would generally increase the progression of the combined tax structure. The precise nature of the change in progression would depend upon state government reaction. Given reaction A or B, progression would generally increase. This is shown in Table 3, column 1. However, the increases in average tax rates for the AGI classes of $500,000-$1,000,000 and $1,000,000 and over would be only 2.6 and 2.0 percentage points respectively, while the increase for the $200,000-$500,000 AGI class would be 2.9 percentage points.

Following reaction A or B, the increase in progression would result from the removal of deductibility, not from the introduction of the credit. Reaction A would result in an increase in the cost of the credit plan as a percentage of AGI as AGI increased, thus tending to decrease progression. The cost of deductibility as a percentage of AGI would increase as AGI increased, thus tending to increase progression. In each AGI class, the cost of deductibility would exceed the cost of the credit as shown in Table 10, column 3. In other words, adoption of plan 5 would increase the combined tax burden for each AGI class.

TABLE 3. Change in Average Tax Rates Due to Adoption of Plans 5–7, by AGI Classes, 1958

(Percent)

AGI Class ($000)	Change in Combined Tax Rate for Reaction A or B to Plan 5 (1)	Change in Combined Tax Rate for Reaction C to Plan 5 or 6 (2)	Change in Federal Tax Rate for Plan 7 (3)
.6– 1	.02	.03	−.5
1– 2	.04	.1	−.3
2– 3	.04	.2	−.3
3– 4	.1	.3	−.3
4– 5	.2	.4	−.3
5– 6	.3	.5	−.2
6– 7	.3	.6	−.2
7– 8	.3	.6	−.1
8– 9	.3	.6	−.1
9– 10	.3	.6	−.1
10– 15	.4	.7	.0
15– 20	.8	1.1	.4
20– 25	1.1	1.4	.6
25– 50	1.5	1.9	1.1
50– 100	2.2	2.7	1.9
100– 150	2.5	3.0	2.2
150– 200	2.8	3.4	2.6
200– 500	2.9	3.5	2.8
500–1,000	2.6	3.5	2.8
1,000 and over	2.0	3.1	2.5
.6 and over	.4	.7	—

Given reaction C, adoption of plan 5 would have the same effect upon progression as would adoption of plan 1; that is, progression would increase over practically the entire income scale, as shown in Table 3, column 2. However, the increase in the average tax rate for the $1,000,000 and over AGI class would be only 3.1 percentage points, while the increases for the $150,000-$200,000, $200,000-$500,000, and $500,000-$1,000,000 AGI classes would be 3.4, 3.5, and 3.5 percentage points, respectively.

Plan 6. Adoption of plan 6 would generally increase progression, but for reaction A or B, the increase would be less marked than for plan 5. Given reaction C, adoption of plan 5 or 6 would have the same effect upon progression as would adoption of plan 1; that is, progression would increase over practically the entire income scale. This may be seen in Table 3, column 2.

Plan 7. As shown in Table 3, column 3, adoption of plan 7 would increase progression over practically the entire income scale. However, the increase in the average tax rate for the AGI class of $1,000,000 and over would be only 2.5 percentage points, while the increases for the classes of $150,000-$200,000, $200,000-$500,000, and $500,000-$1,000,000 would be 2.6, 2.8, and 2.8 percentage points respectively. A reduction in taxes would result for each AGI class below $10,000. For the AGI class of $10,000-$15,000, tax liability would remain unchanged. For each AGI class above $15,000, there would be a tax increase.

Progression would increase for three reasons. First, the credit would be available to persons filing taxable returns with the standard deduction. As AGI increased, the ratio of number of taxable returns with standard deduction to number of taxable returns would decrease from .95 to less than .005. Second, as AGI increased, the ratio of deductible taxes to AGI on taxable returns with standard deduction would decrease from .076 to .001. Third, the stated credit percentage would remain unchanged as AGI increased.

State-by-State Effects

This national view is again supplemented by an analysis of effects state-by-state.

Among the general observations which necessarily precede this analysis, one important distinction must be made about the way in which upper limit of the credit is defined. For a constant-percentage credit, the maximum credit as a percentage of pre-credit federal income tax liability would be the same for each state. Since pre-credit federal tax per capita generally varies directly with state per capita personal income, the maximum credit per capita would generally vary directly with per capita personal income.

Given a flat-amount credit, the maximum credit as a percentage of the pre-credit federal tax would generally vary inversely with state per capita personal income. Pre-credit federal tax per taxable return generally varies directly with state per capita personal income. On the other hand, maximum credit per capita would vary directly with state per capita income. Pre-credit federal tax per capita varies directly with state per capita personal income.

Constant-percentage and flat-amount credits may be regarded as the two polar types of negatively-graduated sliding-scale credits. Thus, for a sliding-scale credit, maximum credit as a percentage of federal tax would vary inversely with state per capita income. Maximum credit per capita would vary directly with state per capita income. For a given maximum credit cost, sliding-scale credits are more favorable to the poor states than constant-percentage credits and less favorable than flat-amount credits.

The distribution of free revenue by states is also important. If one considers credits for state income taxes only, among states without income taxes, the entire maximum credit is free revenue. Among states with income taxes, this is not the case. Given the maximum credit cost, the form of the credit has considerable effect upon the size and distribution of free revenue. Free revenue would be largest for flat-amount credits, next largest for sliding-scale credits, and smallest for constant-percentage credits.

Plan 5. Given reaction A, combined taxes and federal taxes would increase for forty-eight of the fifty-one states.[28] In other words, in forty-eight states, cost of deductibility would exceed offset state tax.[29] This is shown in Table 12, column 5. State-local tax revenue would be unchanged in all states.

For reaction B, combined tax would increase for forty-eight of the fifty-one states; that is, in these states, the cost of deductibility exceeded existing state tax which would be offset by the credit. Federal tax would increase for twenty states and decrease for thirty-one states. As shown in Table 12, column 4, for twenty of the fifty-one states, cost of deductibility would exceed maximum credit. State-local tax revenue would increase for forty-seven states and not change for four states. Forty-seven states would receive free revenue, as shown in Table 11, column 2. Four states would not receive free revenue.[30]

For reaction C, combined tax for each state would increase by the amount of the cost of deductibility. Federal tax would increase for twenty states and decrease for thirty-one states. For twenty of the fifty-one states, cost of deductibility would exceed maximum

[28] Fifty states plus the District of Columbia.

[29] For Idaho, Montana, and Virginia, existing state income tax offset by the credit exceeded cost of deductibility.

[30] Alaska, Hawaii, Oregon, and Vermont would not receive any free revenue.

credit. State-local tax for each state would increase by the amount of the maximum credit, as shown in Table 11, column 1.

Given reaction B or C, adoption of plan 5 would not appreciably narrow interstate differences in per capita personal income. There was no association between maximum credit minus cost of deductibility as a percentage of federal tax and per capita personal income (Spearman r^2 of —.02; not significant at the 5 percent level). Maximum credit minus cost of deductibility would equal the net decrease in federal tax. The association between maximum credit as a percentage of federal tax and per capita personal income was loosely negative (Spearman r^2 of —.58; significant at the 1 percent level). The association between maximum credit per capita and personal income per capita was strongly positive (Spearman r^2 of .92; significant at the 1 percent level).[31]

For reaction B or C, adoption of plan 5 would not appreciably affect the relative treatment of high-effort and low-effort states. The measure of fiscal effort used is the ratio of general revenue of state-local governments from own sources to personal income. There was no association between maximum credit minus cost of deductibility as a percentage of federal tax and fiscal effort (Spearman r^2 of — .01; not significant at the 5 percent level). The positive association between maximum credit as a percentage of federal tax and fiscal effort was extremely weak (Spearman r^2 of .19; significant at the 1 percent level).

In addition, no association existed between free revenue per capita and fiscal effort (Spearman r^2 of —.01; not significant at the 5 percent level).

For thirty-one of the fifty-one states, maximum credit would exceed cost of deductibility. However, maximum credit would exceed cost of deductibility for fifteen of the seventeen states without income taxes. As shown in Table 12, column 4, maximum credit would exceed cost of deductibility for sixteen of the thirty-four states with income taxes. Costs of deductibility as percentages of deductible taxes would be higher for income taxes than for other deductible taxes.

The seventeen states without income taxes could receive $865

[31] This strong positive association is largely explained by the fact that the federal tax per capita was higher for the richer than for the poorer states.

million of free revenue. For these states, free revenue would equal 100 percent of the potential credit. The thirty-four states with income taxes could receive $295 million of free revenue, of which California alone would receive $100 million. For these thirty-four states free revenue would equal only 28 percent of the potential credit. Thus the states with income taxes could receive 55 percent of the total maximum credit, but only 25 percent of total free revenue. Moreover, free revenue as a percentage of the credit would vary widely among states with income taxes.

Plan 6. For reaction B or C, adoption of plan 6 would not appreciably affect interstate differences in per capita personal income. There was no association between maximum credit minus cost of deductibility as a percentage of federal tax and per capita personal income (Spearman r^2 of .01; not significant at the 5 percent level). Maximum credit minus cost of deductibility would equal the net decrease in federal tax. The association between maximum credit per capita and personal income per capita was strongly positive (Spearman r^2 of .95; significant at the 1 percent level).[32]

For reaction B or C, adoption of plan 6 would not appreciably affect the relative treatment of high-effort and low-effort states. There was no association between maximum credit minus cost of deductibility as a percentage of federal tax and fiscal effort (Spearman r^2 of —.05; not significant at the 5 percent level).

Maximum credit would exceed cost of deductibility for only twenty-six of the fifty-one states. However, maximum credit exceeded cost of deductibility for fifteen of the seventeen states without income taxes. Maximum credit exceeded cost of deductibility for eleven of the thirty-four states with income taxes, as shown in Table 13, column 3.

Plan 7. Adoption of plan 7 would not appreciably narrow interstate differences in per capita personal income. There was a weak negative association under plan 7 between credit minus cost of deductibility as a percentage of federal tax and per capita personal income (Spearman r^2 of —.23; significant at the 1 percent level). Credit minus cost of deductibility would equal the net federal tax decrease. The association between credit as a percentage of federal

[32] This strong positive association is largely explained by the fact that federal tax per capita was higher for the richer than for the poorer states.

tax and per capita personal income was very weakly negative (Spearman r^2 of —.18; significant at the 1 percent level). The association between credit per capita and personal income per capita was loosely positive (Spearman r^2 of .52; significant at the 1 percent level).

Adoption of plan 7 would not appreciably affect the relative treatment of high-effort and low-effort states. There was no association between credit minus cost of deductibility as a percentage of federal tax and fiscal effort (Spearman r^2 of —.06; not significant at the 5 percent level). The positive association between credit as a percentage of federal tax and fiscal effort was extremely weak (Spearman r^2 of .15; significant at the 1 percent level).

Adoption of plan 7 would improve the treatment of the states lacking income taxes relative to that accorded the states with incomes taxes. For thirty-eight of the fifty-one states, credit would exceed cost of deductibility. However, credit would exceed the cost of deductibility for all seventeen of the states without income taxes. Credit would exceed cost of deductibility for only twenty-one of the thirty-four states with income taxes, as shown in Table 14, column 4. For one state (Arizona) with income taxes, credit would equal cost of deductibility.

Interstate Income Tax Differentials

Most states are quite sensitive to modifications of income tax laws and rates in other states, largely because politicians and voters believe that changes in interstate income tax differentials significantly affect citizens' choices of residence, place of work, and business location.[33] This belief may or may not be justified. Although the record of discussion of income tax differentials shows a preoccupation with corporate income taxes, the problem of differential also exists for personal income taxes.[34] Thus it is impor-

[33] For example, see Heller, in *Tax Revision Compendium*, pp. 424-25, and Nathan and Hollander, in *Tax Revision Compendium*, p. 222.

[34] It is alleged that personal income tax rate differentials for salary income discourage business firms from locating in high-income-tax states because of the difficulty of attracting executive talent to such states. In addition, it is alleged that personal income tax rate differentials on the profit income of unincorporated business firms significantly affect locations of such firms.

tant to determine how various changes in federal treatment of state-local taxes under the federal personal income tax affect interstate personal income tax differentials, and thus influence decisions about residence, place of work, and business location.

For eight "typical" taxpayers with different net incomes, dollar differentials in combined federal-state income tax liability were computed for various federal treatments of state-local taxes. Each typical taxpayer comprises a family composed of husband, wife, and two dependents. Each taxpayer can reside in state I, II, or III. These three states differ *only* with respect to state income taxation. State I does not have a state income tax. The income tax provisions of state II and state III differ only in that state III grants deductibility for federal income tax, but state II does not. Differentials in combined federal-state tax are more relevant than differentials in state tax, because federal as well as state income taxes may differ among states. The granting of federal allowances for state income taxes, for example, may cause such differentials. In choosing location, dollar (or average rate) differentials are more relevant than marginal rate differentials. For example, suppose a citizen can reside in state X or state Y. For the relevant income range, state X has the lower combined average rate and the higher combined marginal rate. *Ceteris paribus,* the citizen should choose to reside in state X, where his tax bill would be lower.

In the present treatment of deductibility, differentials were found to be rather small. The differential between state II and state I ranged from $41 for the taxpayer with a net income of $5,000, to $6,157 for the taxpayer with a net income of $1,000,000. This is shown in Table 4, column 1. As shown in Table 5, column 1, the differential between state III and state I ranged from $31 to $2,284. The differential between state II and state III ranged from $10 to $3,873, as may be seen in Table 6, column 1.

Under plans 1 or 2, differentials would be much larger than under the present deductibility treatment. For plan 1, the differential between state II and state I would range from $51 for the taxpayer with a net income of $5,000, to $68,412 for the taxpayer with a net income of $1,000,000, as shown in Table 4, column 2. The differential between state III and state I would range from $37 to $22,740, as shown in Table 5, column 2. The differ-

TABLE 4. Dollar Differentials in Combined Income Tax Between Income-Tax State Which Does Not Grant Deductibility and Non-Income-Tax State

Net Income ($000)	Present Deductibility (1)	Plan 1[a] (2)	Plan 2 (3)	Plan 3 (4)	Plan 4 (5)	Plan 5: Reaction A or B (6)	Plan 6: Reaction A or B (7)	Plan 7 (8)
5	$ 41	$ 51	$ 51	$ 41	$ 41	$ 9	$ 23	$ 42
10	183	235	235	183	183	171	151	194
20	582	880	880	581	581	759	643	726
50	1,379	2,934	2,934	1,361	1,498	2,535	1,961	2,421
100	2,235	6,385	6,385	2,235	3,093	5,407	3,878	5,268
200	3,313	13,252	13,252	3,313	5,713	11,803	7,589	10,933
500	3,737	33,972	33,972	3,737	12,904	26,875	17,966	28,027
1,000	6,157	68,412	68,412	6,157	25,449	47,046	33,832	56,440

[a] Also plan 5 or 6 for reaction C.

ential between state II and state III would range from $14 to $45,672, as shown in Table 6, column 2. Plan 1 and plan 2 differentials would be quite similar.

Differentials generally would be the largest for plans 1 and 2, next largest for plan 7, followed by plans 5, 6, 4, and 3 in declining order.

Changes in interstate income tax differentials might affect citizens' choices of place of residence and place of employment. For a

TABLE 5. Dollar Differentials in Combined Income Tax Between Income-Tax State Which Does Grant Deductibility and Non-Income-Tax State

Net Income ($000)	Present Deductibility (1)	Plan 1[a] (2)	Plan 2 (3)	Plan 3 (4)	Plan 4 (5)	Plan 5: Reaction A or B (6)	Plan 6: Reaction A or B (7)	Plan 7 (8)
5	$ 31	$ 37	$ 38	$ 30	$ 30	—	$ 9	$ 32
10	130	160	163	127	128	$ 99	80	136
20	396	567	584	384	385	455	347	481
50	830	1,649	1,717	787	919	1,278	744	1,391
100	1,162	3,073	3,248	1,127	1,963	2,164	742	2,588
200	1,579	5,773	6,169	1,523	3,879	3,756	507	4,863
500	1,564	12,832	13,952	1,505	10,597	7,185	—	10,800
1,000	2,284	22,740	25,161	2,186	21,349	10,575	—	19,156

[a] Also plan 5 or 6 for reaction C.

citizen (hereafter termed passive) who in the absence of change in the differential was not seriously considering a change to a residence and/or job in another state, a change in differential would not induce him to move unless the change more than covered moving costs (broadly defined). In absolute terms moving costs (broadly defined) are likely to be substantial. Thus, under any of plans 1 through 7, the change in the differential would not be likely to have much effect upon the place of residence or employment of a low-income or middle-income passive citizen. In addition, under plan 3, the change in the differential would not be likely to have much

TABLE 6. Dollar Differentials in Combined Income Tax Between Income-Tax States Which Grant Deductibility and Those Which Do Not

Net Income ($000)	*Present Deductibility* (1)	*Plan 1*[a] (2)	*Plan 2* (3)	*Plan 3* (4)	*Plan 4* (5)	*Plan 5: Reaction A or B* (6)	*Plan 6: Reaction A or B* (7)	*Plan 7* (8)
5	$ 10	$ 14	$ 13	$ 11	$ 11	$ 9	$ 14	$ 10
10	53	75	72	56	55	72	71	58
20	186	313	296	197	196	304	296	245
50	549	1,285	1,217	574	579	1,257	1,217	1,030
100	1,073	3,312	3,137	1,108	1,130	3,243	3,136	2,680
200	1,734	7,479	7,083	1,790	1,834	7,327	7,082	6,070
500	2,173	21,140	20,020	2,232	2,307	19,690	17,966	17,227
1,000	3,873	45,672	43,251	3,971	4,100	36,471	33,832	37,284

[a] Also plan 5 or 6 for reaction C.

effect upon the place of residence or employment of a passive citizen with a high income. Under plans 1, 2, 4, 5, 6, or 7 (especially for plans 1 or 2), change in the differential might influence decisions about place of residence or employment of a passive citizen with a high income.

Since states generally tax income both at place of residence and at place of employment, however, a citizen who wished to take full advantage of the increased differential would need both to live and work in the state with the lower state income tax. Thus, in order to take advantage of the increased differential, a citizen who both lived and worked in the state with the higher rate would need to change both his place of residence and his place of employment. A citizen who lived in the state with the higher rate but worked in the state with the lower rate would need to change only his place of residence. A citizen who lived in the state with the lower rate but worked in the state with the higher rate would need to change only his place of employment. Most interstate commuting between job and residence is confined to those urban areas which occupy more than one state (urban border areas).

For a citizen (hereafter termed active) who in the absence of change in the differential was seriously considering change to a residence and/or job in another state, a change in the differential might not have to cover moving costs in order to affect him. In border areas, a citizen who plans to live in the state with the lower rate, and who is planning to change jobs, would not necessarily require that the changed differential cover the cost of changing jobs (a type of moving cost). Similarly, a citizen living in a border area who plans to work in the state with the lower rate and who is planning to change residence would not necessarily require that the changed differential cover the cost of changing residence (this would be a type of moving cost). Under plan 3, a change in differential would not be likely to have much effect upon the place of residence or employment of an active citizen. For plans 1, 2, 4, 5, 6, or 7 (especially for plans 1 or 2), the change in the differential might significantly affect the place of residence or employment of a middle-income or high-income active citizen who lived and worked in a border area. However, in choosing place of residence or employment, other factors (such as differences in income opportunities, property tax rates, or in quality of schools) are likely to be more important than income tax differentials. In addition, many middle-income active citizens probably would not be aware of the magnitude of these changes in income tax differentials. Nevertheless, changes in differentials under plans 1, 2, 4, 5, 6, or 7 (especially under plans 1 or 2) might significantly affect the attitude of state politicians and voters toward future changes in state income tax rates.

Summary and Conclusions

This section brings the findings of the paper up to date, summarizes them, and presents certain conclusions about the course of policy.

Summary of Findings

Table 7 summarizes the revenue effects of the various plans for 1958. In addition, this table lists estimates of revenue effects for 1964, for the two different federal individual income tax rate structures of 1963 and 1965.

TABLE 7. Summary of Findings[a]

(Millions of dollars)

	Change in Revenue		
	1958	*1964: For 1963 Rates*	*1964: For 1965 Rates*
		Changes in Federal Revenue	
Plan 1	1,920	4,250	3,600[b]
Plan 2	0	1,320	1,250
Plan 3	1,460	3,030	2,560
Plan 4	1,070	1,900	1,610
Plan 5: Reaction B	0	1,670	1,240
Plan 6: Reaction B	0	1,320	1,250
Plan 7	0	880	230
		Changes in State-Local Revenue	
Plan 1	—[c]	—[c]	—[c]
Plan 2	—[c]	—[c]	—[c]
Plan 3	—[c]	—[c]	—[c]
Plan 4	—[c]	—[c]	—[c]
Plan 5: Reaction B	1,150	1,300	1,100–1,200
Plan 6: Reaction B	1,000–1,100	1,350–1,450	1,100–1,200
Plan 7	—[d]	—[c]	—[c]

[a] See App. A, item 7.
[b] This $3,600 million includes the $300 million cost of deductibility of alcohol taxes, tobacco taxes, motor vehicle license fees, and motor vehicle operators' license fees.
[c] Slight decrease.
[d] Little change.

An outline of the various types of effects under the different plans and for the various years follows.

PLAN 1. Removal of all deductibility unaccompanied by any change in federal-bracket tax rates.

a. For 1958, federal tax revenue would increase by $1,920 million. Under 1963 and 1965 rates, 1964 federal tax revenue would increase by $4,250 million and $3,600 million, respectively.

b. State-local tax revenue would decrease slightly.

c. Tax progression would increase.

d. Interstate income tax differentials would increase.

PLAN 2. Removal of all deductibility accompanied by a 5.3 percent reduction in all federal-bracket tax rates.

a. For 1958, federal tax revenue would not change. Under 1963 and 1965 rates, 1964 federal tax revenue would increase by $1,320 million and $1,250 million, respectively.

b. State-local tax revenue would decrease slightly.

c. Tax progression would increase.

d. Interstate inequality in per capita personal income would not change appreciably.

e. Interstate income tax differentials would increase.

PLAN 3. Removal of deductibility of state-local taxes other than income taxes unaccompanied by any change in federal-bracket rates.

a. For 1958, federal tax revenue would increase by $1,460 million. Under 1963 and 1965 rates, 1964 federal tax revenue would increase by $3,030 million and $2,560 million, respectively.

b. State-local tax revenue would decrease slightly.

c. Tax progression would increase.

d. Interstate income tax differentials would not appreciably change.

PLAN 4. Removal of deductibility of taxes which do not exceed 3 percent of adjusted gross income, without any reduction in federal-bracket rates.

a. For 1958, federal tax revenue would increase by $1,070 million. Under 1963 and 1965 rates, 1964 federal tax revenue would increase by $1,900 million and $1,610 million, respectively.

b. State-local tax revenue would decrease slightly.

c. Tax progression would increase.

d. Interstate income tax differentials would increase.

PLAN 5 WITH REACTION B. Replacement of deductibility with a credit for 100 percent of state income tax up to 12 percent of the first $200 of federal income tax, 6 percent of the next $300 of federal tax, and 2 percent of federal tax in excess of $500. For persons whose state income tax is less than the maximum potential credit, reaction B requires an increase in state tax just sufficient to fully absorb the maximum credit. For all other persons, state income tax is not changed.

a. For 1958, federal tax revenue would not change. Under 1963 and 1965 rates, 1964 federal tax revenue would increase by $1,670 million and $1,240 million, respectively.

b. For 1958, state-local tax revenue would increase by $1,150 million. Under 1963 and 1965 rates, 1964 state-local tax revenue would increase by $1,300 million and $1,100-$1,200 million respectively.

c. Tax progression would increase.

d. Interstate inequality in per capita personal income would not appreciably change.

e. Free revenue would accrue largely to the states not having state income taxes.

f. Interstate income tax differentials for high-income citizens would increase.

PLAN 6 WITH REACTION B. Replacement of deductibility with a credit for 100 percent of state income tax up to 5.3 percent of federal income tax.

a. For 1958, federal tax revenue would not change. Under 1963 and 1965 rates, 1964 federal tax revenue would increase by $1,320 million and $1,250 million, respectively.

b. For 1958, state-local tax revenue would increase by $1,000-$1,100 million. Under 1963 and 1965 rates, 1964 state-local tax revenue would increase by $1,350-$1,450 million and $1,100-$1,200 million, respectively.

c. Tax progression would increase.

d. Interstate inequality in per capita personal income would not appreciably change.

e. Free revenue would accrue largely to the states not having state income taxes.

f. Interstate income tax differentials for high-income citizens would increase.

PLAN 7. Replacement of deductibility with a credit for 17.5 percent of deductible taxes.

a. For 1958, federal tax revenue would remain unchanged. Under 1963 and 1965 rates, 1964 federal tax revenue would increase by $880 million and $230 million, respectively.

b. State-local tax revenue would remain unchanged or decrease slightly.

c. Tax progression would increase.

d. Interstate inequality in per capita personal income would not appreciably change.

e. The treatment of states not having state income taxes would improve slightly relative to that of states having income taxes.

f. Interstate income tax differentials for high-income citizens would increase.

Policy Conclusions

The following policy conclusions may be drawn about equity and other aspects of the problem.

IMPROVING TAX EQUITY. Large-scale broadening of the base of the federal individual income tax is urgently needed in order to increase tax equity and to improve taxpayer morale. In this context it has been argued that the present treatment of deductibility of state-local nonbusiness taxes is quite inequitable. Various alternative proposals have been suggested for improving the equity of deductions currently permitted. Deductibility could be partially or completely removed. Alternatively, deductibility could be replaced by some form of federal credit for state-local tax.

Given the recent sizeable reductions in federal statutory bracket rates, complete removal of deductibility of state-local nonbusiness taxes would be a desirable means of improving tax equity. Removal of deductibility would clearly achieve greater equity than would replacement of deductibility with a credit device. In the absence of substantial rate reduction, a first step could have been taken by limiting deductibility to state income taxes which exceed 3 percent of adjusted gross income. Such partial deductibility of state income taxes would have moderated interstate income tax differentials and prevented excessive combined marginal income tax rates for upper-income taxpayers.

AIDING STATE-LOCAL GOVERNMENTS. Credits against the federal individual income tax for state individual income taxes have been proposed as a method of providing federal aid for state-local governments. Credits could either replace or supplement deductibility.

As a means of federal aid the credit is more efficient per dollar of cost to the federal government than the present method which works through deductibility, but less efficient than direct federal grants.

Substitution of such a credit for deductibility would cause a considerable increase in state-local tax collections (provided the maximum cost of the credit approximately equals the cost of deductibility). For plans 5 and 6, increases in state-local revenue would exceed $1,200 million for 1958. But for such a credit the resulting increase in state-local revenue would be considerably less than the revenue cost of the credit to the federal government. For plans 5 and 6, increases in state-local revenue would probably be about two-thirds of the cost of the credit to the federal government. About one-third of the cost of the credit would be used to provide decreases in the combined federal-state-local tax burden. Thus, per dollar of cost to the federal government, such a credit would provide less aid to state-local governments than would direct federal grants.

The greatest revenue benefit, in terms of free revenue, would accrue to those states which do not as yet impose income taxes. For plan 5, the seventeen states without income taxes could receive 75 percent of total free revenue (estimate for 1958); and for plan 6, these states could receive 75 to 85 percent of total free revenue.

The direct revenue benefit from such a credit would go entirely to state rather than to local governments, but local governments probably would receive increased state aid. It has been argued that because of the under-representation of urban areas in state legislatures such areas would not receive their fair share of the increase in state aid to local governments. But recent court decisions which are forcing reapportionment of state legislatures should result in a more equitable distribution of state aid.

The credit approach represents a combination of freedom and coercion. It would strongly encourage if not force those states not having state income taxes to adopt them. In addition, it would have some effect upon the tax structures of states already having income taxes. On the other hand, such a credit would increase somewhat the financial independence of state governments by enabling them more fully to exploit their tax bases. The credit would leave room under state income tax laws for variations in definitions of income, exemptions, tax rates, and so forth. Furthermore, states would be free to differ in their degrees of reliance upon state income taxation. All in all, such a credit offers states a large gain in fiscal independence in exchange for a relatively small loss in freedom of tax action. The element of federal control involved in such credit proposals would be small compared to that involved in *conditional* federal grant programs, but not small compared to that involved in an *unconditional* federal grant program.

The credit could be a constant-percent credit or a sliding-scale credit. Since free revenue would accrue largely to the states without income taxes, for two credits of equal maximum cost free revenue would be only slightly larger for the sliding-scale credit than for the constant-percent credit. The sliding-scale credit would be only slightly more favorable to the poor states and only slightly less favorable to the rich states than would the constant-percent credit. A sliding-scale credit, moreover, would decrease tax progression less sharply than would a constant-percent credit. While the balance of these differences favors the sliding-scale credit, a choice between them is not a matter of crucial importance.

The present treatment of deductibility is a source of considerable inequity and an ineffective means of aiding state-local governments. To improve tax equity, deductibility should be removed. To secure a more effective means of aiding state-local governments, a credit for state income taxes and/or a program of *unconditional* federal grants should be introduced.

APPENDIX A

Data and Methods

This appendix is a presentation of sources and methods of estimation for various parts of the analysis.

1. The cost of deductibility for all allowed taxes by AGI classes was estimated as follows: Amounts of tax deductions by AGI classes were taken from *Statistics of Income: Individual Income Tax Returns for 1958,* Table 5. The marginal tax rates applicable to tax deductions were computed separately for joint returns and for single returns. For the upper AGI classes for each of the two kinds of returns, separate marginal rates were computed for returns with and without income subject to the alternative capital gains tax rate. Weighted marginal rates were then computed. For 1958, my estimate of cost of deductibility is $1,920 million.

For 1958, James Maxwell estimates the cost of deductibility at $2,020 million. Maxwell's marginal tax rate for a given income class was computed by dividing the difference in average tax liability between the given income class and the next *higher* income class by the difference in average taxable income between the same two income classes.[35] This method of estimation causes Maxwell's marginal tax rates to be too high.

2. Estimates of state-local revenue derived from deductible tax were derived by a method similar to that used by Maxwell.[36]

3. The 1958 cost of deductibility of state and local income taxes

[35] Maxwell, *Tax Credits,* pp. 117-18.
[36] *Ibid.,* App. C.

was estimated on the basis of deductions of state income taxes by AGI classes for 1960, as shown in *Statistics of Income: Individual Income Tax Returns for 1960,* Table 0. For each AGI class, it was assumed that deductions of state income tax on taxable returns for 1958 were 60 percent (70 percent multiplied by 85 percent) of the corresponding deductions for 1960. Deductible state income tax for 1958 was approximately 70 percent of deductible state income tax for 1960. The ratio of deducted state income tax to deductible state income tax for 1958 was approximately 85 percent of the corresponding ratio for 1960. An attempt was made to estimate by AGI classes the deductions of local income taxes on taxable returns. The marginal tax rates used were the same as those used in estimating the revenue effects of plans 1 and 2.

4. The revenue effect of plan 4 was estimated as follows: It was assumed that for each AGI class, adoption of plan 4 would cause taxable income to increase by 2.8 percent of the AGI of that class's taxable returns with tax deductions. The marginal tax rates used were the same as those used in estimating the effects of plans 1-3.

5. Cost of deductibility by states was estimated as follows: First, estimates of deductible taxes by type of tax by state were derived by a method similar to one recently used by Maxwell. Second, estimates of cost of deductibility by state were derived from the estimates of deductible taxes. *Ceteris paribus,* costs of deductibility as percentages of deductible taxes tend to vary directly with state per capita income. *Ceteris paribus,* costs of deductibility as percentages of deductible taxes tend to vary with the percentage composition of deductible taxes among different types of taxes. In estimating costs of deductibility on a state-by-state basis, an attempt was made to take account of these two factors.

For 1957 Maxwell estimated deductible tax by state, but did not estimate cost of deductibility by state.[37]

6. Maximum federal credits and state income taxes were computed by applying federal credit provisions and 1958 state income tax provisions to the state-by-state distributions of returns, income, and tax by AGI classes which appear in *Statistics of Income: Individual Income Tax Returns for 1958,* Table 16, and *Statistics of Income: Individual Income Tax Returns for 1959,* Table 17. Walter Heller estimated maximum credit by state for a more costly sliding-scale credit for twenty-one states for 1956.[38] Maxwell estimated maximum credit by state for this

[37] *Ibid.*

[38] Heller, in *Tax Revision Compendium,* p. 426, Table 3.

more costly credit for all states for 1958.[39] However, neither Heller nor Maxwell estimated maximum credit, offset tax, or free revenue by AGI classes. Moreover, my estimates of maximum credit, offset tax, and free revenue by state are somewhat more accurate than the estimates of Heller or Maxwell.

7. In estimating 1964 revenue effects the following assumptions were made:

a. The federal revenue increase resulting from the adoption of plan 1 rose by 25 percent between 1962 and 1964. For 1962, amounts of tax deductions by AGI classes were available in the preliminary *Statistics of Income: Individual Income Tax Returns for 1962*.

b. The federal revenue increase resulting from plan 3 rose by 70 percent between 1960 and 1964.

c. For 1963 and 1965 rates, the 1962-64 federal revenue increases resulting from plan 4 were $300 million and $250 million, respectively.

d. For 1963 and 1965 rates, the 1962-64 increases in the maximum cost of the plan 5 credit were $240 million and $300 million, respectively.

e. The amount of tax eligible for the plan 7 credit which was paid by persons not filing taxable federal income tax returns did not change between 1958 and 1964.

[39] Maxwell, *Tax Credits,* App. B.

APPENDIX B

Tables

TABLE 8. Change in Federal Tax Liabilities Due to Adoption of Plans 1–4, by AGI Classes, 1958

(Amounts in millions of dollars)

AGI Class ($000)	*Plan 1* (1)	*Plan 2* (2)	*Plan 3* (3)	*Plan 4* (4)
.6– 1	.7	– 1.3	.58	.25
1– 2	12.9	–14.1	10.8	4.96
2– 3	39.9	–22.6	34.1	17.7
3– 4	81.1	–29.6	72.6	40.3
4– 5	138	–25	125	71.4
5– 6	186	– 1	169	96.8
6– 7	175	– 3	159	93.9
7– 8	144	–11	128	78.0
8– 9	118	– 9	102	64.0
9– 10	84.1	–16.9	71	46.3
10– 15	213	–26	169	117
15– 20	113	14	81	62.5
20– 25	81.9	15.6	55	46.3
25– 50	231	54	137	136
50– 100	163	43	91	99.8
100– 150	48.9	9.7	23	31.4
150– 200	22.5	5.8	10.0	13.7
200– 500	39.2	9.8	15.0	24.9
500–1,000	12.5	2.5	4.4	8.76
1,000 and over	15.3	2.2	4.6	12.2
All Classes	1,920	—	1,460	1,070

Note: Totals are rounded to the nearest $10 million.

TABLE 9. Costs of Deductibility and Net Decrease in Federal Tax Under Plan 2, by States, 1958

State	Cost of Deductibility (Millions of dollars) (1)	Cost of Deductibility ÷ Before-Tax-Deduction Federal Tax (Percent) (2)	Cost of Deductibility ÷ Population (Dollars) (3)	Net Decrease in Federal Tax Due to Adoption of Plan 2 ÷ Before-Tax-Deduction Federal Tax (Percent) (4)
Alabama	$ 18.4	5.11	$ 5.73	.19
Alaska	2.5	6.05	11.79	− .75
Arizona	11.8	5.73	10.35	− .43
Arkansas	9.1	5.97	5.15	− .67
California	274.8	6.72	19.17	−1.42
Colorado	21.0	5.99	12.27	− .69
Connecticut	29.6	3.95	12.78	1.35
Delaware	9.7	5.94	21.37	− .64
District of Columbia	15.2	6.17	18.42	− .87
Florida	36.0	4.77	8.10	.53
Georgia	26.6	5.74	6.97	− .44
Hawaii	12.3	10.78	19.74	−5.48
Idaho	4.2	4.29	6.34	1.01
Illinois	110.6	4.05	11.18	1.25
Indiana	43.0	4.95	9.39	.35
Iowa	25.1	5.44	8.89	− .14
Kansas	17.4	4.58	8.22	.72
Kentucky	20.4	5.49	6.62	− .19
Louisiana	21.1	4.87	6.78	.43
Maine	6.6	4.89	6.93	.41
Maryland	39.1	5.40	13.23	− .10
Massachusetts	70.4	5.89	14.48	− .59
Michigan	93.3	5.49	11.86	− .19
Minnesota	35.8	5.96	10.61	− .66
Mississippi	9.4	6.86	4.30	−1.56
Missouri	37.7	4.60	8.83	.70
Montana	3.7	3.56	5.38	1.74
Nebraska	5.6	2.44	3.84	2.86
Nevada	2.7	3.42	10.11	1.88
New Hampshire	4.2	3.96	7.19	1.34
New Jersey	50.8	3.19	8.84	2.11
New Mexico	8.6	6.20	10.21	− .90
New York	348.0	7.19	21.44	−1.89
North Carolina	28.0	6.46	6.16	−1.16
North Dakota	3.6	4.68	5.54	.62
Ohio	89.2	4.19	9.55	1.11
Oklahoma	17.7	5.16	7.75	.14
Oregon	29.6	7.93	16.69	−2.63
Pennsylvania	106.5	4.30	9.59	1.00
Rhode Island	6.9	3.86	7.89	1.44
South Carolina	11.7	6.04	4.87	− .74
South Dakota	2.9	3.49	4.15	1.81
Tennessee	21.2	4.97	6.11	.33
Texas	34.4	2.18	3.67	3.12
Utah	9.1	6.65	10.52	−1.35
Vermont	4.1	7.98	11.02	−2.68
Virginia	27.1	4.63	6.89	.67
Washington	38.7	5.85	13.98	− .55
West Virginia	12.8	5.12	6.50	.18
Wisconsin	49.8	6.64	12.65	−1.34
Wyoming	2.2	3.54	6.88	1.76
All States	1,920.0			

Note: Totals are rounded to the nearest $10 million.

TABLE 10. Credits and Changes in Taxes Under Plans 5 and 7, by AGI Classes, 1958

(Amounts in millions of dollars)

AGI Class ($000)	Maximum Plan 5 Credit	Existing State Tax Offset by Plan 5 Credit	Change in Combined Tax for Reaction A or B to Plan 5	Plan 7 Credit	Change in Federal Tax for Plan 7
	(1)	(2)	(3)	(4)	(5)
.6– 1	4.64	.27	.42	14	– 13
1– 2	60.9	8.5	4.4	50	– 37
2– 3	127	32	8	93	– 53
3– 4	200	57	24	156	– 75
4– 5	255	86	52	228	– 90
5– 6	269	93	93	249	– 63
6– 7	216	86	89	222	– 47
7– 8	161	73	71	170	– 26
8– 9	117	55	63	133	– 15
9– 10	84.6	40.4	43.7	98	– 14
10– 15	169	92	121	213	0
15– 20	56.2	32.1	81	71	42
20– 25	33.5	18.8	63.1	46	36
25– 50	78.5	43.2	188	94	137
50– 100	48.4	26.9	136.0	46	117
100– 150	15.2	7.9	41.0	12.2	36.7
150– 200	6.4	3.72	18.7	5.1	17.4
200– 500	11.3	6.5	32.0	8.4	30.8
500–1,000	3.76	2.11	9.5	2.5	10.0
1,000 and over	4.97	2.83	9.9	3.0	12.3
All Classes	1,920	770	1,150	1,910	

Note: Totals are rounded to the nearest $10 million.

TABLE 11. Maximum Plan 5 Credit, Free Revenue, and Free Revenue as a Percentage of Maximum Plan 5 Credit, by States, 1958

State	*Maximum Plan 5 Credit (Millions of dollars)* (1)	*Free Revenue (Millions of dollars)* (2)	*Free Revenue ÷ Maximum Plan 5 Credit (Percent)* (3)
Alabama	$ 20.4	$ 9.8	48
Alaska	1.95	—	—
Arizona	11.3	5.9	52
Arkansas	9.14	4.76	52
California	203	100	49
Colorado	19.0	6.9	36
Connecticut	37.0	37.0	100
Delaware	6.62	.47	7
District of Columbia	11.9	.8	6
Florida	40.2	40.2	100
Georgia	26.8	14.1	53
Hawaii	6.40	—	—
Idaho	5.87	.30	5
Illinois	138	138	100
Indiana	48.6	48.6	100
Iowa	27.4	7.5	21
Kansas	21.7	4.4	20
Kentucky	21.6	1.5	7
Louisiana	23.7	18.7	79
Maine	8.46	8.46	100
Maryland	38.7	2.0	5
Massachusetts	65.6	9.4	14
Michigan	88.7	88.7	100
Minnesota	34.2	2.6	8
Mississippi	8.61	7.75	90
Missouri	44.6	19.1	43
Montana	6.16	1.57	26
Nebraska	13.6	13.6	100
Nevada	3.97	3.97	100
New Hamsphire	6.51	5.43	83
New Jersey	82.5	82.5	100
New Mexico	7.67	4.01	52
New York	236	24	10
North Carolina	26.4	2.9	11
North Dakota	4.95	2.13	43
Ohio[a]	115	115	100
Oklahoma	19.4	10.1	52
Oregon	20.2	—	—
Pennsylvania[a]	135	135	100
Rhode Island	10.6	10.6	100
South Carolina	12.9	3.7	29
South Dakota	5.34	5.34	100
Tennessee	24.1	20.1	83
Texas	83.7	83.7	100
Utah	8.17	2.16	26
Vermont	3.30	—	—
Virginia	33.3	1.9	6
Washington	35.0	35.0	100
West Virginia	14.9	14.9	100
Wisconsin	42.6	1.7	4
Wyoming	3.95	3.95	100
All States	1,920	1,160	60

Note: Totals are rounded to the nearest $10 million.

[a] Introduction of a state income tax may cause a considerable decrease in revenue from local income taxes.

TABLE 12. Effects of Credits Under Plan 5, by States, 1958

State	Maximum Plan 5 Credit ÷ No-Allowance Federal Tax[a] (1)	Maximum Plan 5 Credit ÷ Population (2)	Free Revenue ÷ Population (3)	(Maximum Plan 5 Credit — Cost of Deductibility) ÷ No-Allowance Federal Tax[a] (4)	(Cost of Deductibility — Existing State Tax Offset by Plan 5 Credit) ÷ No-Allowance Federal Tax[a] (5)
Alabama	5.66%	$ 6.35	$ 3.05	.55%	2.16%
Alaska	4.72	9.20	—	−1.33	1.21
Arizona	5.49	9.91	5.13	− .24	3.11
Arkansas	5.99	5.18	2.70	.02	3.08
California	4.96	14.18	6.95	−1.76	4.20
Colorado	5.42	11.10	4.01	− .57	2.54
Connecticut	4.94	15.98	15.98	.99	3.95
Delaware	4.06	14.58	1.04	−1.88	2.14
District of Columbia	4.83	14.42	.91	−1.34	1.66
Florida	5.33	9.05	9.05	.56	4.77
Georgia	5.78	7.02	3.69	.04	3.00
Hawaii	5.61	10.27	—	−5.17	5.17
Idaho	6.00	8.87	.46	1.71	−1.43
Illinois	5.05	13.99	13.99	1.00	4.05
Indiana	5.59	10.61	10.61	.64	4.95
Iowa	5.94	9.71	2.64	.50	1.13
Kansas	5.71	10.26	2.09	1.13	—
Kentucky	5.81	7.01	.49	.32	.01
Louisiana	5.47	7.62	6.03	.60	3.71
Maine	6.27	8.89	8.89	1.38	4.89
Maryland	5.34	13.09	.69	− .06	,33
Massachusetts	5.49	13.49	1.94	− .40	1.19
Michigan	5.22	11.28	11.28	− .27	5.49
Minnesota	5.69	10.13	.77	− .27	.70
Mississippi	6.28	3.94	3.55	− .58	6.20
Missouri	5.44	10.44	4.47	.84	1.49
Montana	5.92	8.95	2.28	2.36	− .87
Nebraska	5.93	9.33	9.33	3.49	2.44
Nevada	5.03	14.87	14.87	1.61	3.42
New Hampshire	6.14	11.15	9.30	2.18	2.92
New Jersey	5.19	14.35	14.35	2.00	3.19
New Mexico	5.53	9.11	4.76	− .67	3.53
New York	4.87	14.54	1.49	−2.32	2.81
North Carolina	6.09	5.80	.63	− .37	1.04
North Dakota	6.43	7.62	3.28	1.75	1.04
Ohio	5.40	12.27	12.27	1.21	4.19
Oklahoma	5.66	8.49	4.42	.50	2.45
Oregon	5.41	11.39	—	−2.52	2.52
Pennsylvania	5.46	12.17	12.17	1.16	4.30
Rhode Island	5.94	12.11	12.11	2.08	3.86
South Carolina	6.66	5.37	1.53	.62	1.29
South Dakota	6.43	7.64	7.64	2.94	3.49
Tennessee	5.65	6.95	5.79	.68	4.03
Texas	5.31	8.93	8.93	3.13	2.18
Utah	5.97	9.45	2.50	− .68	2.27
Vermont	6.42	8.87	—	−1.56	1.56
Virginia	5.68	8.46	.48	1.05	− .73
Washington	5.29	12.64	12.64	− .56	5.85
West Virginia	5.96	7.57	7.57	.84	5.12
Wisconsin	5.68	10.82	.42	− .96	1.19
Wyoming	6.36	12.34	12.34	2.82	3.54

[a] Federal tax with no deductions or credits for state-local nonbusiness taxes.

TABLE 13. Maximum Credits Under Plan 6, by States, 1958

State	Maximum Plan 6 Credit (Millions of dollars) (1)	Maximum Plan 6 Credit ÷ Population (Dollars) (2)	(Maximum Plan 6 Credit — Cost of Deductibility) ÷ No-Allowance Federal Tax[a] (Percent) (3)
Alabama	19.1	5.95	.19
Alaska	2.2	10.38	− .75
Arizona	10.9	9.56	− .43
Arkansas	8.1	4.59	− .67
California	216.8	15.12	−1.42
Colorado	18.6	10.87	− .69
Connecticut	39.7	17.14	1.35
Delaware	8.6	18.94	− .64
District of Columbia	13.1	15.88	− .87
Florida	40.0	9.00	.53
Georgia	24.6	6.44	− .44
Hawaii	6.0	9.63	−5.48
Idaho	5.2	7.85	1.01
Illinois	144.8	14.64	1.25
Indiana	46.1	10.06	.35
Iowa	24.4	8.65	− .14
Kansas	20.1	9.50	.72
Kentucky	19.7	6.40	− .19
Louisiana	23.0	7.40	.43
Maine	7.1	7.46	.41
Maryland	38.4	12.99	− .10
Massachusetts	63.3	13.02	− .59
Michigan	90.1	11.45	− .19
Minnesota	31.8	9.42	− .66
Mississippi	7.3	3.34	−1.56
Missouri	43.4	10.16	.70
Montana	5.5	7.99	1.74
Nebraska	12.2	8.37	2.86
Nevada	4.2	15.73	1.88
New Hampshire	5.6	9.59	1.34
New Jersey	84.3	14.66	2.11
New Mexico	7.4	8.79	− .90
New York	256.6	15.81	−1.89
North Carolina	23.0	5.06	−1.16
North Dakota	4.1	6.31	.62
Ohio	112.9	12.08	1.11
Oklahoma	18.2	7.96	.14
Oregon	19.8	11.17	−2.63
Pennsylvania	131.1	11.81	1.00
Rhode Island	9.5	10.86	1.44
South Carolina	10.3	4.28	− .74
South Dakota	4.4	6.29	1.81
Tennessee	22.6	6.51	.33
Texas	83.5	8.90	3.12
Utah	7.3	8.44	−1.35
Vermont	2.7	7.26	−2.68
Virginia	31.1	7.90	.67
Washington	35.1	12.68	− .55
West Virginia	13.2	6.70	.18
Wisconsin	39.8	10.11	−1.34
Wyoming	3.3	10.31	1.76
All States	1,920		

Note: Totals are rounded to the nearest $10 million.

[a] Federal tax with no deductions or credits for state-local nonbusiness taxes.

TABLE 14. Effects of Credits Under Plan 7, by States, 1958

State	Plan 7 Credit (Millions of dollars) (1)	Plan 7 Credit ÷ No-Allowance Federal Tax[a] (Percent) (2)	Plan 7 Credit ÷ Population (Dollars) (3)	(Plan 7 Credit — Cost of Deductibility) ÷ No-Allowance Federal Tax[a] (Percent) (4)
Alabama	20.5	5.69	6.38	.58
Alaska	2.3	5.57	10.85	− .48
Arizona	11.8	5.73	10.35	− .00
Arkansas	10.8	7.08	6.12	1.11
California	267.8	6.55	18.68	− .17
Colorado	21.1	6.02	12.33	.03
Connecticut	30.0	4.00	12.95	.05
Delaware	5.4	3.31	11.89	−2.63
District of Columbia	11.5	4.67	13.94	−1.50
Florida	38.0	5.04	8.55	.27
Georgia	29.9	6.45	7.83	.71
Hawaii	12.4	10.87	19.90	.09
Idaho	4.3	4.39	6.50	.10
Illinois	117.0	4.28	11.83	.23
Indiana	52.1	6.00	11.37	1.05
Iowa	28.4	6.16	10.06	.72
Kansas	19.6	5.16	9.26	.58
Kentucky	19.3	5.19	6.27	− .30
Louisiana	21.2	4.89	6.82	.02
Maine	9.0	6.67	9.45	1.78
Maryland	36.0	4.97	12.18	− .43
Massachusetts	88.6	7.41	18.22	1.52
Michigan	105.3	6.19	13.39	.70
Minnesota	33.6	5.59	9.96	− .37
Mississippi	11.6	8.46	5.31	1.60
Missouri	39.1	4.77	9.15	.17
Montana	3.5	3.37	5.09	− .19
Nebraska	6.8	2.96	4.67	.52
Nevada	3.1	3.92	11.61	.50
New Hampshire	5.0	4.72	8.56	.76
New Jersey	54.1	3.40	9.41	.21
New Mexico	9.8	7.07	11.64	.87
New York	263.4	5.44	16.23	−1.75
North Carolina	30.7	7.09	6.75	.63
North Dakota	4.7	6.10	7.23	1.42
Ohio	94.9	4.46	10.16	.27
Oklahoma	19.6	5.72	8.58	.56
Oregon	24.0	6.43	13.54	−1.50
Pennsylvania	107.8	4.36	9.71	.06
Rhode Island	8.2	4.59	9.37	.73
South Carolina	14.3	7.38	5.95	1.34
South Dakota	4.1	4.93	5.87	1.44
Tennessee	24.8	5.81	7.15	.84
Texas	36.8	2.34	3.92	.16
Utah	9.5	6.94	10.98	.29
Vermont	4.5	8.75	12.10	.77
Virginia	26.4	4.51	6.71	− .12
Washington	46.4	7.01	16.76	1.16
West Virginia	16.7	6.68	8.48	1.56
Wisconsin	46.0	6.13	11.68	− .51
Wyoming	2.7	4.35	8.44	.81
All States	1,910			

Note: Totals are rounded to the nearest $10 million.

[a] Federal tax with no deductions or credits for state-local nonbusiness taxes.

WILLIAM C. BIRDSALL*

A Study of the Demand for Public Goods

THIS ESSAY is an attempt to identify and analyze the factors which influence the preferences of citizens for public goods.[1] As a first

* Woodstock College, on leave from Marquette University. This paper is based upon the author's dissertation, "Public Finance Allocation Decisions and the Preferences of Citizens: Some Theoretical and Empirical Considerations" (Johns Hopkins, 1963).

[1] In order to avoid confusion the following terminology will be used consistently throughout this essay: A *public good* is any good or service which is *de facto* provided for or subsidized through government budget finance. All other goods are *private goods* (or *private market goods*). These empirical definitions are distinct from though related to the following theoretical definitions (based directly on Richard A. Musgrave, *The Theory of Public Finance* [McGraw-Hill, 1959], p. 8ff.): *Social goods* are goods which are consumed in equal amounts by all, or those whose benefits people cannot be excluded from enjoying. The opposite of a social good is a *purely private good. Merit goods* are goods which could be provided through private markets, but which are in fact provided or subsidized by budget finance. *Mixed goods* are goods which, while not strictly consumed in equal amounts by all, nevertheless bear *social* characteristics to a large extent. Most of the *public goods* dealt with in this paper are "mixed goods," such as education and police protection, which partake of the nature both of social and purely private goods. Others are *merit goods,* such as public housing, which are subsidized through the budget. (Musgrave differs with me in that he defines

step, reflection on the contrast between the supply and demand relationship for private market goods and that for public budget goods will clarify the basis for developing a positive theory of "public demand," and for devising a feasible empirical test of such a theory.

The supply of and demand for private goods are brought together by a market. The consumer, if one of many, is assumed to decide what quantity to purchase at the given price, thus expressing his "demand"; the supplier, again, if one of many, is assumed to determine what quantity to produce at the given price, thus expressing his "supply." Similar statements may be made about all types of markets, however different. In each, quantity or price, or both, will be the operative variables. Provided the supply and demand equations are identifiable, and provided the correct market theory is assumed to apply, empirical estimates can be made of the dependence of supply on its factors (demand "held constant") and similarly of demand on its factors (supply "held constant").

The Problem of Demand for Public Goods

By definition, the supply of and demand for public goods are not brought together by a market. Individual consumers (citizens) neither bid for a given supply nor decide what quantity to purchase at a given price. Suppliers do not offer their goods directly to citizens. Rather, what correspond to market decisions are budgetary decisions made by government. On the supply side, a department supplies a given quantity of a public good; the quantity supplied depends upon the department's budget allocation for the period in question, the form of the production function, the prices of factors, the characteristics of the locale, and the efficiency of the department. If a department supplies a set of goods rather than a single good, the particular *mix* of these goods may be decided by the wisdom and experience (or less admirable qualities) of the departmental decision-makers, or it may be decided according to the prefer-

---

public goods as those produced under public management [*Public Finance*, p. 42]. In this essay there is no occasion for using this concept, so I have borrowed the term for the concept given above. Perhaps a better term for the empirical concept I used would have been "budget good," but this seemed awkward.)

ences of the "administration" or of the citizenry as interpreted by the administration. In this last case, of course, demand has direct influence upon supply.

How does the individual express his demand for public goods when he cannot do so independently by deciding the quantity he will purchase and consume? He does so through political action—by voting for representatives or on referenda, and by less formal "civic" action which may range from angry letters and personal campaigns to lobbying and outright bribery. There are many citizens who will enjoy public goods and help pay for them, thus there are many "demand functions." The necessary aggregation of demand functions may be determined directly by a voting decision, as in the case of a referendum, or it may be determined indirectly, as when an elected representative decides what his constituency "wants" or "needs."

A market and a well-developed economic theory of markets mediate between the supply of and the demand for private goods. The complex process of political intermediation[2] and the discipline of political science mediate between the supply of and the demand for public goods. The problem of mediation is complicated by the fact that public goods are supplied by a federal system of governments. Furthermore, none of these governments is run by a "party team" which possesses a clear mandate from the electorate and unencumbered powers to pursue policy. Rather, each level of government is normally divided into branches whose limited powers are interdependent. Finally, goals, programs, and financing are decided by legislatures whose members may represent geographically distinct electorates.

The solution to the problem of estimating demand for public goods is represented in this paper by a study of the vote on popular finance referenda. This solution is based upon the assumption that the complexities of informal political intermediation are at least minimized in a study of a direct popular vote. The validity of this assumption is reconsidered below, in light of the results of the empirical study.

[2] The term "political intermediation" is used in a broad sense, encompassing the legal decisions of formal governmental bodies, and the complex, informal actions and pressures of leadership, parties, and interest groups, all of which mediate between the "demand" of citizens and ultimate tax and expenditure decisions.

A Simple Theoretical Model

An individual's demand for public goods can be symbolically described as follows:

$$\text{Equation 1.} \quad g_{ij} = d_{ij}(X, C, p, G, t, L),$$

where, g_{ij} is the quantity of public good i demanded by the individual j; X is a matrix in which row k contains all the "traits" of individual k upon which the demand of the individual j (or of any other individual) depends ($k = j$ is the row of traits of the individual whose own demand is in question); C is a matrix of quantities of private market goods in which row k contains the quantities of each good consumed by individual k; p is a vector of prices of the private market goods; G is a matrix of quantities of all public goods (except g_i) in which row k contains the quantities consumed by citizen k (the columns of this matrix are partitioned according to which level of government provides the good); t is a vector of tax rates for different types of taxes (partitioned according to which level of government levies the taxes); and L is a matrix of locational characteristics in which row k contains the characteristics of the political subdivision k.

It cannot be determined *a priori* what traits of individual j will influence his own demand for a public good and comprise important elements in row j of the X matrix. To some extent, the relevance of one trait over another will depend upon the good in question. Almost certainly, income will be an important variable for most goods. In the case of education, a mixed (and partially merit) good, the number and age of the individual's children would surely be operative variables and religion would probably constitute an important variable. For state-subsidized housing, a merit good, the individual's housing situation (condition of the dwelling, and whether he owns or rents it) would be important. It is assumed that each row of X contains an individual's (or family's) income, property ownership, housing situation, and an indeterminate number of other characteristics, such as religion, age, number and age of children, occupation, and so forth.

Similarly, the extent to which an individual's demand depends upon other individuals' trait-profiles is not ascertainable *a priori*.[3] But since it would be unrealistic to assume that an individual's demand for public goods is independent, I have assumed, in the case of public education, that an adult bachelor expresses a positive demand which depends upon the number of children of his fellow citizens. In the case of public housing, I have assumed that the wealthy home owner expresses a positive demand which depends upon the housing needs of his fellow citizens.

In the matrix C, which shows the quantities of each private market good enjoyed by each individual, each row refers to an individual, each column to a given good; the vector p represents the prices of these goods. The demand functions for some private and public goods, such as automobiles and highways, will affect each other in a positive complementary fashion. Other private market goods, notably private education and housing, are apt to be substitutes for their public counterparts. Again, the demand of individual j for a public good may depend upon others' consumption of particular private goods. For example, the bachelor's demand for public education will depend on others' consumption of private education.

The matrix G expresses in a given row the quantities of each public good (excluding g_i) enjoyed by a given individual. In this matrix, the first n goods would be those provided by the smallest political subdivision (city, town, or village), the next m those provided by the county, and so on up to the federal government. (In the real world, strict definition of levels is complicated by quasigovernmental units, such as school districts and special districts, and by intergovernmental aid.) Clearly, an individual may demonstrate an entirely different demand function for a given service depending upon which level of government offers the service. The preferences implicit in the controversy over federal aid to education provide a case in point. In contrast to the clear relationship between particular private goods in the C matrix and their individual prices in the p vector, the relationship between particular public goods in the G matrix and particular tax rates in the t vector is usually tenuous at

[3] When honest revelation of preferences cannot be assumed, the *revealed* demand of an individual depends not only upon the trait-profile of others, the X matrix ($k \neq j$), but also upon the individual's *expectations* about others' true demand and how honestly they will reveal it. See Musgrave, *Public Finance*, Chap. 6, p. 136, and *passim*.

best. Except in the rare cases of attempted benefit taxation, as for example when highways are financed exclusively by earmarked fuel-tax revenue, there is seldom any direct relation between the "amount" of a given service which is provided and the rate of a particular tax.

The matrix L contains "aggregative" characteristics of localities which cannot be derived directly from the X matrix. Thus, the demand of citizen j for police or fire protection may well depend upon population density or housing density. The location and size of his city relative to other cities, particularly whether his city is a satellite, central, or independent city, are likely to influence his demand for many services. Similar variables, based upon characteristics of the larger geographical areas, are relevant to the demand for state and national services.

Feasibility of Estimating Public Demand

The model described above is only a framework for conceptualizing the demand for public goods. The important question is whether or not it can serve as a basis for estimating public demand.

Most of the independent variables present no intrinsic problems. If the cost of research is ignored, all the data in three of the matrices (X, C, and L) and in the two vectors (p and t) are available, both for individuals and in aggregated form. The data in the G matrix, including g_i, the dependent variable, present the serious problems. Ordinarily, public goods are not produced in physical units, or if they are, externalities of consumption limit the appropriateness of quantified output as the measure of actual output. Thus it is virtually impossible empirically to quantify national defense, police or fire protection, or public health—all typical public services. Some mixed and merit goods can be quantified; public education can be expressed in terms of pupils' years of education, public housing in terms of number of apartments or rooms, or square feet of floor space. But even these goods cannot be accounted for entirely by quantification. Part of the justification for providing or subsidizing them through government budgets, rather than through private markets only, is that they benefit not only the student or tenant directly affected, but others as well.

The lack of quantified data is only part of the problem. Suppose one could determine the "quantity" of police protection (as a set of probabilities which measured the likelihood of various crimes) supplied by the local government, and further, that such protection was afforded all citizens equally (the pure case of a social good). Even if one possessed all the data in C, L, X, t, and p, and had *a priori* certitude about what variables were relevant to the demand for police protection, he would find it very difficult to estimate demand by using the quantity of police protection supplied as the dependent variable. Since the dependent variable is a *constant* among individuals, its variance is zero, and it cannot be explained by *variables* which differ among individuals. This problem is precisely parallel to the conditions of a competitive market (many sellers and many buyers), about which it is assumed that the price of a good is given as a parameter to all buyers and sellers. In this market, price, a constant, cannot be explained by variations in preference, and thus in demand, among individuals.

Although price in a competitive market is parallel to the quantity of a social good supplied by a government—that is to say, both are constant among individuals—the quantity purchased by individuals in a private market is not parallel to the price (or tax) paid by individuals for a government service. The quantity purchased in a private market is decided by the individual; thus, given sufficient data, the theory of consumer behavior justifies explaining the quantity an individual purchases by reference to his characteristics and those of the world he lives in (X, C, L, G, p, and t); in so doing, *demand* is explained. On the other hand, the government, not individual taxpayers, decides the price of a public service. This price derives from a tax formula, such as $T_i = 0.04Y_i$ or $T_i = 0.03F_i$ (where T is the tax paid, Y is income, F is gasoline consumption, and i signifies the individual). Unless the formula is (miraculously) a perfect benefit formula, it cannot be argued that differences in demand for a public good are accounted for by differences in the prices paid for services.[4]

[4] Interestingly enough, if citizens were not forced to pay taxes, but paid for individual public goods voluntarily, and if each honestly paid his marginal evaluation of the services, one could explain the demand for public services by explaining price paid. This should not be surprising. In a private auc 'on market where consumers bid for fixed quantities of a good, one could similarly explain each individual's demand by explaining the final bid of each individual, regardless of which bidder purchased the good. Of course, this is assuming that the bidders

The problem, then, is that both the quantity and price of public goods are government parameters. This, of course, is the problem of political intermediation between supply and demand noted above. There are at least two basic ways in which one can attempt to circumvent the problems.

Just as we study markets over time or cross-sectionally in order to observe variations in both the quantity and the price of private goods, so we can study a level of government, such as a municipal government, over time or cross-sectionally in order to observe variations in the output of the government service.[5] In such a study, the explanatory variables can be used from t, L, G, and p and can be aggregated from X and C. Initially, an investigation was made of the possibility of a cross-sectional study using city expenditure data as surrogate for unavailable quantity data, and subjecting them to multiple regression analysis. It seemed clear, however, that a demand interpretation of such a study would be tenuous at best.

The most important objection to interpreting expenditure differences as demand or preference differences is not the difficulty of defining the good, the quantity-quality problem, or the problem of accounting for the supply side—the three difficulties which arise from having to use per capita expenditures as a surrogate for the output variable. Even if the quantity and quality of public services were as clearly defined as they are in the case of cement, and the cost differences could be allowed for, a final difficulty is crucial. Service level differences cannot be interpreted as effects of preference differences of citizens without a theory to explain how successfully citizens express their preferences and how representatives aggregate such preferences in deciding budget levels and allocation of the budget among types of services.

---

are not strategists, that the final bid of each represents his marginal evaluation of the good. Thus, where the private market has a parallel with the demand for public goods, strategy is a problem in both. The "voluntary exchange" approach to public goods was developed by Eric Lindahl early in this century; it is criticized by Musgrave and others because of the unreality of its assumptions. See Musgrave, *Public Finance,* Chap. 4, and references cited therein.

[5] Of course, we could also observe variations in tax rates (price); but this aspect of the problem is not as important as it would be in a study of demand for a market good because there is no direct relation between a given type of service and a given tax rate. The weakness of this relationship would diminish the significance of any estimate of a "tax-elasticity" of demand.

Because of these problems of interpreting expenditure differences, the decision was made to obtain data, not on expenditures for public goods, but on the preferences of citizens regarding public goods.[6] This decision helps to insure that the study is not explaining supply instead of demand, but it leaves the problem of whether or not demand is explained in any meaningful sense of that word. This problem is discussed later.

Interview Data Versus Aggregated Voting Data

Given the decision to obtain preference data as such, a choice still remains. One alternative is to interview individuals, asking them to express their preferences between different levels of provision of one service or between different public services. This approach is similar to private market studies in which consumers are interviewed about their tastes by firms and advertising agencies; that is, preferences expressed may be explained by characteristics individuals reveal in the interviews. An alternative to interviewing is to collect aggregated voting data on finance referenda and use explanatory variables available in aggregated data of the federal census and state studies.[7]

The latter alternative was chosen for several reasons. First, interviewing is costly and presents its own peculiar difficulties in for-

[6] Besides attempting to explain public demand by explaining expenditure levels or citizens' preferences, there is a third possible approach to the problem of public demand. This is to study the finance decisions of a legislature (and the votes of individual representatives in it), attempting to explain its (and their) behavior either by the objective characteristics of the constituencies or by the revealed preferences of the constituencies. While this approach probably can and will be fruitful, it was not pursued in this study because it is extraordinarily difficult to isolate the public finance decision (or any aspect of the decision) in an actual legislative body. Nearly every decision has some element of finance in it and finance decisions are modified (if not hidden) in the formal and informal avenues of decision. Examples of the former would be bicameral legislatures, committees and subcommittees, and voice votes; examples of the latter would be caucuses and logrolling agreements. For a discussion of these and related problems, see Anthony Downs, *An Economic Theory of Democracy* (Harper, 1957), and James M. Buchanan and Gordon Tullock, *The Calculus of Consent* (University of Michigan, 1962).

[7] Both interview data and secret ballot referendum data are quite likely to be honest revelations of preferences because in these cases the revelation of preference (or the intensity of the preference) of an individual is not going to be revealed to the government for purposes of taxation, and so forth. The one situation in which strategy might arise in referendum voting is discussed below, p. 286.

mulating proper questions and interpreting results.[8] Second, there is no unambiguous measure of the relative intensity of preference among individuals. If interview preferences were elicited, one would either have to assume intensities of preference were "equal" (or unimportant), or else devise a sophisticated method of measuring differences in intensity. Third, it is possible that more stability and consistency could be found in voting data than in interview-elicited preferences regarding fiscal questions.[9] Finally, aggregation may result in a minimizing of the random elements found in individual preferences, and it permits examination of the relationship between preferences and several independent variables simultaneously by multiple regression analysis.[10]

[8] See George Katona, *Psychological Analysis of Economic Behavior* (McGraw-Hill, 1951), p. 330, and *passim*. The problem of formulating proper questions for interviews is a crucial difficulty in light of a key assumption made in this study: Because of the nature of public goods, namely their social and merit character, one cannot expect the demand of an individual for them to be as much a function of immediate personal need and benefit as it would be for a private good; rather, one would expect the demand of an individual to be significantly related to his *judgment* of others' needs for and expected benefits from public goods; these others include citizens of his own city, and more generally (for state programs), citizens of the whole state. This assumption applies particularly to a merit good such as public housing. If the assumption is taken seriously, an effort would have to be made in the interview to elicit this judgment because it would be important as an explanatory variable. Formulating interviews to test for the relationship sought is difficult because an individual's preference may, in fact, influence and color his judgment. Thus one might be testing a theory of perception as much as a theory of demand.

[9] Regarding interview-elicited preferences, Mueller points out that "certain aspects of the preference system for public goods and services are not clearly crystallized in the consumer's mind; hence these attitudes have elements of inconsistency and may change easily under the impact of new information or new circumstance." See Eva Mueller, "Public Attitudes Toward Fiscal Programs," *Quarterly Journal of Economics,* Vol. 77 (May 1963), pp. 210-35.

[10] Regarding the question of correlation of aggregated data ("ecological correlation"), it should be mentioned that Robinson and others have strongly objected to using such results for conclusions about individuals. This is at least a wise caution. But as it relates to the broader question of the value of ecological correlations as such, the criticism is not as well founded. Although it is a fact that in empirical tests the same data result in greater correlation the more they are aggregated, this phenomenon is not necessarily objectionable. As Yule and Kendall have pointed out, it may be caused by the reduction in the variance of random elements. See W. S. Robinson, "Ecological Correlation and the Behavior of Individuals," *American Sociological Review,* Vol. 15 (1950), pp. 351-57; and G. Udny Yule and M. G. Kendall, *Introduction to the Theory of Statistics,* 14th ed., rev. (London, Hafner, 1950), pp. 310-15.

The availability of voting data also influenced the choice. Since 1955 the New York State electorate has voted on some forty-four statewide referenda,[11] many of which are of a fiscal nature. For twenty-six of these referenda, Percent Yes Vote was obtained for each of the fifty-five cities of New York with population of ten thousand or more. The Percent Yes Vote of a city is defined as the vote "for" (multiplied by 100) divided by the sum of the vote "for" and "against." Cities of less than ten thousand population were excluded solely because of the difficulty of obtaining data, especially data on voting in villages, and data on the independent variables for towns and small cities. (There are seven cities in New York State with population under ten thousand, and ninety-one towns with population over ten thousand; within those towns are twenty-eight villages with population over ten thousand.)

In terms of demand function, the aggregated form of the preference data prevents explaining g_{ij} by any of the data on distinct individuals in the X matrix. Percent Yes Vote is an expression of the intensity of preference of a city between the *status quo* and a given fiscal change. On the side of the explanatory variables are data aggregated from the columns of the X matrix, for example, Percent Students in Private Schools; also, city characteristics from the L matrix and a few city tax rates from the t vector. It is not possible to relate the preference or vote of an *individual* either to his own trait-profile, or to his evaluation of the traits and needs of others, or to his perception of X, L, and t. This loss should not be underestimated.[12]

Nevertheless, the realism of referendum voting is an advantage over responses to hypothetical alternatives. The contradictions and instability that Eva Mueller finds in the interview-elicited preferences on hypothetical alternatives suggest that these preferences are expressions of "habitual ways of thinking" rather than "genuine decisions."[13] There are *a priori* reasons why the preferences re-

[11] The term "referenda" includes any question submitted to the general electorate, whether in the form of a constitutional amendment or a proposition.

[12] In Campbell's term, this is the "social approach" to voting. For his reservations about the fruitfulness of this approach to studies of presidential voting, see Angus Campbell and others, *The American Voter* (Wiley, 1960).

[13] See Mueller, in *Quarterly Journal of Economics,* p. 212. For the distinction between habitual attitudes and decisions, see George Katona, *Economic Behavior,* Chap. 4.

vealed in the actual voting situation should be more stable and consistent. The referenda to be voted on are published well in advance of election day; information in the form of discussion, debate, and editorials may be available; finally, a voter's preference will be counted and will thus "help" effect an actual group decision. Attention over time, information, and the realistic voting situation are all conducive to transforming attitudes into decisions.

A Voting Study of Public Finance Referenda

The New York State Referenda

In Table 1 the referenda studied are listed in chronological order and the arithmetic mean and standard deviation of Percent Yes Vote are given. Generally the questions were submited as popular referenda because no state debt can be incurred in New York without popular approval; the state constitution contains explicit provisions regarding state debt, its limits for particular programs and the method of repayment; and the constitution limits the fiscal powers of local governments.

In Table 5 the referenda are grouped according to subject matter. The first ten referenda involve publicly supported *housing;* the next two are local *sewage* finance enabling referenda; then three on *education;* five on *highways* (two on highway finance, three on the use of forest preserves for highways); an enabling referendum on *local pension* expenditures; one *recreation* expenditure referendum; two *"business cycle"* referenda; one on the definition of *taxable income;* and lastly, one on *public officials'* testifying regarding their official conduct. Referenda 10, 3, 4, 18, and 19 are another subgroup: local autonomy questions. The referenda were chosen to obtain as great a mix of similarities and differences as possible, in types of programs, methods of finance (debt vs. current revenue), and level of government financing (local vs. state).[14]

The Statistical Hypothesis

Given the aggregated *yes* and *no* votes on these referenda as preference data, the basic question can be stated more explicitly: Can the revealed preferences of citizens, formulated as Percent Yes

[14] The last, Referendum 17, "public officials," was chosen to determine whether or not the same variables which explain public finance referenda would also explain a purely political referendum.

Vote by city, be explained by observable characteristics of cities, by differences between cities in property value, local public expenditures and tax levels, population growth and mobility rates, education levels and needs, housing values and needs, and so forth?

Symbolically, the basic hypothesis can be written in the form of a set of linear regression equations, one for each referendum:

$$\text{Equation 2.} \qquad y_k^i = b_o^i - \Sigma b_j^i x_{jk}^i + u_k^i,$$

where y_k^i is the Percent Yes Vote of city k on referendum i; b_o^i is the constant term in regression equation i; b_j^i is the regression coefficient of independent variable j in regression equation i; x_{jk}^i is the value of independent variable j for city k in the regression equation i; u_k^i is the value of the random term for city k in the regression equation i; $i = 1, \cdots, 26$, signifying referenda and regression equations; $k = 1, \cdots, 55$, signifying cities; $j = 1, \cdots, n$, signifying independent variables.

Stepwise Regression: Hypotheses and Results

Even when the hypothesis is formulated as a multiple regression equation, there are alternative statistical methods of testing it. The most common is standard multiple regression in which the investigator himself chooses the independent variables and tests their explanatory power *as a group,* looking of course for those independent variables which have statistically significant regression coefficients. Other methods are available which to some extent leave the "choosing" up to the empirical data.

One of these methods is stepwise regression analysis. In stepwise analysis a multiple regression equation is built up from a set of potentially independent variables, (a maximum of fifty-nine in the program used); at each step the "best" (in terms of explaining the remaining variance) of the remaining independent variables is brought into the equation. When none of the remaining independent variables can satisfy a test of minimum explanatory power, the analysis stops. The initial analysis was made using this stepwise method.[15]

[15] For an explanation of the computer routine by its author, see M. A. Efroymson, "Multiple Regression Analysis," in *Mathematical Methods for Digital Computers,* Anthony Ralston and Herbert S. Wilf (eds.), (Wiley, 1960).

TABLE 1. New York State Referenda: Mean and Standard Deviation of Percent Yes Vote, Fifty-Five Cities

Referenda[a]	Percent Yes Vote	
	Arithmetic Mean[b]	Standard Deviation[c]
Voted on, November 1955		
1. Authorize a maximum of $750 million state debt for highway construction (had controversial fuel-tax rider; lost; see Referendum 6)	46%	10%
2. Raise the maximum annual subsidy for low-rent public housing to $34 million (passed)	45	13
3. Authorize local governments to exclude sewage debt from local debt limit (lost)	41	12
4. Authorize local governments to carry on joint sewage operations (passed)	53	13
5. Authorize the state to loan capital to limited-profit housing corporations (passed)	42	13
Voted on, November 1956		
6. Authorize a maximum of $500 million state debt for highway construction (no fuel-tax rider; not controversial; passed)	66	9
7. Authorize $100 million state debt for limited-profit housing corporations (only controversial housing referendum; lost; repeated as Referendum 14)	35	12
Voted on, November 1957		
8. Authorize $250 million state debt for expansion of state university complex (passed)	67	7
9. Authorize slower amortization of state debt incurred for reloan to housing corporations (passed)	57	9
10. Authorize towns and villages to exclude housing debt from local debt limit (cities already enjoyed this exclusion; passed)	55	10
11. Authorize the relocation of 50 miles of hazardous roads in forest preserves (passed)	63	8
Voted on, November 1958		
12. Allow the state more time in which to repay temporary housing finance notes (passed)	43	15

Referendum		
13. Authorize $100 million state debt for public housing and urban renewal (passed)	38	15
14. Authorize $100 million state debt for limited-profit housing corporations (repeat of Referendum 7 without change; not controversial; passed)	36	15
15. Raise maximum annual subsidy for housing and urban renewal to $39 million (passed)	38	15
Voted on, November 1959		
16. Allow the "Northway" highway to be routed through a forest preserve (controversial conservation question; passed)	60	10
17. State officials must testify to grand juries regarding their official conduct or lose office (passed)	70	7
18. Authorize New York City to exclude $500 million school debt from local debt limit (lost)	48	11
19. Authorize local governments to raise pension benefits for retired employees (passed)	65	9
20. Adopt the federal definitions of taxable income (both business and personal income; passed)	63	8
Voted on, November 1960		
21. Authorize $75 million in state debt for recreation facilities (passed)	67	8
22. Raise maximum annual subsidy for housing and urban renewal to $44 million (passed)	43	15
Voted on, November 1961		
23. Authorize $100 million in loans for plant construction in depressed areas (passed)	60	9
24. Authorize the submission of multi-purpose debt referendum in a recession (lost)	42	9
25. Authorize $500 million state debt to aid public and private college construction (controversial church-state question; lost)	50	9
26. Relocate a 10-mile section of highway in a Hamilton County forest preserve (controversial conservation question; lost)	46	10

[a] For a fuller description of the referenda, of the reasons for choosing these particular referenda, and of the controversies about some of them, see Chap. 6 of my dissertation. For official summaries of each of the referenda submitted between 1955 and 1961, see New York Secretary of State, *Manual for the Use of the Legislature of the State of New York* published annually); the referenda are indexed under Amendments and Propositions; the vote by county is given in the *Manual* of the year following submission.

[b] The arithmetic mean of Percent Yes Vote is not to be confused with the percentage of the total residents of the state who voted *yes*. Mean Percent Yes Vote is how the "average city" voted. Thus Referendum 1 (as well as many others) *passed* because *total state* Percent Yes Vote exceeded 50 percent, even though the "average city" voted only 43 percent *yes*.

[c] Standard Deviation is measured in percentage points of deviation because the observations themselves are percentages.

One reason for using stepwise regression is that little theory exists to guide the choice of independent variables for standard multiple regression. The lack of theory is due to the fact that an attempt is being made here to explain preferences, the "givens" of so much of economic research; it is also due to the type of preferences under study—that is, preferences expressed through voting on public programs. Aggregation, the lack of locational or temporal specificity of benefits from the programs at the time the referenda are voted on, and the assumption of interdependent demand for public goods—all of these make it difficult to predict explanatory effects and their direction with confidence. In this situation it is not easy to choose a small set of independent variables and then defend that choice.

The second reason for using a non-standard regression method arises from the nature of the twenty-six referenda available—from the number itself and from the similarities and differences among subsets of the referenda. By allowing the data to "choose" the explanatory variables, it is possible to distinguish both *general* determinants of referenda voting and intelligibly *specific* determinants of individual referenda (or subsets of them), and simultaneously to eliminate alternative explanations.

For the stepwise analysis, fifty-two independent variables were chosen or constructed from New York State studies of local taxes and expenditures and from various federal censuses.[16] Insofar as possible, variables were chosen which might be expected to explain distinguishable subsets of the referenda and support the "specific theory." The fifty-two variables are listed in Table 2.[17] The results of the stepwise analysis are given in Table 3; in Table 4 the hypothesized relationships and the empirical results are summarized. The overriding conclusion of the stepwise analysis is that with few ex-

[16] Since the intention of this research was to investigate the fruitfulness of studying cities' intensity of preference, the empirical work was oriented toward exploration, rather than toward testing a highly specified hypothesis. This goal led to an investigation of the explanatory value of a large number of independent variables. Although this fairly exhaustive approach of trying many variables greatly increases the possibility of Type I Error (the error of adopting an hypothesis on the evidence of a relationship which arose by chance), the exploratory nature of the goal encouraged concentration on minimizing the probability of Type II Error (the error of rejecting a hypothesis when a relationship does exist).

[17] For a description of all the variables and a fuller discussion of how and why particular variables were expected to be related to the referenda, see Chap. 8 of my dissertation.

TABLE 2. Independent Variables for Stepwise Regression: Means and Standard Deviations, Fifty-Five Cities

Variable[a]	*Arithmetic Mean*	*Standard Deviation*
X1 Local Capital Expenditures (per person)	$16.1	$14.4
X2 Local Current Expenditures (per person; adjusted to exclude health and hospital, welfare, and education expenditures)	$59.4	$15.2
X3 General Government Expenditures (as percentage of X2)[b]	13.4%	2.6%
X4 Police Protection Expenditures (as percentage of X2)[b]	17.1	3.1
X5 Fire Protection Expenditures (as percentage of X2)[b]	15.2	3.7
X6 Sanitation Expenditures (as percentage of X2)[b]	11.8	4.2
X7 Highway Expenditures (as percentage of X2)[b]	18.7	7.0
X8 Recreation Expenditures (as percentage of X2)[b]	6.2	2.3
X9 "All Other" Expenditures (as percentage of X2)[b]	17.5	4.5
X10 Interest Expenditures (per person)	$ 1.82	$ 2.16
X11 Net Current Education Expenditures (per Average Daily Attendance, ADA, net of pension and transportation expenditures)[c]	515.	75.
X12 Total Current Education Expenditures (per ADA)[c]	597.	102.
X13 Instructional Education Expenditures (per ADA; salaries, books, and supplies)[c]	336.	47.
X14 School Tax Rate (per $1,000 equalized full valuation of taxable property)	13.6	2.3
X15 Municipal Tax Rate (per $1,000 full valuation of taxable property; includes both the city and county rates)	22.8	4.1
X16 Overall Tax Rate (per $1,000 full valuation of taxable property; the sum of X14 and X15)	36.4	4.6
X17 Percentage of Private School Students (private elementary school enrollment as a percentage of total elementary school enrollment)	27.3%	11.2%
X18 Percentage of Adults Who Completed High School	39.9	8.2
X19 Median Education of Adults (years completed)	10.6 years	0.9 years
X20 Percentage of Students in College (college enrollment as a percentage of total school enrollment)	9.7%	11.9%
X21 Percentage of Families with Children (under 18)	52.8	4.2
X22 Median Gross Rent (renter-occupied dwellings)	$72.3	$12.5
X23 Median Home Value (owner-occupied dwellings)[d]	13,300.	4,880.
X24 Median Family Income (annual)[d]	6,150.	990.
X25 Equalized Full Valuation of Taxable Property (per person)[e]	3,320.	990.
X26 Percentage Residential Property (the equalized full valuation of taxable residential property as a percentage of X25)	55.4%	10.7%

TABLE 2. Continued

Variable[a]	*Arithmetic Mean*	*Standard Deviation*
X27 Percentage of Low-Income Families (families with a total income of less than $3,000 as a percentage of all families)	14.6%	3.3%
X28 Percentage of Labor Force Unemployed	6.2	2.0
X29 Percentage Near-Unemployed (the percentage of the labor force that worked less than 13 weeks in 1959)	10.8	4.2
X30 Percentage of Employed Who Travel to Work by Private Automobile	59.8	9.8
X31 Percentage Retail Sales Made by Service Stations	5.2	1.8
X32 Percentage of Homes Occupied by Non-Whites	3.8	4.1
X33 Percentage Crowded Dwellings (dwellings with 1.01 or more persons per room)	6.0	2.4
X34 Percentage Sound Dwellings (dwellings which are not dilapidated and have adequate plumbing, as a percentage of all dwellings)	78.5	11.3
X35 Percentage Stable Population (the percentage of the population over the age of 5 who had lived in the same dwelling since 1955)	56.5	6.4
X36 Percentage Migrant (persons who lived in a different county in 1955 as a percentage of total population over the age of 5)	12.7	6.1
X37 Percentage of the Population Born in New York State	73.4	8.0
X38 Percentage Locally Employed (the percent of total employed who work in residence county)	82.6	8.0
X39 Population Growth (1960 population as a percentage of 1950 population)	105.0	16.0
X40 Percentage of Public School Students (students enrolled in public elementary and secondary schools as a percentage of the total school enrollment)	67.6	13.5
X41 Percentage Unskilled (the sum of males employed as operative and kindred workers, service workers, except those in private households, and laborers, except farm and mine laborers, as a percentage of total employed)	35.6	7.0
X42 Percentage Who Work in Industry (the sum of all employed in mining, manufacturing, construction, transportation, communication, and utilities, as a percentage of total employed)	44.2	10.6
X43 Percentage of Population Under 18 years of age	31.6	3.0
X44 Percentage of Population over 65 years of age	12.1	2.4
X45 Percentage of Male Adults Who Are Married	67.8	5.5
X46 Percentage of Male Adults Who Are Veterans	41.0	4.0
X47 Population Density (per square mile)[f]	5,797 persons	4,044 persons
X48 The Log of Population	4.55	0.55

TABLE 2. Continued

Variable[a]	*Arithmetic Mean*	*Standard Deviation*
X49 Percentage Democrats (total Democratic enrollment for the spring primary as a percentage of total registration for the following fall election)		
1955	36.0%	17.0%
1956	28.2	13.6
1957	42.9	17.2
1958	35.4	14.9
1959	37.7	14.9
1960	30.6	13.9
1961	47.3	18.2
X50 Percentage Republicans —1 (total Republican enrollment for the spring primary as a percentage of the sum of Democratic and Republican enrollment)		
1955	60.3	17.7
1956	58.9	17.6
1957	59.6	17.4
1958	57.9	18.0
1959	57.5	17.3
1960	56.8	17.7
1961	54.1	16.6
X51 Percentage Republicans —2 (total Republican enrollment for the spring primary as a percentage of total registration for the following fall election)		
1955	55.7	23.4
1956	39.8	12.9
1957	60.9	26.8
1958	49.6	17.9
1959	52.4	19.2
1960	39.9	13.9
1961	57.0	22.6
X52 Percentage Participating (the sum of vote for and against as a percentage of the total vote including blank votes in that particular general election)		
1955: Referenda: 1	58.9	7.4
2	44.7	8.0
3	40.7	8.0
4	40.3	8.0
5	39.0	8.3
1956: Referenda: 6	41.8	8.2
7	39.8	8.0
1957: Referenda: 8	52.6	9.4
9	46.5	7.2
10	45.3	9.6
11	47.0	7.9

TABLE 2. Continued

Variable[a]			Arithmetic Mean	Standard Deviation
1958:	Referenda:	12	38.9%	7.6%
		13	38.3	7.7
		14	37.5	7.7
		15	37.5	7.4
1959:	Referenda:	16	53.4	8.3
		17	48.2	8.4
		18	49.2	9.3
		19	50.1	12.4
		20	46.5	12.1
1960:	Referenda:	21	43.1	7.9
		22	41.2	7.5
1961:	Referenda:	23	40.0	9.7
		24	38.2	10.0
		25	42.3	9.8
		26	40.0	10.1

Sources:

Variables X1 through X10, X25, X39, and X47: New York State Department of Audit and Control, *Comparison of Revenues, Expenditures, and Debt: 1949–1959*, Comptroller's Studies in Local Finance, No. 1 (1961).

Variables X14 through X16: New York State Department of Audit and Controls, *1959 Tax Atlas of New York State*, Comptroller's Studies in Local Finance No. 2 (1961).

Variables X11 through X13: The University of the State of New York, *Annual Education Summary, New York State, 1959–1960, Statistical and Financial Data on Elementary, Secondary, Higher and Cultural Education in New York State for the Year Ending June 30, 1960* (1961), Table 59.

Variable X31: U. S. Bureau of the Census, *U. S. Census of Business: 1958, Retail Trade, New York*, BC58-RA32 (1960), Table 102.

Variables X43 through X48: U. S. Bureau of the Census, *U. S. Census of Population: 1960. General Population Characteristics, New York*, Final Report PC(1)-34B (1961), Tables 13 and 72.

Variables X49 through X51: New York Secretary of State, *Manual for the Use of the Legislature of the State of New York* (published annually); see "enrollment" and "registration" in the index.

Variables X17 through X21, X24, X27 through X30, X35 through X38, X40 through X42, X46: U. S. Bureau of the Census, *U. S. Census of Population: 1960; General Social and Economic Characteristics, New York*. Final Report PC(1)-34C (1962), Tables 1, 32, 33, and 72–76.

Variables X22, X23, and X32 through X34: U. S. Bureau of the Census, *U. S. Census of Housing: 1960, Volume I, States and Small Areas, New York*, Final Report HC(1)-34 (1962), Table 1.

Variable X26 is not published; it was obtained through the courtesy of the Department of Audit and Control of the State of New York.

Variable X52 is not published; this variable, and the dependent variable, Percent Yes Vote, were constructed from data collected from County Boards of Election in New York.

[a] Tables of simple correlation coefficients between these independent variables (and between them and the dependent variables) are available from the author in limited quantities on request.

[b] Variables X3 through X9 were formulated as a percentage of Local Current Expenditures to measure relative emphasis in the local budget. Walker hypothesizes that on the local level there is little scope or reason for decision on per capita expenditures by function; but that there is scope for decision on the relative proportion to be spent on different functions. See Mabel Walker, *Municipal Expenditures* (Johns Hopkins, 1950), p. 5ff.

[c] In the standard regressions the decimal point for these variables was displaced one to the left; thus in Table 5 they should be read as units of $10 per student.

[d] In the standard regressions the decimal point for these variables was displaced three integers to the left; thus in Table 5 they should be read as units of $1,000.

[e] In the standard regressions, the decimal point for this variable was displaced two integers to the left; thus In Table 5 it should be read in units of $100 per person.

[f] In the standard regressions the decimal point for this variable was displaced two integers to the left; thus in Table 5 it should be read in units of 100 persons per square mile.

ceptions, the hypothesized relation between individual referenda or groups of referenda and particular variables is not confirmed. This is evidenced by the frequency of the word "none" in the right-hand column of Table 4.

There are innumerable possible reasons why few specific hypotheses were confirmed in the stepwise analysis. One reason may be aggregation itself and the use of Percent Yes Vote as a measure of preference. This and other general assumptions of the study are discussed below.

Another possible reason is that the particular independent variables are frequently more gross than one would like and/or their expected effects more complex than a summary table can explain. Thus there may be reasons for expecting a variable to be both positively and negatively related to Percent Yes Vote.

An outstanding example of this is the relation between Median Family Income and the finance referenda. This variable is listed as a wealth variable with a positive effect expected on the hypothesis of the existence of a positive income elasticity of demand for public goods. This variable may not have entered the stepwise equations (it entered only one of the twenty-six) because in measuring income, a tax base for state taxes is being measured (some 40 percent of the tax revenue of New York State comes from the state personal income tax). A tax base variable should be negatively related to demand because it is a measure of those who will pay the cost. Thus the negative tax-base effect may cancel the positive income effect, with the net result that Median Family Income does not enter the equations with either a positive or negative sign.

In the case of the Related Expenditures Effects, no direction of effect was given in Table 4 because it is difficult to decide whether these local *current* expenditure items are likely to be complements or substitutes for the related state *capital* expenditure programs. Again it may be that they are something of both and the two effects cancel.

Other expected effects may not have been confirmed because preferences were expressed by voting. Voting studies have shown, for example, that nonwhites and persons of low income (thus also the unemployed) tend not to go to the polls at general elections (and *a fortiori* not to vote on referenda submitted at general

TABLE 3. Simple Stepwise Regressions; Percent Yes Vote for Twenty-Six Referenda

Independent Variables	*Housing Referenda*[b]									
	2	*5*	*7*	*14*	*12*	*13*	*15*	*22*	*9*	*10*
1. Capital Expenditures (per person)	−14*						−18			−16
2. Current Expenditures (per person)	−12		−13*							
3. Percent General Government Expenditures				−11	−11		−16			−15
4. Percent Police Protection Expenditures						+16*	+20*	+17*	−7*	
5. Percent Fire Protection Expenditures	(−)2	(−)3								
6. Percent Sanitation Expenditures										
7. Percent Highway Expenditures					(+)5	(+)5	(+)5			
8. Percent Recreation Expenditures										+20
9. Percent Expenditures for "All Other"				−10	−12	−11	−11	−11		
10. Interest Expenditures (per person)	+13		−5*							
11. Education Expenditures per A.D.A. (Net)			+12							+14
12. Education Expenditures per A.D.A. (Total)	−7	−7	−10	−4*	−4	−4	−4	−9		−10
13. Education Expenditures per A.D.A. (Instr.)				−12		−13	−13*			
14. School Tax Rate					−18*			+13	−5	(−)5
15. Municipal Tax Rate										
16. Overall Tax Rate										
17. Percent Students in Private Schools				−8				−4		
18. Percent Completed High School			+9*					−15*		+19*
19. Median Years of Education of Adults				+13*				+16*		−18
20. Percent Students in College			−7							
21. Percent Families with Children										
22. Median Gross Monthly Rent	+10	+12*		+7	+9*		+15			
23. Median Home Value			+1*	+1	+1	+1	+1	+1		
24. Median Family Income										
25. Equalized Taxable Property Value (per cap.)	+6	+6	+11			+10	+10	+12		+6
26. Percent Residential Property			+15			+9	(+)9			+4*
27. Percent Low Income Families										
28. Percent Unemployed										
29. Percent Near-Unemployed								+7		
30. Percent Travel to Work by Private Car			−3						−6	−9
31. Percent Service Station Sales										
32. Percent Homes Occupied by Non-Whites						−15	−17	−14		−13
33. Percent Crowded Dwellings		+14*	+6	+6	+6	+6	+6		+2*	+3
34. Percent Sound Dwellings		+9			+17					+23*
35. Percent Stable Population				+5	+8	+7	+7	+8*	+3	+21
36. Percent Migrant (lived in different county 1955)										
37. Percent Born in New York State		+11			−15			(+)6		+7*
38. Percent Locally Employed										(−)2
39. Population Growth			(+)4						+4	
40. Percent Students in Public Schools		+10*								
41. Percent Unskilled Workers	(−)1	(−)1			−14					
42. Percent Work in Industry	−3	−2		−3	−3	−3	−3	−2	−1	−1
43. Percent Population Under 18 Years of Age										
44. Percent Population Over 65 Years of Age										−17
45. Percent Married Male Adults	+4	+4								
46. Percent Veterans	−9	−8	−8							−12*
47. Population Density			−14	+9	(+)10	+14	+14	+5		
48. Log of Population										
49. Percent Democrats										−22
50. Percent Republicans (1)										
51. Percent Republicans (2)					+7	+8	+8			
52. Percent Participating	−8		−2	−2	−2	−2	−2	−3		
Multiple Coefficients of Determination	.66	.76	.85	.85	.82	.87	.87	.81	.50	.65

* The regression coefficient is *not* significant (at the 5 percent level) in the final regression equation.

[a] Explanation: Each entry consists of the *sign* of the regression coefficient of the variable entering and the *step* at which it entered. Parentheses around the *sign* indicate that the variable was removed at a later step.

[b] Housing Referenda:

2. Raise the maximum annual subsidy for low-rent public housing to $34 million.
5. Authorize the state to loan capital to limited-profit housing corporations.
7. Authorize $100 million state debt for limited-profit housing corporations (lost).
14. Repeat of number 7 (passed).
12. Allow the state more time in which to repay temporary housing finance notes.
13. Authorize $100 million in state debt for public housing and urban renewal.
15. Raise the maximum annual subsidy for housing and urban renewal to $39 million.
22. Raise the maximum annual subsidy for housing and urban renewal to $44 million.
9. Authorize slower amortization of state debt incurred for reloan to housing corporations.
10. Authorize towns and villages to exclude housing debt from the local debt limit.

[c] Sewage Referenda:

3. Authorize local governments to exclude sewage debt from local debt limit (lost).
4. Authorize local governments to carry on joint sewage operations.

[d] Education Referenda:

18. Authorize New York City to exclude $500 million school debt from local debt limit (lost).

in Relation to Fifty-Two Independent Variables[a]

Sewage Referenda[c]		Education Referenda[d]			Highway Referenda[e]					Other Finance Referenda[f]		"Business Cycle" Referenda[g]		Other Referenda[h]		
3	4	18	8	25	1	6	11	16	26	19	21	23	24	20	17	
−9			−5	+13				−3	+20*		−4*	−6		−9*		1
				−11									−15			2
													−18*			3
		−3							−17							4
							−3*					(+)3				5
			−16*		−2	−12					−6			−10		6
		+5		−21*									−17			7
			+4													8
									+5		−8					9
			+6	−14												10
			+13		−11									+5*		11
−4	−8	−11	−12								−10			−4		12
																13
		−1				(−)7				−2					−8	14
−11		+8		+8					+6		−13*				+2	15
	−5									+3	+11					16
				−3		−2		+1			+3			+8		17
	+1*			−15		+4				+11						18
(+)1		+7			+6*											19
				−2	−7											20
+10									−7				−12*			21
		+10							+8							22
			+10							−10			+9	+1	+1	23
													+16			24
+3	+6		+8	+9	+4					+6	+12					25
						+13			(−)11		+9		−13	−6		26
		+9											+4		+10*	27
						+5*										28
						(−)6				−12					−6	29
								−7			−1	−1*				30
					+16*			+8					+8	+3	+5	31
	(+)2				+9*	+11*				+4						32
	+10*	+6		(+)4		+16		+4	+14							33
+7*	+9	−4						−5		−8		+2*	−14*			34
				+19	−1				(+)1			+9	+5			35
		(+)2	+14	+20									+10			36
			+7	(+)5					+3	+7	−7					37
				+7	+3	+9		+10		−1	+5		+6			38
−14								+11*		+9	+2		+3			39
+6	+3			−1						−5						40
−13			+9													41
−5	−4		−1	−6	−13	(−)1	−1		(−)2			−4	−1	−2	−4	42
				+16					+18				+11			43
								+9								44
									−15					+7		45
			−11								−14*				+7	46
				+12	(−)10								+7			47
					−14*			−6	−12*							48
			+17*	+10*		+3						(+)5			(+)3	49
−15*			(−)3		−5				−13			−10				50
		−13					−2*				+16		−2			51
(−)12			+2			−8		+2	+4		−15*	+7				52
.66	.71	.74	.68	.82	.57	.47	.22	.44	.56	.49	.70	.35	.75	.64	.56	

8. Authorize $250 million in state debt for the expansion of the state university complex.
25. Authorize $500 million in state debt to aid public and private college construction (lost).

[e] Highway Referenda:
1. Authorize a maximum of $750 million in state debt for highway construction (lost).
6. Authorize a maximum of $500 million in state debt for highway construction.
11. Authorize the relocation of 50 miles of hazardous roads in forest preserves
16. Allow the "Northway" highway to be routed through a forest preserve.
26. Relocate a 10 mile section of highway in a Hamilton County forest preserve (lost).

[f] Other Finance Referenda:
19. Authorize local governments to raise pension benefits for retired employees.
21. Authorize $75 million in state debt for recreation facilities.

[g] Business Cycle Referenda:
23. Authorize $100 million in loans for plant construction in depressed areas.
24. Authorize the submission of a multi-purpose debt referendum in a recession (lost).

[h] Other Referenda:
20. Adopt the federal definitions of taxable income.
17. State officials must testify to grand juries regarding their official conduct or lose office.

elections).[18] Variables related to race, unemployment, and poverty (X27, X28, X29, and X32) were included as potentially explanatory variables. The hypothesis was that they measure need for public housing and for recession or depressed areas aid, and should thus be positively related to Percent Yes Vote for these referenda (and negatively related to other finance referenda because of lack of ability to pay). The fact that this hypothesis was not confirmed does not refute it; the lack of significance might result from the possibility that these persons do not express their need by voting.

Whatever the reasons why particular hypotheses were not confirmed, the fact remains that, in general, the results of the stepwise analysis were disappointing. There is simply not sufficient intelligibility in the set of referenda equations which a given variable enters, nor in the set of variables that enter the equation of a given referendum. This lack of intelligibility is attributable, at least in part, to the stepwise analysis itself as used here. At each step in the analysis it is the difference between the explanatory power of the remaining independent variables that determines which variable will enter at that step. This difference is quite likely to be statistically insignificant.[19] Since the variables in the equation influence the size of the partial correlation coefficients of the remaining variables, the *order* in which the early variables enter can influence (and with some likelihood, in an arbitrary fashion) which variables will enter the equation later. The problem is compounded by the fact that there were fifty-two independent variables potentially capable of entering each regression equation.[20]

[18] See Bernard R. Berelson, Paul F. Lazarsfeld, and William N. McPhee, *Voting; A Study of Opinion Formation in a Presidential Campaign* (University of Chicago, 1954), p. 336, items 42 and 43. See also V. O. Key, Jr., *Politics, Parties, and Pressure Groups* (Crowell, 1952), p. 571ff. and references cited therein.

[19] For example, given the sample size (fifty-five), if the simple correlation coefficient between each of two independent variables and the dependent variable is around .50, they are significant at the 1 percent level, but the *difference between them* must be greater than .09 (in the range of .50) if that difference is to be significant *at the 44 percent level.* Furthermore, at each successive step in the regression analysis, that difference must be greater than at the previous step to be significant at the same level.

[20] Furthermore, the minimum significance level which an independent variable must meet to enter the regression was set relatively low ($t^2 = 1.65$), so that the probability of a variable's entering because of *chance* correlation at a given step is further increased. Suffice it to say that neither ignoring entries after, say, the fifth step, nor setting the t^2 level high, causes the relationship between the particular variables and the given referendum to become more intelligible.

Standard Regressions Estimated

Since the stepwise method proved weak, a standard regression analysis was made of each of the twenty-six referenda. Several independent variables seemed to be pervasive general determinants of Percent Yes Vote in the stepwise regressions, and all of these were included in each standard regression; any intelligibly specific determinants were included in the appropriate subgroup of equations whether they had originally been hypothesized as such or not; finally, some other variables were included in all or some of the equations on the basis of interesting relationships in simple correlation or simply out of my stubborn determination to give them every possible chance to be "useful;" in particular, two political variables, Percent Republican (X50) and Percent Participating, were included in all the equations lest the "political" explanation of referenda voting be prematurely ignored.

The standard regressions are given in Table 5 and a summary of the results by "effects" is given in Table 6. Many of these "effects" are interesting and enlightening.

Results of the Standard Regression Analysis

ISSUE-CONTROVERSY EFFECT. The relationship between School Tax Rate and Referendum 18, the New York City school finance referendum, is called an issue-controversy effect in Table 6 because the result was intelligible only after an examination of the *New York Times*' accounts of the controversy over this referendum.[21] School Tax Rate is the outstanding determinant[22] of Percent Yes Vote on this referendum, with a negative regression coefficient. The coefficient is relatively very large, and significant at the 5 percent level. The reaction of cities to the highly publicized New York City school efficiency debate on this referendum is apparently related to

[21] See my dissertation, p. 69ff.

[22] The relationship between Referendum 18 and School Tax Rate is outstanding in two ways. First, the tax rate explains Referendum 18 better than any other independent variable does. (That is, in simple correlation, the correlation coefficient between these two is larger than the coefficient between Referendum 18 and and any other variable; in the standard multiple regression the β coefficient and elasticity coefficient of School Tax Rate are larger than those of any other independent variable in the equation.) Second, the tax rate is a poor determinant of the other referenda in both simple correlation and multiple regression, with the exception of the two cases noted in the text.

TABLE 4. Summary of Main Stepwise Hypotheses and Results by Independent Variable

Variables		Referenda[a] in Question	Expected Direction of Effect	Empirical Effect
Need and User Effects				
X21	Percent Families with Children	Referenda 8 and 25	positive	none
X43	Percent of Population under 18	Referenda 8 and 25	positive	positive (?)
X17	Percent Private School Students	Referendum 25	positive	negative
X40	Percent Public School Students	Referendum 25	negative	negative
X20	Percent Students in College	Referenda 8 and 25	positive	negative (?)
X30	Percent Go to Work by Car	Highway Referenda	positive	negative (?)
X31	Percent Service Station Sales	Highway Referenda	positive	positive (?)
X32	Percent Homes Occupied by Non-Whites	Housing Referenda	positive	negative (?)
X33	Percent Crowded Dwellings	Housing Referenda	positive	positive
X34	Percent Sound Dwellings	Housing Referenda	positive	positive (?)
X27	Percent Low-Income Families	Housing Referenda	positive	none
X28	Percent of Labor Force Unemployed	Housing Referenda	positive	none
X27	Percent Low-Income Families	Business Cycle Referenda	positive	positive (?)
X28	Percent of Labor Force Unemployed	Business Cycle Referenda	positive	none
X27	Percent Low-Income Families	Other Finance Referenda	negative	none
X28	Percent of Labor Force Unemployed	Other Finance Referenda	negative	none
Related Expenditure Effects				
X1	Local Capital Expenditures	Capital Expenditure Referenda	uncertain	negative (?)
X10	Local Interest Expenditures	Capital Expenditure Referenda	uncertain	none
X2	Local Current Expenditure	Current Expenditure Referenda	uncertain	none
X6	Sanitation Expenditures	Sewage Referenda	uncertain	none
X7	Highway Expenditures	Highway Referenda	uncertain	none
X8	Percent Recreation Expenditures	Recreation Referendum 21	uncertain	none
X12	Education Expenditures per ADA	Education Referenda	positive	negative

Wealth Effects				
X22	Median Gross Rent	Finance Referenda (especially Housing Finance Referenda)	positive	positive
X23	Median Home Value		positive	positive
X24	Median Family Income		positive	none
X25	Property Value per person		positive	positive
Tax Effects				
X14	School Tax Rate	Education Referenda	uncertain	negative (?)
X15	Municipal Tax Rate	Other Finance Referenda	uncertain	none
X16	Overall Tax Rate	Other Finance Referenda	uncertain	none
Education Attainment Effect				
X18	Percent Adults Completed High School	Education Referenda	positive	negative (?)
X19	Median Education of Adults	All Referenda (?)	positive (?)	none
Benefit Spillover Effects				
X26	Percent Residential Property	Housing Referenda	positive	positive
X35	Percent Stable Population	Housing Referenda	positive	positive
X20	Percent Students in College	Referenda 8 and 25	positive	negative (?)
Mobility Effects				
X36	Percent Migrant	All Referenda	uncertain	none
X37	Percent Born in New York State	All Referenda	uncertain	none
X38	Percent Locally Employed	All Referenda	uncertain	none
X39	Population Growth	Referenda 3, 4, and 21	positive	none
City-Size Effect				
X48	Log of Population	All Referenda	uncertain	none

[a] The *groups* of referenda mentioned are made up as follows:
Highway Referenda: Nos. 1, 6, 11, 16, 26.
Housing Referenda: Nos. 2, 5, 7, 14, 12, 13, 15, 22, 9, 10.
Business Cycle Referenda: Nos. 23, 24.
Finance Referenda: *all except* Nos. 11, 16, 17, 18, 19, 20, 26.
Capital Expenditure Referenda: Nos. 5, 7, 14, 12, 13, 9, 10, 3, 18, 25, 1, 6, 21, 23, 24.
Current Expenditure Referenda: Nos. 2, 15, 22, 19.
Sewage Referenda: Nos. 3, 4.
Education Referenda: Nos. 18, 8, 25.

local education costs. This may indicate that the issue in this referendum was not simply the scandals and asserted inefficiency of New York City public school administration, but that to some extent the issue became the cost and efficiency of the school system in all the cities. One would feel more confidence in this explanation, however, if the relationship between School Tax Rate and Referendum 22 (to raise the subsidy on public housing), which is significant, almost as strong, and of opposite sign, were equally understandable.

The relatively large significant regression coefficient of School Tax Rate in the regression on Referendum 19 could be interpreted as a substitution effect since Referendum 19 is a referendum to enable cities to raise a competing *local* expenditures item, pensions.[23]

CITY SIZE EFFECT. The negative explanatory power of Log of Population for the highway referenda is a purely *a posteriori* result. Log of Population was included in the standard highway regressions because in the stepwise regressions it entered only highway equations, and only three in five of those, always with negative sign. This relationship is not open to an obvious interpretation. However, there are two possible interpretations of the fact that Log of Population is significant for Referendum 1 (the highway finance referendum with the controversial fuel tax rider) and not for Referendum 6 (the highway finance referendum without the controversial fuel tax rider). One is that the incidence of the state fuel tax falls relatively more heavily on larger cities (unfortunately at present this cannot be checked empirically). The other interpretation is that the vigorous campaign against Referendum 1 was focused (effectively) on larger cities—an eminently rational strategy when expending limited funds to defeat a popular referendum in a large state. The latter interpretation is supported by the statistical significance of the regression coefficient of Log of Population for the three conservation referenda, particularly since the size of the regression coefficient is larger for the two referenda against which conservationists waged a campaign, Referenda 16 and 26.

BENEFIT-SPILLOVER EFFECTS. The two benefit-spillover effects noted on Table 6 were expected. Percent Residential Property (the

[23] Regarding this regression equation, it should be noted that $R^2 = .37$, significant at the 10 percent level only, and that School Tax Rate becomes insignificant if Overall Tax Rate is dropped from the equation.

percentage of the value of total taxable property that is residential) was used in an attempt to measure how much of the wealth of the community belongs to residents (and thus voters or potential voters). It is not precisely the most ideal variable, because the residential property (especially apartments and rented homes) may not be owned by residents, while commercial and industrial property may be owned by residents. Also, the *distribution* of ownership is an important variable and this may differ among cities. To the extent that Percent Residential Property does approximate locally owned wealth, a positive wealth effect is to be expected.[24] A stronger positive effect was expected for the housing referenda because the higher the residential percentage of property, the greater the possibility that the spillover benefit of public housing on local property value (both financial and subjective benefit) will fall on residents and thus on voters. In the standard regressions in Table 5, the regression coefficients are generally positive, and for the housing referenda, all significant ones are positive.[25]

Percent Stable Population was included on the hypothesis that greater housing stability would characterize communities in which residents, by their permanence, would have a greater human and material investment in local prosperity, and thus the Percent Yes Vote would be higher for housing referenda in these stable cities.[26]

WEALTH EFFECT. Equalized Full Valuation of Taxable Property per Person[27] is the best measure of the relative wealth of the cities.

[24] This variable also measures the proportion of the tax base on which residents pay *local taxes* as homeowners and renters, probably without being able to shift the burden of incidence. See Seymour Sacks, Robert Harris, and John J. Carroll, *The State and Local Government . . . The Role of State Aid,* Comptroller's Studies in Local Finance, No. 3 (New York State Department of Audit and Control, 1963), p. 54. Thus one would expect a mixed effect between this variable and demand for local public goods—that is, a positive wealth effect and a negative tax-base effect. Again, because property is not a state tax base, there is no reason to expect the latter effect for state-financed public goods.

[25] If Percent Stable Population, which also measures housing "commitment," is dropped from these housing equations, Percent Residential Property becomes consistently positive and more significant.

[26] Percent Stable Population may also measure the age of housing and thus be a need variable. However, this interpretation is weakened by the fact that Percent Sound Dwellings (X34) was a potential explanatory variable in the stepwise regresssions and entered only two housing-finance regressions, both with an unexpected positive sign.

[27] For a discussion of how the equalized full valuations are derived see New

TABLE 5. Regression Coefficients: Percent Yes Vote for Twenty-Six Referenda in

	Constant Term	Median Home Value (X23)	Population Density (X47)	Percent Stable Population (X35)	Percent Residential Property (X26)	Percent Travel to Work by Private Car (X30)	Population Growth (X39)
Housing Referenda:							
2. Raise the annual subsidy for public housing	57	− .70	−.02	.26	.48[a]	−.30	.08
5. Subsidize Limited-Profit Housing Corporations	52	−1.22[a]	−.03	.28	.49[a]	−.36[b]	.07
7. $100 million for Limited-Profit Housing Corporations (lost)	49	.45	−.09[a]	.28[b]	.40[a]	−.61[a]	.05
14. $100 million for Limited-Profit Housing Corporations	10	1.09[a]	.04	.70[a]	.33[b]	.01	.09
12. Allow the state more time to repay housing notes	10	1.09[a]	.02	.66[a]	.34[b]	.08	.01
13. $100 million for public housing and urban renewal	14	1.00[a]	.03	.61[a]	.33[b]	.12	.07
15. Raise the annual subsidy for housing and renewal	11	1.01[a]	.03	.64[a]	.40[a]	.11	.01
22. Raise the annual subsidy for housing and renewal	89	1.89[a]	.11[a]	.17	−.18	.00	.24[b]
9. Slower amortization of debt incurred for Housing Corporations	65	− .43	−.01	.43[a]	.31[b]	−.12	.07
10. Let towns and villages exclude housing debt from their legal debt limit	51	− .11	−.01	.29	.22	−.25	.08
Sewage Referenda:							
3. Exclude sewage debt from local legal debt limit	29	—	—	—	.20	.38[a]	−.18
4. Allow local governments joint sewage operations	63	—	—	—	.35[a]	.09	−.11
		Percent Students in Private Schools (X17)	*Percent Families with Children (X21)*	*Percent Migrant (X36)*			
Education Referenda:							
18. Let N.Y.C. go in debt for school construction	71	− .15	.70[b]	.34	−.38[a]	−.30[b]	−.03
8. $250 million for expansion of the state university	84	− .09	.29	.39[b]	.12	−.16	−.03
25. $500 million for public and private school construction	49	.32[a]	1.03[a]	.26	.02	−.01	−.25[a]
		Log of Population (X48)	*Percent Service Station Sales (X31)*	*Percent Locally Employed (X38)*			
Highway Referenda:							
1. $750 million for highway construction	61	−7.02[a]	.45	.37[a]	−.06	−.19	.02
6. $500 million for highway construction	63	−3.05	.39	.26[a]	.25[b]	−.19	−.02
11. Allow relocation of some roads in forest preserves	102	−3.81[b]	.21	.05	.33[a]	−.14	−.12
16. Route "Northway" through a forest preserve	87	−8.36[a]	1.98[b]	.15	.09	−.27	−.07
26. Relocate 10 miles of road in a forest preserve	124	−5.06[b]	.96	−.16	−.04	−.06	−.24[b]
				Overall Tax Rate (X16)			
Other Finance Referenda:							
19. Allow local governments to raise pension benefits	65	—	—	.83[a]	−.10	−.23	.09
21. $75 million for recreation facilities finance	66	—	—	.24	.23[a]	−.21[b]	.02
			Percent Low Income Families (X27)	*Percent Unemployed (X28)*			
"Business Cycle" Referenda:							
23. $100 million for industry aid in depressed areas	73	—	.31	.21	.14	−.30[b]	.03
24. Allow multi-purpose debt referendum in a recession	42	—	.67	−.49	.24[b]	.15	.01
Other Referenda:							
20. Adopt the Federal definition of taxable income	66	—	—	—	−.01	−.04	.01
17. Officials must testify or lose their office	70	—	—	—	.07	−.01	−.01

Note: For units of measurements for variables 11, 12, 13, 23, 24, 25, and 47, see footnotes to Table 2.

Relation to Selected Variables

Local Total Current Education Expenditures per A.D.A. (X12)	Local Capital Expenditures per capita (X1)	School Tax Rate (X14)	Percent Adults Completed High School (X18)	Equalized Taxable Property Value per capita (X25)	Percent Crowded Dwellings (X33)	Percent Work in Industry (X42)	Percent Republican (X51)	Percent Participating in this Referendum Vote (X52)	Coefficient of Determination R^2
−.75[a]	−.01	.30	.16	1.18[a]	1.98[a]	−.73[a]	.09	−.51[a]	.69[a]
−.73[a]	.04	.39	.25	1.20[a]	2.08[a]	−.83[a]	.13[b]	−.41[a]	.77[a]
−.33[b]	.01	−.34	.03	.48[a]	2.36[a]	−.22[b]	.04	−.53[a]	.81[a]
−.53[a]	−.01	−.42	.14	.56[a]	2.30[a]	−.75[a]	.19[a]	−.94[a]	.85[a]
−.51[a]	−.01	−.67	.40[b]	.52[a]	3.04[a]	−.59[a]	.20[a]	−1.08[a]	.83[a]
−.54[a]	−.01	−.69	.38[b]	.52[a]	2.78[a]	−.76[a]	.17[a]	−1.03[a]	.86[a]
−.58[a]	−.01	−.58	.34	.63[a]	2.93[a]	−.74[a]	.17[a]	−1.08[a]	.86[a]
−.95[a]	−.12	1.53[a]	−.23	.68[a]	−1.67[a]	−.95[a]	.11	−.78[a]	.81[a]
−.44[a]	.00	−.47	.23	.56[a]	1.66[a]	−.57[a]	.00	−.52[a]	.63[a]
−.31	−.12[b]	−.22	.01	.41[b]	1.18	−.35[a]	−.09	.15	.57[a]
−.88[a]	−.18[a]	.81	.63[a]	1.21[a]	1.53[a]	−.46[a]	−.06	−.22	.66[a]
−.89[a]	−.06	.79	.10	1.26[a]	1.30[b]	−.71[a]	.07	−.16	.67[a]
−.41[a]	−.10	−2.09[a]	.18	.23	−.23	−.37[a]	−.16[a]	.28[b]	.69[a]
−.22	−.10[a]	−.21	−.56[a]	.44[a]	.13	−.32[a]	−.09[b]	.30[a]	.60[a]
−.09	−.04	−.07	−.46[b]	.32[b]	.08	−.49[a]	−.10	.02	.62[a]
−.60[a]	.00	−.01	.29	.48[a]	.92	−.32[b]	−.14[a]	.26	.52[a]
−.36[b]	−.09	.25	.38	.34[b]	1.23[b]	−.32[a]	−.03	−.21	.50[a]
−.45[a]	−.01	.13	.08	.44[a]	1.42[a]	−.31[a]	−.06	−.24	.42[b]
−.10	−.10	.13	−.49	.14	1.43[b]	−.32	−.17[b]	.66[a]	.41
−.03	−.06	−.89	−.39	.05	.38	−.37[b]	−.10	.67[a]	.30
−.09	−.08	−1.51[a]	.14	.16	.06	−.01	−.10	.04	.37[b]
−.27[b]	−.04	−.21	.07	.41[a]	.89[b]	−.08	−.06	−.12	.54[a]
.01	−.21[a]	−.35	−.22	.17	−.02	−.17	−.20[a]	.43[a]	.43[a]
−.42[a]	.04	.57	−.14	.60[a]	1.31[a]	−.46[a]	−.13[a]	−.21[b]	.58[a]
−.21	−.05	.01	.31	.15	1.12[a]	−.21[b]	−.07	.03	.45[a]
−.09	−.01	−.01	−.03	.17	.65	−.18[b]	−.12[a]	.21[b]	.38[a]

[a] Coefficients significant at the 5 percent level.
[b] Coefficients significant at the 10 percent level.

It was included in the expectation of both a general positive wealth elasticity of preference for public goods and a stronger effect for housing referenda because of the spillover effect on local property values. This variable (in contrast to Median Family Income) entered fourteen of the twenty-six stepwise regressions, always with a positive sign. In order to check the pervasiveness of the effect, this property value variable was included in all the standard multiple regressions. As shown in Table 5, the relationship is always positive and is significant except in the cases of Referenda 18, 16, 26, 23, 19, 20, and 17. Note here that the issue was one of *finance* in only two out of these seven exceptions—Referenda 23 and 19—and that passage of Referendum 19 would have meant a possible increase in *property tax.*

Thus property value, rather than income, is the strong positive determinant of demand for public goods. This is understandable. It measures wealth, and (for housing referenda) it is some measure of likely spillover benefits. Furthermore, property is not a state tax base, so the negative tax-base effect associated with income is not present.[28]

EDUCATION EXPENDITURES EFFECT. Local current education expenditure variables (X11, X12, X13) were originally included in the stepwise regressions in the expectation of a positive complementary effect between the level of local education service and preferences for increased state higher education service. With the reservations mentioned above about interpreting local public expenditure levels as expressions of preference on the part of the populace, the hypothesis for this variable was that cities which, *ceteris paribus,* prefer more or better pre-college education would prefer greater expenditures on higher education. Thus a positive relationship is to be expected between Total Current Education Expenditures per ADA and Referendum 8, aid to state colleges, and (with less certitude) Referendum 25, aid to public and private colleges. There is

---

York State Board of Equalization and Assessment, *Principles and Procedures Used in Establishing State Equalization Rates* (The Board, 1961).

[28] The property value effect is a positive wealth elasticity of preference consonant with Mueller's determination that, for individuals, it is not true that "upper income groups are less favorably disposed toward the extension of government programs than lower income groups" (Mueller, in *Quarterly Journal of Economics,* p. 228).

little reason to expect that local education expenditures and the programs of the other referenda are complementary goods;[29] if the relationship is negative, the obvious interpretation is that the two are substitutes.

Because Total Current Education Expenditures per ADA entered some fifteen of the twenty-six stepwise regressions, always with a negative sign, it was included in all the standard regressions. The result is a pervasive negative effect, as shown in Table 5. The regression coefficient is negative twenty-five out of twenty-six possible times, and significant seventeen times. It should be noted that in simple correlation all three of the education expenditure variables (X11, X12, and X13) are highly correlated (positively) with the property value variable (X25) and are generally positively correlated with Percent Yes Vote in simple correlation. This result can be stated as follows: A wealthy city tends to vote *yes* and also have high education expenditures, but when wealth (along with the other variables in the standard regression) is held constant, the higher education expenditures are, the lower is Percent Yes Vote, even on higher education referenda.

Three things encourage interpretation of the general negative effect of the education expenditure variable as a *substitution effect*. The variable is not a significant negative determinant of the two education *finance* referenda (8 and 25), the two referenda which were expected to be its complements;[30] it is not a significant determinant of five out of seven of the non-finance referenda. The seven non-finance referenda are Referenda 11, 16, 17, 18, 19, 20, and 26. Finally, education expenditures are a very large item of local expense—indeed, the item one would expect citizens to be most

[29] To the extent that there are distinct preferences regarding the use of the *public* sector of the economy to provide goods and services, or regarding what level of government should provide them, empirical relationships which can be interpreted as complementary or substitution effects between goods, may, in fact, arise because of these "political" preferences. For example, it may happen that cities with relatively high local education expenditures per student may also be cities which are repelled by state higher education or state debt finance because the citizens believe that education is a local matter or that debt finance is "bad."

[30] The regression coefficient is significant only for Referendum 18, an understandable relationship if this were a protest vote on school efficiency. But it should also be noted that dropping the left three or six variables from these three equations does not change the relationship between the education expenditures variable and these three referenda in either sign or significance.

TABLE 6. Standard Regression Results by Independent Variable[a]

Type of Effect and Variable	*Referenda*	*Direction of Effect*
Issue-Controversy Effect		
School Tax Rate	Referendum 18[b]	negative
City Size Effect		
Log of Population	Highway Referenda Highway Referenda (except 6)[b]	negative
Benefit-Spillover Effects		
Percent Residential Property	Housing Referenda (except 22) Housing Referenda (except 22 and 10)[b]	positive
Percent Stable Population	Housing Referenda Housing Referenda (except 2, 5, 22, and 10)[b]	positive
Wealth Effect		
Property Value per person	All Referenda All Referenda except 18, 16, 26, 19, 23, 20, and 17[b]	positive
Education Expenditures Effect		
Education Expenditures	All Referenda except 23 All Referenda except 10, 8, 25, 16, 26, 19, 23, 20, and 17[b]	negative
Living Density Effect		
Percent Crowded Dwellings	All Referenda except 22, 18, and 23 All Referenda except 10, 18, 8, 25, 1, 26, 19, 23, and 17[b]	positive
Occupation Effect		
Percent Work in Industry	All Referenda All Referenda except 16, 19, 21, and 23[b]	negative
Political Effects		
Percent Republicans — 2	All Housing Referenda except 10 Housing Referenda 5, 12, 13, 14, and 15[b]	positive
	All Non-Housing Referenda except 4 Non-Housing Referenda 18, 8, 1, 16, 23, 24, and 17[b]	negative

Percent Participating	Housing Referenda except 10[b]	negative
	Referenda 18, 8, 16, 26, 23, and 17[b]	positive
Need and User Effects		
Percent Service Station Sales	Highway Referenda Highway Referendum 16[b]	positive
Percent Private School Students[c]	Referendum 25[b]	positive
Percent Families with Children	Education Referenda Education Referenda 18 and 25[b]	positive
Tax Rate Effect[d]		
Overall Tax Rate	"Other Finance" Referenda Referendum 19[b]	positive
Education Level Effect[e]		
Percent Completed High School[e]	Education Referenda 8 and 25[b]	negative
Mobility Effects		
Percent Locally Employed	Highway Referenda except 26 Referenda 1 and 6[b]	positive
Percent Migrant	Education Referenda Referendum 8[b]	positive[b]

[a] Even in the standard regressions the following hypothesized *general* explanatory variables were insignificant or were mixed and unclear in their effect: Population Growth, Percent Travel to Work by Car, Capital Expenditures, School Tax Rate (but see above), and Percent Completed High School. The same is true for the following *specific* determinants: Percent Unemployed, Percent Low-Income Families, Population Density, and Median Home Value.

[b] The regression coefficients are significant for each of these referenda.

[c] The specificity of this effect is supported by the negative (insignificant) regression coefficients for Referenda 18 and 8.

[d] The "effect" is questionable because of the low R^2 for Referendum 19.

[e] This variable becomes insignificant if the three left hand variables are dropped from these equations.

aware of.[31] However, any interpretation should be made with caution because the precise determinants of expenditures for education are not yet fully or clearly understood.

LIVING DENSITY EFFECT. Percent Crowded Dwellings—dwellings with 1.01 or more persons per room—was originally included in the stepwise study as a need variable for public housing. It entered more of the stepwise equations than was expected, and so was included in all twenty-six standard regressions. In these it is quite consistent in its positive effect on Percent Yes Vote (twenty-three of the regression coefficients are positive and sixteen of these are significant).[32] The pervasiveness of this effect leads one to question the *need-for-housing* interpretation of this variable. If the norm for "crowded" were higher—1.5 or more persons per room, for example (such data were not available for all fifty-five cities)—one would more confidently assert that need for housing was measured.

The magnitude of the regression coefficients of this variable for the housing referenda as compared to the rest of the referenda (see Table 5) offers some foundation for arguing that Percent Crowded Dwellings is more important for housing referenda. However, its explanatory significance for the eight non-housing referenda is not so easily interpreted. It is insignificant for the three education referenda, but there is no particular grouping common to the eight significant ones.

OCCUPATION EFFECT. Percent Work in Industry was constructed with the intention of measuring relative unionization of the labor force. In a preliminary regression study it was a pervasive *negative* determinant of Percent Yes Vote. In the final stepwise regressions Percent Unskilled (X41) was included to determine whether the earlier negative result was a matter of skill, or of industry as such.

[31] Even with state subsidies for local public education, the school tax rate is an average of $13.60 per $1,000 equalized full property value, while the tax rate for all other local functions, city and county, is less than twice that—$22.80 per $1,000.

[32] The significant *negative* coefficient for Percent Crowded in Referendum 22 is an anomaly. However, the sign of this coefficient depends upon the presence of Median Home Value in the equation. When that variable is dropped from the equation, the sign of the regression coefficient for Percent Crowded in Referendum 22 becomes positive, although small (+ .04), and insignificant.

The results of the final stepwise regressions in Table 3 show that this strong negative effect is a phenomenon of industry, rather than of skill. Percent Work in Industry entered twenty-one of the twenty-six regressions (more than any other variable entered), and remained in nineteen regardless of what other variables entered. In the standard regressions shown in Table 5 the effect of Percent Work in Industry was always negative and was significant twenty-two out of twenty-six possible times. The regression equations in which it was not significant have only one thing in common—for all of them the percent of variance explained was less than 55 percent.

There is good reason not to interpret this negativism as a phenomenon of unionization. First, the AFL-CIO publicly supported most of the referenda; second, there is evidence that in upstate New York little political solidarity exists among union members.[33]

This strong negative effect may be what sociologists and political scientists have characterized as political negativism or alienation. Thus Horton and Thompson[34] find that powerlessness and the feeling of being threatened by the powers-that-be are factors which cause negative voting and the defeat of local referenda. Unfortunately the results of their study are not directly comparable with the data at hand, but the pervasiveness of this industry effect in both types of regression results—and particularly its significance in the regressions of Referendum 17 (officials must testify regarding official conduct or lose office)—leads to the conclusion that this is a negativism related to the industrial city rather than to spending. Perhaps the type of job held by a large portion of the labor force in industrial cities is a factor which helps to produce the sense of "threatened powerlessness" that Horton and Thompson found non-voters to feel. But before a more nearly economic explanation of this negativism is abandoned as hopeless, further investigation is called for.

POLITICAL EFFECTS. Percent Republicans and Percent Participating are two general determinants of referenda voting, though neither of

[33] See Berelson and others, *Voting,* Chap. 3.

[34] John E. Horton and Wayne E. Thompson, "Powerlessness and Political Negativism: A Study of Defeated Local Referendums," *American Journal of Sociology,* Vol. 67 (March 1962), pp. 485-93.

them is consistent in the direction of its effect. In general, Percent Republicans is positively related to the housing referenda and negatively related to the others (with one exception, Referendum 4, insignificant); just the reverse is true of Percent Participating. (There are only five instances in which the two variables do not have opposite signs in a given equation, and in only one of those five cases is either variable significant. See Table 5.)

Two difficulties arise in explaining this phenomenon. One is the meaning of Republican enrollment for the spring primary of the year in question. The relative strength of the Republican party *philosophy* in each city was the variable desired. In retrospect the gubernatorial or presidential vote might have been better. (Both of these variables are also open to question. For example, persons who are Democratic nationally but Republican locally, or vice versa, are not unusual.) To the extent that primary enrollment is a function not of party philosophy, but of local issues, or of local, state, or national personalities, the variable is not what is desired. The pattern of the explanatory power of Percent Republicans—positive for public housing, negative for the rest—certainly does not encourage the conclusion that the strength of party philosophy was measured.[35] The fact that some but not all cities were permitted permanent personal registration (and thereby permanent party enrollment), and the fact that enrollment is a matter of public information in a heavily Republican state cast further doubt on the reliability of this variable for the purpose for which it was intended.[36]

With respect to Percent Participating—defined as *yes* vote plus *no* vote as a percent of total (*yes* plus *no* plus *blank*) vote in that election—there is independent evidence that defeat of municipal referenda is associated with high turnout.[37] Thus high participation

[35] Since the two major parties did not normally take a stand regarding the referenda, a direct party involvement cannot be argued. Of course, the referenda were put on the ballot by a legislature which was predominantly Republican. The governor was never recorded as being against any referendum, and was usually recorded as being for each of them. There is no pattern by years that indicates that the change from a Democratic to a Republican governor in 1958 had any effect.

[36] An explanation of the New York State system of registration and enrollment can be found in either Lynton K. Caldwell's *The Government and Administration of New York* (Crowell, 1954); or *New York State and Local Government* (University of the State of New York, 1959).

[37] See Horton and Thompson, in *American Journal of Sociology*, p. 488, and

should be negatively related to Percent Yes Vote; for only nine housing referenda was it significantly so related.

The fact that Percent Participating and Percent Republicans have opposite signs in nearly all of the equations leads one to suspect that the sign of one of them is a function of interaction between them. The two are relatively strongly correlated in simple correlation.

It is unfortunate that a clear interpretation cannot be given of these two independent variables and of the relation of each to Percent Yes Vote for the different referenda. Because of this, the study does not shed any clear light on the *political* element of finance referenda voting.

OTHER EFFECTS. The three need and user effects noted in Table 6 were expected prior to even the stepwise analysis; they are immediately understandable and an opposite result would have been surprising.[38] The relation of service station sales (as a percent of total retail sales) to the highway referenda is too weak to be relied on. This is also true of the relation between Overall Tax Rate and the "Other Finance" referenda.

Two effects went counter to *a priori* expectations. It is rather surprising that a variable measuring education of adults (X18) has a negative significant regression coefficient for two of the three education referenda (Table 5); nor does the sign change when as many as the first six of the independent variables (starting from the left) are dropped from the equations (although both negative coefficients lose their significance). While the controversy over the church-state question might explain a negative regression coefficient for Referendum 25, it cannot do so for the non-controverted Referendum

---

the references cited therein. *Turnout* in a *special* election is the concept to be compared with *participation* when the referenda are submitted at a *general* election. No attempt was made in the study to collect turnout data because it was assumed that turnout would be mainly a function of the popularity of candidates at these general elections.

[38] With respect to the relationship between Percent Families with Children and the education referenda, the regression coefficient is positive for all three regressions and significant in two or the three: the regression of Referendum 18, to exclude New York City school debt, and of Referendum 25, aid to public and private colleges. The regression coefficient for the noncontroversial education finance referendum (Referendum 8, aid to public colleges) is smaller than for the other two and insignificant. This suggests that need is expressed and perhaps felt in proportion to the controversy over the referendum.

8, and for the latter the coefficient is more significant. Certainly the hypothesis that, *ceteris paribus,* preference for education (for others) is a positive function of one's own education is not confirmed. More evidence would be needed before drawing the opposite conclusion which these results suggest.

With respect to the other unexpected effect—the positive relation between Percent Locally Employed and the highway referenda —it would be surprising only if Percent Locally Employed were *inversely* related to highway use. It may not be so related, particularly in New York State where many of the people who work outside their county of residence travel to work by train (those who commute to work in New York City). In New York it may be true that those who work within their home county use highways more intensively than those who work outside their home county.[39]

Correlation Between the Referenda

The lack of *specific* determinants of referenda was noted above, and it was just observed that four of the *general* determinants are quite consistent (over the referenda) in the sign of their regression coefficients.[40] The combination of these two observations implies that Percent Yes Vote is apt to be highly (positively) correlated between different referenda. Simple correlations were calculated between Percent Yes Vote for every pair of referenda and it was found that many of the referenda tend to form a positively "inter-correlated" group. Table 7 shows an ordering of the referenda according to how deeply imbedded they are in the correlated group.

Two questions arise from the results given in Table 7. First, five out of six of the least imbedded referenda (Referenda 1, 25, 18, 28, and 16) were controversial, leaving only one controversial referendum (Referendum 7) imbedded in the correlated group. The question is, does the grouping of the controversial referenda *outside* the correlated group suggest that Katona's distinction between habitual attitudes and genuine decisions might explain the ordering of Table 7? Secondly, does our ability to explain referenda (the size of R^2 in

[39] It is also possible that the benefit incidence of the *particular* highways to be built was expected to fall more on those cities where a high percentage of workers were employed within the residence county.

[40] The four *general* determinants are Total Current Education Expenditures per ADA, Equalized Full Valuation of Taxable Property per person, Percent Crowded Dwellings, and Percent Work in Industry (see Table 5).

TABLE 7. Correlation Between Percent Yes Votes for Pairs of Referenda

Referenda[a]	*Smallest Simple Correlation Coefficient in the Cumulative Group*[b]
13	. . . .
15	r (15, 13) = .997
14	r (14, 13) = .985
12	r (12, 13) = .983
22	r (22, 12) = .84
7	r (7, 22) = .76
2	r (2, 22) = .72
5	r (5, 22) = .68
9	r (9, 2) = .68 = r (9, 7)
10	r (10, 5) = .66
6	r (6, 9) = .54
11	r (11, 7) = .53
4	r (4, 9) = .51
8	r (8, 4) = .48
24	r (24, 11) = .41
20	r (20, 4) = .41
21	r (21, 6) = .37
23	r (23, 4) = .33
17	r (17, 4) = .32
3	r (3, 17) = .16
16	r (16, 8) = .07
19	r (19, 3) = .01
26	r (26, 3) = −.03
18	r (18, 7) = −.04
25	r (25, 4) = −.05
1	r (1, 19) = −.16

[a] The first two referenda at the top (13 and 15) are the two with the highest correlation. Referenda were successively brought into the group according to the following criterion: A given referendum was brought into the group if, when it was in, the *lowest* simple correlation coefficient between members of the group was greater than (or equal to) the lowest correlation coefficient if any alternative referendum was brought in. Thus, the higher the position of a given referendum in the column, the more deeply it is imbedded in the correlated group.

[b] If the referenda are ordered by smallest r *in absolute value*, the ordering is the same down to referendum 16. Below that it would be:

18	r (18, 7) = −.04
26	r (26, 4) = −.02
19	r (19, 3) = .01
1	r (1, 9) = .01
25	r (25, 3) = .00

the stepwise and standard regressions) depend merely upon the degree of correlation between the referenda? A positive answer to this second question considerably weakens any argument that some

TABLE 8. Rank of the Referenda According to Five Criteria[a]

Referenda	Ordering of Table 7 (1)	Size of R^2 in the Stepwise Regressions[b] (2)	Size of R^2 in the Standard Regressions[c] (3)	Mean Percent No Vote[d] (4)	Aggregated Percent No Vote[e] (5)
1.	26	18	18	12	12
2.	7	14	8	10	10
3.	20	15	11	5	5
4.	13	11	10	15	15
5.	8	8	7	7	7
6.	11	23	19	23	23
7.	6	3	5	1	1
8.	14	13	14	25	22
9.	9	21	12	17	17
10.	10	16	16	16	16
11.	12	26	22	21	20
12.	4	5	4	9	9
13.	1	1	1	4	4
14.	3	4	3	2	2
15.	2	2	2	3	3
16.	21	24	23	19	19
17.	19	20	24	26	26
18.	24	10	9	13	13
19.	22	22	25	22	25
20.	16	17	20	20	21
21.	17	12	17	24	24
22.	5	7	6	8	6
23.	18	25	21	18	18
24.	15	9	15	6	8
25.	25	6	13	14	14
26.	23	19	26	11	11

[a] The Spearman rank correlation coefficient, ρ, between the orderings of each of the following pairs of criteria is:

Cols. (1) and (2): $\rho = .54$
Cols. (1) and (3): $\rho = .63$
Cols. (2) and (3): $\rho = .87$
Cols. (4) and (2): $\rho = .71$
Cols. (4) and (3): $\rho = .75$

All are significant at the 5 percent level.

[b] From Table 3.

[c] From Table 5.

[d] From Table 1.

[e] Col. (5) contains the ranking of the referenda according to how negative all cities (except New York) were when their vote was aggregated *before* obtaining Percent No Vote. It was calculated to determine whether variations in Percent No Vote *by city size* were possible determinants of the variations found in the average Percent No Vote as derived from Col. (4). Clearly, city size is not the explanation, for the value of ρ between the orderings of Cols. (4) and (5) $= .99$.

variables are general determinants *because* they are significant in many or most of the regressions.

The answer to the first question is not clear. On the one hand, there are *a priori* reasons why the vote on controversial referenda is more likely to be a "decision" than the vote on noncontroversial referenda. Also, the great diversity found within the well-correlated group supports the hypothesis that only a vague attitude could be the basis of such similar voting on such diverse questions. On the other hand, no criterion of preference (such as attitude toward spending or attitude toward incumbents)[41] could be found which would satisfy both the correlation between the correlated referenda and the lack of it between them and the rest, nor could the presence of a controversial referendum in the well-correlated group be explained. If each of the controversial referenda had been well explained in the regressions by a variable clearly related to the issue of the controversy, this would have supported the conclusion that controversy elicited decisions. However, only in two cases were *specific* determinants directly related to the controverted issue. These were the positive explanatory power of Percent Private School Students for Referendum 25, aid to public and private higher education, and the explanatory power of School Tax Rate for Referendum 18, the New York City bond issue referendum with its controversy over public school efficiency. The other four controversial referenda (16, 26, 1, and 7) do not have specific determinants, perhaps because there are no determinants related to the particular issues available among the fifty-two *potential* determinants.

With respect to the second question, Table 8 shows that although correlation between the referenda is positively related to the degree to which referenda can be explained, a better explanation is found in the degree to which the cities as a whole were *against* the referendum (whether the measure of negativism is mean Percent No Vote or Percent No Vote of the aggregated vote of the cities, excluding New York City).[42] This rather surprising result means that the

[41] If attitude toward the "government" or administration were the relevant "habitual attitude," one would expect some systematic difference in the regressions before and after Rockefeller displaced Harriman as governor in 1958. As was earlier noted, no systematic difference was found.

[42] This can be seen by comparing the rank correlations between the columns of Table 8. Negativism of the cities, col. 4, is a stronger determinant of the relative size of the coefficients of determination, cols. 2 or 3, than is "intercorrelation" between the referenda, col. 1.

more nearly the cities as a whole oppose a referendum, the more reliable are *economic*[43] variables as determinants of the vote.[44]

Empirical Limitations of the Results

Before the theoretical relationship between voting and economic demand for public goods is examined, the limitations of the empirical results in themselves should be noted.

First, linear approximations were made of relationships which are probably not linear in the real world; certainly one cannot assume that they are.[45]

Second, although a reasonably high percentage of the variance has been explained in many of the equations (see the last column of Table 5), the equations cannot be used to predict the outcome of future referenda. Outcome depends on the total *yes* and *no* vote in the state; to predict this, estimates should be made from samples drawn from all areas of the state and drawn in proportion to the size of expected vote (a separate regression for New York City based on wards, a regression for villages, rural areas, etc.). Furthermore, there is serious question about which equation would be used to predict even cities' Percent Yes Vote on, say, a new housing referendum. A glance at the variations in size of the constant terms and regression coefficients in Table 5 shows the importance of

[43] The extent to which the variables should be called economic is debatable; Percent Private School Students is one case in point. The only interpretation given of the Percent Work in Industry effect is sociological. It would be more accurate to speak not of economic variables, but of "variables which can be understood and interpreted economically, or by economists."

[44] There are not sufficient years covered in the sample of referenda to make any judgment about whether or not trough years of the business cycle might explain the negativism of cities as a whole. 1958 and 1960 were mild trough years in the time-span studied. Although Referenda 12, 13, 14, and 15, which were voted on in 1958, have the lowest mean Percent Yes Vote of all the referenda, they are also all housing referenda (and very highly correlated with one another). In the other trough year, 1960, another housing referendum was voted on and the mean Percent Yes Vote for that referendum (Referendum 22) was relatively very high.

[45] In order to insure that the presence of New York City among the cities did not distort the results, a calculation was made of all simple correlation coefficients between the fifty-two independent variables and Percent Yes Vote without New York City. Also the stepwise regressions were recalculated without it. The results differ only slightly, and not systematically. The reason for this, no doubt, is that all of the variables were normalized in some way, by per capita, percent, and so forth.

choosing the right equation (even from this fairly consistent group of housing referenda). In fact, one of the conclusions that follows from these variations and from the lack of specific determinants is that neither the kind of program, nor the type of finance, nor the presence or absence of controversy has proved to be a reliable *a priori* indicator of *similar* referenda.

A third limitation of the empirical results are the systematic deviations from the regression equations. For each set of regression studies, the stepwise and standard residuals (and a preliminary stepwise residual with thirty-five variables) from the regressions were studied. For each of the sets it was observed that particular cities had residuals of a given sign for more of the twenty-six equations than chance predicts. For both the stepwise and standard regressions, the probability that the pattern arose from chance was only 10 percent.

No explanation was found for the pattern of residuals. Several possible explanations were investigated. For example, the presence or absence of public housing was checked as an explanation of the residuals for the housing referenda. There are seven cities whose predicted affirmative vote was consistently higher (in both standard and stepwise regressions) than their actual vote for the ten housing referenda; that is, for eight or more of the ten referenda, they voted more heavily against the referenda than the equation predicted. Of these cities only three did not have some form of state-subsidized housing either completed, under construction, or planned (as of 1961). Of the ten cities which consistently voted more heavily than predicted for the housing referenda (by the same test), four had no form of state-subsidized housing.[46]

The Validity of the Demand Interpretation of Voting

In the voting study which has just been described, the empirical relationships have been interpreted in terms of demand for public goods. Thus the positive relationship between property value and Percent Yes Vote was interpreted as a positive wealth elasticity of demand, and negative relationship between local education expen-

[46] For a list of these "deviate" cities, see my dissertation, p. 137ff.

ditures and Percent Yes Vote as a substitution effect. The next step is to ask under what assumptions it is economically meaningful to interpret vote on a referendum as a measure of demand for a public good.

This question involves a series of problems: the economic meaning of a referendum and of an individual's vote, and the justification for aggregating individuals' votes into Percent Yes Vote. The assumptions implicit in the demand interpretation can best be understood in relation to (or in contrast with) an "ideal" referendum and "ideal" preference data for a study of demand for a public good.

THE IDEAL DATA. Assume that the proposal is to build a monument to the dead of World War II in front of the state capitol in Albany. This constitutes a nearly pure social good, the only qualification being that consumption may be partially a function of citizens' locations. The monument is to be paid for by a head tax of fifty cents on every state resident. (Assume that drawings of the proposed monument are widely circulated with all the factual details.) This referendum question is ideal in that the voter should be able to make a clear calculation of benefit and cost.

The question of what kind of data would ideally express demand for this public good was mentioned above, where the comparison is made between the market situation and the budget situation (see footnote 4). There it is pointed out that if citizens voluntarily paid for public goods, and paid their marginal evaluation of each public good, then demand could be explained by explaining price paid. This system of voluntary taxation is obviously unrealistic, but it provides a basis for interpreting the economic meaning of a referendum vote. Hereafter it will be assumed that for each citizen there exists a "price-offer" (or "price-demand") which is the amount of money he would have to give up (or receive) to make him indifferent as between the *status quo* and the given fiscal change.[47] This "price," of course, is not empirically available, and

[47] Since the fiscal change proposed in the ideal referendum involves both a good and a predetermined cost (fifty cents per person), the possibility of "price-demands" has to be included. Unless someone objects to the monument, no price-demand should exceed the cost to the individual. The concept of price-offers and price-demands was developed by the writer in order to examine the conditions for arriving at the Pareto frontier when honest revelation of preferences is assumed. See my dissertation, Part I.

only an honest revelation of preferences by all citizens would make it available. All citizens, however, are strongly motivated by the social nature of most public goods to dissemble their preferences; once social goods exist, no citizen can be excluded from enjoying them.[48]

THE MEANING OF INDIVIDUAL VOTING DATA. In the real world, where a citizen is not asked to reveal his demand for public goods in monetary terms, the only data available which reveal individual preferences are the vote (of yes, no, or abstention) of each individual on fiscal proposals. This vote itself does not have the direct economic meaning that a voluntary price-offer has. Furthermore, the taxes the particular individual pays (or will pay) are not directly a function of his voting decision. Finally, the vote of an individual on a popular referendum does not have the exchange value over a series of proposals that the vote of a legislator has.

Even though a citizen's vote is not a price-offer, and though it does not have a logrolling exchange value, it certainly has meaning; regardless of who pays for the proposal if it passes, and of how others vote, a *no* vote counts for a defeat of a referendum and a *yes* vote for its passage. On the basis of this statement, a calculation can be made on the way in which the "rational man" will vote.[49]

The citizen's voting decision is similar to the decision he would face if given a one-shot possibility of making a market purchase of a good (a painting, for example) for which both quantity and price are fixed. He would make such a purchase if the exchange would result in a net benefit for him—that is, if the benefit of the good (net of the cost of purchasing it and net of the cost of telephoning or reaching the market) is positive.

Similarly, in that ideal referendum for which costs and benefits should be easily calculable, a voter could be expected to vote *yes* if

See Musgrave, *Public Finance,* p. 116. This insight into the essential problem of the social nature of public goods goes back to Knut Wicksell, "Ein neues Prinzip der gerechten Besteuerung," in *Finanztheoretische Untersuchengen* (Jena, 1896), translated by James M. Buchanan in *Classics in the Theory of Public Finance,* Richard A. Musgrave and Alan T. Peacock (eds.), (Macmillan, 1958), pp. 72-118.

[49] The term "rational man" is used here in its customary economic sense; that is, the rational man is he who manifests a consistent preference system, defined over all possible bundles of goods including public goods of all types. Downs, *Economic Theory of Democracy,* Chap. 3, describes the rational calculation such a man would make before voting for a party or candidate.

the benefit of the war memorial (net of the cost to him in future higher taxes—fifty cents) exceeds the cost of voting; he would vote *no* if the cost of the memorial to him, net of benefit, exceeds the cost of voting; and he would abstain if neither net cost nor net benefit exceeded the threshold voting cost. An attempt is made, below, to relate the empirical results of this and other studies to the validity of these assumptions about the "rational" voter, but for the present it is useful to assume that he behaves as described.

It is clear that the above expression of rational demand in terms of a *yes* or *no* vote (or abstention) is a very gross measure of intensity of preference or demand. Of two voters who both vote *yes,* one may be almost indifferent, the other wildly enthusiastic; or—to express the intensity of preference in the way which is most meaningful in this context—one individual's honest price-offer may be very small while the other's is very large, yet both are expressed by a *unit* vote of *yes.* If differences within the group of *yes*-voters and within the group of *no*-voters were unimportant in comparison to the differences between the two groups, then voting data on individuals could be used as the surrogate variable for the "true demand" of these individuals.[50] The problem would be to select the proper explanatory variables from the group of potential variables.

THE MEANING OF AGGREGATED VOTING DATA. Where the secret ballot is used, voting data on identifiable individuals are normally not available; for this reason, the empirical study was made using aggregated voting data. What is the economic meaning of aggregated votes?

In discussing the individual's decision to vote *yes* or *no* on a finance referendum, a parallel was drawn between that decision and a market-purchase decision; that is, whether an individual should buy when faced with an opportunity in a market in which price and quantity are fixed. On the theoretical plane, the parallel is not an exact one, even for the individual. In the market situation, the individual has only two alternatives—to purchase or to abstain; in the voting situation he has not two, but three alternatives—to vote *yes,* abstain, or vote *no.* The reason votes of *no* are present in the referendum decision is obvious. The decision is not just the individual's, as it is in the case of the market good; it is ultimately a group

[50] The statistical method of estimation would be discriminate regression analysis in which the dependent variable can assume only discriminate values.

decision. Thus, no matter how a given individual votes, he may be forced to "consume" the good and help pay the cost.

A *no*-vote is easy enough to interpret in terms of a group decision, but it is not so easily interpreted in terms of demand. Presumably, in terms of demand, one who votes *no* indicates that he is potentially willing to give up an amount of money (less than or equal to his honest price-demand) to prevent the referendum from passing, or conversely, that he would have to be compensated to make him even indifferent as between the *status quo* and the proposed change. These price-demands implied by *no*-votes are a serious problem when one is trying to determine the true demand of the community. In the terms of welfare economics, the problem is less difficult, for the true communal demand is the sum of price-offers minus the sum of price demands.[51] In the terms of economic reality, compensation is normally not paid (particularly not to an individual citizen dissatisfied with a public expenditure and/or his tax bill), and the meaning of a community's demand is not as clear. For the purposes of empirical study, one is virtually forced to accept the voting system by which group finance decisions are made as an approximation of the reality of public-goods demand. Without taking up the question of the desirability of majority voting as a way of making group decisions,[52] it can be said that demand is *defined* for purposes of decision (when the decision is made by majority voting on a popular referendum) by *yes* minus *no* votes, with each citizen allowed one vote. Thus, *yes* minus *no* votes are the best available measure of a community's net total demand, crude as that estimate is when compared either to the ideal revelation of price-offers and price-demands or to an estimate made on the basis of a more sophisticated voting system, such as point voting.

Summary of Assumptions

The assumptions implicit in an interpretation of this voting study in terms of economic demand can now be listed. They are: (1) that it is possible for the citizen to make a rational calculation of

[51] Welfare economists are interested in changes which can meet the Pareto criterion; that is, changes which leave at least one person better off and have a neutral effect on all others. When the sum of price-offers exceeds the sum of all price-demands plus physical costs, then the change meets this criterion.

[52] See Musgrave, *Public Finance,* Chap. 6, and my dissertation, Part I. The latter assumes honest revelation of preference.

the benefits and costs of proposals; (2) that individuals, in fact, make such a calculation and "rationally" behave (vote) according to the resulting preference; (3) that both strategy on the part of individual voters, and "politics"—in the broad sense of the intermediation of both the state and local governments—can be safely ignored; and (4) that the preferences of citizens are symmetrical in the sense that *yes* and *no* votes reasonably approximate their true preferences.

The Realism of the Assumptions

Obviously the calculation of the relevant cost and benefit of the programs in the referenda studied is not as simple as in the case of the war memorial. Several serious problems arise. First, what is voted on is usually the long-range maximum expenditure on a program. Within this maximum the legislature will later decide the actual spending level. (Realistically, a New York voter should soon learn that the legislature will shortly be spending or borrowing the maximum, at least for programs of subsidized housing.) Second, the location within the state where the capital expenditure will be made is normally not specified in referenda. Third, cost calculation involves estimating the incidence of the present and future state tax structure. When a tax increase is implicit in raising the spending (or borrowing) maximum, the voter should know *which* tax will be increased, but normally he does not. Finally, the problems of reloaning the borrowed funds to local governments or to housing corporations, of self-liquidation of debt, and of present and future interest rates, further complicate the cost calculation. Even though these problems differ only in degree from the problems the consumer faces in calculating the probable cost and benefit of buying, say, a used car "on time," the difficulties the voter faces are still likely to diminish his chances of making the necessary rational calculations.

Some of the referenda have little or nothing to do with cost and benefit to cities in the normal economic meaning of these terms. Referendum 17, requiring officials to testify, was chosen for its nonfinance character. Referendum 10, the town and village housing-debt exclusion question, is another example. Referendum 18 seems to be another example for all cities except New York City. Yet if the interpretation of the regression result for Referendum 18 is correct —that the vote was a protest vote on school administration efficiency—then this, it would seem, is an instance where the other cities used an "innocent" question to express demand. Referendum 25, aid to public and private schools, with the church-state controversy it aroused, may be considered a "philosophical" question. Yet it can be said that the interpretation of Referendum 25 as demand for a good is quite straightforward. The question was: "Do you wish a new public service—publicly-supported private college education?" It is possible that this referendum was explained well in the regressions because one factor was clearly understood by the voters —namely, the differential net gain or burden accruing to those planning to send their children to a private college as opposed to those who were not so planning.[53]

EMPIRICAL EVIDENCE REGARDING RATIONAL BEHAVIOR. There is some evidence for the conclusion that voters do not make a rational calculation of cost and benefit. It has been seen that on the basis of interview data on preferences for federal programs, Mueller found evidence for inconsistency and instability in individuals' attitudes. Rational calculation should result in stable, consistent preferences. The fact that little specificity was found between particular referenda and *a priori* appropriate independent variables also weakens any argument that voters made *decisions* on the basis of the particulars of the individual referenda. Finally, David's study of preferences for several types of taxes (income, sales, and property) supports this conclusion on the cost side. She finds that low-income groups, rather than high, favor the property tax.[54]

The tendency of non-whites and persons of low income not even to go to the polls is also relevant to this problem. When the

[53] Ideal referenda for a study such as the above, then, are not necessarily ones like the unrealistic "ideal" example of the monument financed by a head tax, but rather referenda which make as explicit as possible the incidence of their benefit and cost. For example, if it was true that Referendum 20, the adoption of the Federal definitions of taxable income, would have caused a determinable change in tax burden, then, if that change had been explicitly described, the referendum might well have been as well explained as Referendum 25. Thus even for purposes of research (not to mention for rational government), the ideal referendum is one which is as explicit as possible *in its effects*.

[54] She attributes this to misinformation about the regressive nature of the property tax. See Elizabeth J. L. David, "Public Preferences and the Tax Structure: An Examination of Factors Related to State and Local Tax Preferences" (Doctoral dissertation, University of Michigan, 1961), p. 66.

ballot includes one or more referenda likely to benefit these groups particularly, then their failure to vote weakens the validity of the assumption about rational calculation and behavior.

STRATEGY AND POLITICS. The vote on these popular referenda is assumed to be an honest revelation of preference because it is difficult to see any motive for deliberately voting contrary to one's true preference (between the *status quo* and the given fiscal change). A voter knows that his vote is anonymous, and thus that it cannot be used as the basis of a tax (or some other form of "reprisal") on him. The possibility of "selling" his vote on one referendum in exchange for a vote by another on a different referendum (logrolling) is most unlikely.[55]

There is one circumstance, however, in which strategy is apt to arise in referendum voting. If a voter thinks that the defeat of a given referendum will be followed by a vote (the following year) on a similar but preferable referendum, then he may vote *no* on the former even though he prefers it to the *status quo*. In the vote on only one case did it seem likely that this type of strategy was involved; that was in Referendum 1, the highway finance referendum which included the controversial fuel-tax-increase rider to finance repayment if the debt were approved. The fact that the highway program and the funds to begin it were necessary warranted the assumption by voters that the defeat of Referendum 1 would mean a vote on a modified highway finance referendum the following year, as was the case. The campaign against this referendum was not directed at the highway construction itself, but at the method of funding it; one group was against it because the fuel-tax revenue was not earmarked for highway finance, the other because of the fuel-tax increase itself.

Referendum 1 was very controversial, and was defeated. Referendum 6, similar to Referendum 1 but without the tax rider, was not controversial, and it passed one year later. These facts alone do not indicate that the type of strategy described was involved, only that it was likely to have been. But the standard regression equations for these two referenda lead one to conclude that the strategy,

[55] The complexity of the problem of a citizen's attempting to exchange votes with other citizens on referenda makes logrolling costly and unfeasible; the secret ballot and large number of voters make it impossible to check "payoffs." See Buchanan and Tullock, *Calculus of Consent,* p. 132.

if it was present and varied systematically by city, was a function of city size. As was remarked, this conclusion is consistent with the rational use of a campaign fund. It is worthy of note that Referendum 1, the only referendum of the twenty-six which provided for payment (not formally in the referendum, but in the well-known rider), was defeated and was considered the most controversial referendum up to that date. This is particularly interesting in relation to Wicksell's belief that the decision on spending for a program and on the means to pay for it should be made together.[56]

There are several grounds for the assumption that the "politics" of state and local government can be ignored in explaining voting on referenda. There were three principal reasons for ignoring the politics of state government. First, the initial passage of a referendum bill by the Assembly and Senate was usually very routine[57] and was reported to the public as an accomplished fact; the manner of passage, the supporters and dissenters, were normally not reported, and hence were assumed not to be known to the voters and thus not to be determinants of the popular vote. Second, as has already been noted, neither of the two major parties ever formally opposed a referendum, nor did any of the governors during the pe-

[56] See Wicksell, in *Classics of Public Finance.* The defeat of Referendum I might be interpreted in several ways. A normative interpretation would be that its defeat shows that either the expenditure or the type of tax which would finance it would not have effected a change which would meet the Pareto criterion; thus the defeat was salutary. The passage the following year of a similar referendum without specified means of payment argues against this interpretation. One can hardly assert that general revenue (mainly income tax) better approximates benefit taxation for highway funding than does a fuel tax. If this normative interpretation is rejected in favor of the argument or assumption that the fuel tax is an appropriate benefit tax for financing highways, two possible interpretations of the facts remain. One is that the preferences of citizens are quite open to influence, and thus the campaign waged by the automobile associations and other highway-user groups influenced the voters to vote against their own best interest. The other is that citizens tend to forget about taxes; that is, they will vote for an increase in expenditures if they are not reminded (by a tax rider or some other means) that the expenditure must be paid for. If the first of these two alternatives is true, it is important to determine the extent to which preferences can be influenced by such campaigning. If the second is true, the problem is then how to insure that citizens are aware of the relation between expenditures and taxes. Both of these hypotheses, if they are true, suggest that finance decisions, especially tax decisions, should not be made by popular referendum. Mueller, in *Quarterly Journal of Economics,* p. 216, supports the second hypothesis.

[57] Of all the referenda, only the passage of the bill to put Referendum 6 on the ballot caused any stir. The reason was that the governor wished a tax rider on this referendum also.

riod. Third, interest groups, not parties, campaigned against the referenda; this was taken into consideration whenever it was known.

So far as local government is concerned, the only significant variable for explaining the vote seemed to be whether a local housing authority existed and was functioning.[58] This variable was tested as an explanation of the residuals of consistent direction and was found not to explain them, as has been noted.

None of these observations imply that the study of legislatures, their internal functioning, and their relation to constituents' preferences, and the study of political leadership are not important for understanding how supply and demand for public goods are (and should be) related.[59] Rather, what is argued here is only that politics in these areas did not systematically affect popular referendum voting in New York State.

SYMMETRY IN PREFERENCES OF CITIZENS. No one would ever argue that all *yes*-voters feel equally intense in their preferences, let alone that a *yes* vote equals a *no* vote (in the sense that the implicit price-offer of the *yes*-voter equals the implicit price-demand of the *no*-voter). Nor is it necessary that so stringent an assumption accurately describe reality in order for voting data to be a reasonable basis for estimating demand. It is only necessary that intensities of preference not vary systematically between cities except insofar as they are captured in the measure Percent Yes Vote and are related to the variables used to explain Percent Yes Vote. One could say that one is not interested in the intensity of preference of individuals, but only of cities, as measured by Percent Yes Vote. It is preferable to try to see how the two sorts of preference are related theoretically, and whenever possible to compare results based on two levels of study.

The assumption that variations in intensities are not "too" important poses a problem not unique to this study. If one uses a general term rather than the term "intensities," the problem can be said to arise whenever individual factors are aggregated prior to compari-

[58] Unfortunately, the creation of a local housing authority was never the subject of a local referendum. Other local referenda are available for study, a few of which are directly related to the state referenda analyzed here. (Most of these local referenda concern a decision in a given city about a pension increase, as authorized by Referendum 19.) The referenda were too few to be of significant help in understanding preferences on the state referenda.

[59] See note 6.

son. In general terms, the problem is one of quality in an ordinary cross-section demand study of a private good; it is a problem even when data are gathered by interview, because such data are almost always aggregated prior to analysis.

Percent Yes Vote and Public Demand

With the above background, the economic meaning of Percent Yes Vote can be seen more clearly, as can its meaning and limitations as a measure of demand. What have been aggregated and normalized here are, at best, gross measures of preference—individual *yes* and *no* votes—expressed as Percent Yes Vote. This variable is not an approximation of a city's *total* "net demand," for which total *yes* minus total *no* is the best estimate.[60] Rather, Percent Yes Vote is an estimate of a city's *normalized* net demand.[61] Although it is an

[60] *Yes* minus *no* could not be used as the dependent variable for statistical reasons. If the preference data are left in this gross form, the dependent variable's distribution would be extremely skewed; even the weaker condition for an unbiased linear estimate will not be fulfilled, because the error term is apt to be correlated with population, an independent variable which would be of overriding importance.

[61] Not directly, but by a linear transformation; where Y is *yes* vote, N is *no* vote, D is normalized demand, and P is Percent Yes Vote,

$$D \equiv \frac{Y - N}{Y + N}$$

$$P \equiv \frac{100 \cdot Y}{Y + N};$$

then,

$$D = \frac{2Y - Y - N}{Y + N},$$

$$D = \frac{2Y}{Y + N} - 1,$$

$$D = \frac{1}{50} \cdot P - 1,$$

or

$$P = 50\,D + 50$$

The relative size of the regression coefficients (and their significance levels) are invariant in such a transformation. All regression coefficients would be multiplied by the same constant.

estimate of a *city's* demand, interpretation is almost invariably made in terms of individual behavior, just as is done in the case of the aggregate consumption function. In the present case, the subject is an abstract, representative individual who, because he lives in a particular city with its particular characteristics, has a preference with respect to a fiscal change (he is, say, "40 percent for" the change), a preference which can be compared to the 20 percent or 80 percent preference of another abstract, representative individual from another city.[62]

While no amount of argument can *prove* that the "true intensities" are not the inverse of (or unrelated to) Percent Yes Vote, the likelihood of this seems quite small. For one thing, citizens with strong aversions to a program can get their intensity registered in the formal vote of their city by convincing potentially weak *yes*-voters to vote *no* (or vice versa).[63] Further, it seems unlikely that Percent Yes Vote and "true intensity" can be inversely related or unrelated, because for either to be true there have to be rather sharp differences between citizens of different cities (independent of all the characteristics of the cities included in this study). Thus another way to state the assumption implicit in using Percent Yes Vote as a measure of demand, is to say that the urban population of the state is assumed to be basically homogeneous, that the differences among individuals (which are not random) will be due at least principally to differences in the population and locational characteristics which have been included as variables in this study.

[62] It is possible, of course, that the "true" intensities of preference of the cities (or of the representative individuals) are in fact precisely the reverse of what the Percent Yes Vote indicates. For example, on Referendum 15, the Percent Yes Vote of Long Beach, New York, is 72 percent, while the Percent Yes Vote of Niagara Falls is only 18 percent. The explanation of the regression results is based on the assumption that, in this case, Long Beach exhibits a stronger preference for Referendum 15 than does Niagara Falls. It is possible that *yes*-voters in Long Beach have weak preferences, and *no*-voters very strong aversions, and that the opposite is true in Niagara Falls. The result of this possibility, then, could be a large negative sum of net price-offers in Long Beach and a large positive sum in Niagara Falls, if such "dollar preferences" were known. But it is difficult in terms of economic demand to interpret this statement as meaning that Long Beach has a stronger preference for Referendum 15 than has Niagara Falls.

[63] Thus if the hypothesis of note 62 were true, many of the weak *yes*-voters of Long Beach would probably have been influenced by the strong *no*-voters to vote against the referendum.

This examination of the validity of Percent Yes Vote as a measure of public demand does not imply a definitive conclusion about validity; rather, its purpose was to clarify the several assumptions implicit in the interpretation of Percent Yes Vote. While there seems to be no basic objection to the assumption that Percent Yes Vote is a reasonable estimate of the intensity of preference between the *status quo* and a given fiscal change, only further studies of public demand on both the aggregate and individual levels will show how reasonable the assumption is.

A Note Concerning Future Research

A serious question must be faced in future research, particularly if that research is mainly in the form of interview studies—namely, should the goal of research in this area be to explain *actual* public demand, however that be defined? Perhaps a more important problem is the extent to which the preferences of citizens for public goods are based on true or false information about facts which should be relevant to the preferences in question, and second, the extent to which preferences based on erroneous information can be changed by supplying correct information.

The problem arises from the failure of some of the variables to explain Percent Yes Vote on the relevant referenda. Consider Percent Sound Dwellings (X34) and Percent Low-Income Families (X27). These two variables are central to the decision by a city to build or subsidize housing and to the decision by the New York State Division of Housing to subsidize housing in a given city. "Unsound," or dilapidated and/or unsanitary dwellings, define a slum. Low income is the criterion for residence in public housing. If the interview method were used to determine and explain citizens' preferences regarding public housing (and an analogous argument would hold for other government programs, such as highways, welfare, foreign aid, or education), the value of the results would be considerably increased if questions were formulated to determine the interviewee's knowledge of the facts which are relevant to the decision.

It is one thing for a consumer not to know the relevant objective differences between apples and oranges or between two makes of automobile; the consequences of error on his part are probably minor, and further, since they will affect him directly, he will be motivated to improve his knowledge.

It is quite another thing for a voter to lack information relevant to a proposed program, such as public housing. He should know the conditions under which household residents live in his city (or, in the context of this study, his state), the ability of low-income families to pay the cost of adequate private housing, and the cost of public housing to himself and to the state. The consequences of error, and of an expressed *vote preference* based on error, do not have an immediate or clear impact on the voter himself; thus he is not directly motivated to obtain correct information.

To elicit preferences from a citizen and to explain them by his age, income, or occupation without determining whether he has any opinion (correct or incorrect) about the relevant facts, is to fail to approach what may be the most significant research question about public preferences: Is public demand based on *true* information? If it is based on error or lack of knowledge, can it be changed by correcting the error or adding new facts?

These observations are not meant as criticisms of the interview studies of preferences regarding types of taxes and government programs. The interview studies by David and Mueller previously cited in fact support the conclusion that the *basis* of these preferences is itself an important area of research. Rather, the intention of this note is to emphasize that the failure of relevant variables to explain the appropriate preferences should not constitute a reason for ignoring these variables in future research but should argue for research to determine *why* they are not significant explanations, and how they can be made the significant variables which they should be in such a decision.

Conclusion

In this essay, one approach to the study of public demand has been exemplified and evaluated. Percent Yes Vote by cities on New York State finance referenda was explained in terms of city characteristics by multiple regression analysis. The characteristics of cities explain between 50 and 85 percent of the variance of Percent Yes Vote for most of the referenda. Several general, consistent determinants have been found. Percent Yes Vote on all referenda is negatively related to the percent of the labor force which works in industry, an effect which may be related to the sociological concept of political alienation. Percent Yes Vote on state *finance* referenda is negatively related to local expenditures on education, which can be explained as a substitution effect. It is positively related to a wealth variable, namely, equalized full valuation of taxable property per person, and to the percent of occupied dwelling units with 1.01 or more persons per room. There are specific determinants for public housing referenda, as well as for two controversial education referenda. It was found that the percent of variance explained—the size of R^2—depends upon how negative the vote was for the cities as a group.

On the other hand, the number of referenda studied and similarities and differences between them according to program, type of finance, and so forth, generally did not add to the intelligibility of the explanations and interpretations; in few cases were explanatory variables found which were intelligibly specific to a referendum or a subset of similar referenda. Because a large number of potentially independent variables were tested, this failure is an important weakness. Nothing in the empirical results suggests that the vote on non-controversial referenda is more likely than interview-elicited preferences to be based on genuine decisions; in fact, high correlation of Percent Yes Vote between non-controversial referenda of diverse types encourages the conclusion that the Percent Yes Vote of cities on these referenda is not a function of the specific cost and benefit of each referendum, but rather a function of some vague attitude.

Two aspects of referenda voting make it less likely that Percent Yes Vote will approximate demand for a public good. One is that a rational calculation of future costs and benefits of the change state finance referenda would cause is frequently difficult. The other is that there is evidence such calculation is not made, particularly by low income persons, or at least that the resulting preferences to be expected are not translated into votes.

Because of the empirical limitations of the multiple regression results and because of the problem involved in the theoretical interpretation of the aggregated voting data, it may be that the method of multiple regression analysis on aggregated data will not prove particularly fruitful in future research, except for purposes of clarifying, rechecking, and broadening some of the conclusions and hypotheses of this study. But the weakness of the aggregate approach does not affect the importance of the problem of public demand.

The ultimate goals of research into public demand are several. One is simply to understand citizens' preferences and what they depend upon. Another is to *inform* citizens if it is found that their preferences (and votes) are based on ignorance, or false information. The final goal is to bring government decisions more into accord with the enlightened preferences of citizens. All of these are important; their attainment depends upon understanding the empirical (and normative!) relationship between tax and expenditure decisions and the preferences of citizens. This is a difficult and intriguing task for students of public finance. The intention of this essay has been to pose the problem of the empirical study of the demand for public goods and to exemplify and evaluate one approach to the solution of that problem.

Index*

* References to tables and figures are in italics.